REMEMBERING FIREBASE RIPCORD

CHRISTOPHER J. BRADY

outskirtspress
DENVER, COLORADO

The opinions expressed in this manuscript are solely the opinions of the author and do not represent the opinions or thoughts of the publisher. The author has represented and warranted full ownership and/or legal right to publish all the materials in this book.

Remembering Firebase Ripcord
All Rights Reserved.
Copyright © 2015 Christopher J. Brady
v4.0

Cover Image by Ben Rice

This book may not be reproduced, transmitted, or stored in whole or in part by any means, including graphic, electronic, or mechanical without the express written consent of the publisher except in the case of brief quotations embodied in critical articles and reviews.

Outskirts Press, Inc.
http://www.outskirtspress.com

ISBN: 978-1-4787-6178-5

Outskirts Press and the "OP" logo are trademarks belonging to Outskirts Press, Inc.

PRINTED IN THE UNITED STATES OF AMERICA

This book is dedicated to those who served in Vietnam. Their stories deserve to be heard, their heroism and sacrifice admired.

Contents

Introduction i

1: A Not-So Welcome Home 1

2: Kill or Be Killed 6

3: Frustrations Mount 10

4: The Initial Assault 16

5: April Fool's Day 47

6: Sporadic Contact 62

7: Ahead of the Siege 87

8: Meeting of the Minds 93

9: Hill 902 108

10: Lightning Strikes 132

11: Lifelines 140

12: The Delta Raiders 158

13:	Hill 1,000	177
14:	Missing in Action	207
15:	The Beginning of the End	218
16:	From the NFL to the 101st	231
17:	Nowhere to Go	242
18:	Delta Makes a Daring Rescue	291
19:	Evacuating the Firebase	300
Acknowledgments		329
Bibliography		353
Index		357

Introduction

A Huey lands atop one of the chopper pads on Firebase Ripcord in early July 1970. Photo provided by James Saller.

As the son of a Vietnam combat veteran, I did not live through this period of American history. However, like with each of these men who live today, my existence is proof that the Vietnam War lives today on nearly every street, and in each corner store and community throughout the United States and beyond.

It has always served as a point of interest to those connected to it and over time that interest has only grown with each passing year and each subsequent revelation. It seems the more one learns about this volcanic time in history, the more the questions flow. Despite being born in an Army hospital on an Army base, my questions routinely outnumbered answers when it came to this war.

Given that, the accounts provided in this book came from the men who were on the ground in South Vietnam, serving in the most deadly area of Vietnam for American troops – I Corps, the northern most section of South Vietnam. Their Area of Operation was attainable only through flight – the Hueys that became the iconic symbol of the Vietnam War – and was closer to neighboring Laos and the Ho Chi Minh Trail than Camp Evans, home to the 2nd Battalion, 506th Infantry of the 101st Airborne Division.

This is their story, their accounts of a horrific time in a horrific war. This is not an evaluation of strategy nor is it an overall recount of specific campaigns. This is not a historical recounting of the battle. This is the story of warfare in the Ripcord Area of Operation in 1970, as relayed by those who were there.

Laos was technically off limits to American soldiers, and the Ho Chi Minh Trail, coupled with the high-speed trails snaking through the jungles of the A Shau Valley just west of the trail in South Vietnam provided a launching point for the North Vietnamese Army. The 101st Airborne Division, dating back to 1969 and action at Dong Ap Bia, was tasked with thwarting the advances from the north southward through the A Shau. While many know the battle at Dong Ap Bia, more famously known as Hamburger Hill, subsequent action just a bit north at Ripcord was left secret and remains a mystery to far too many.

While action associated with the war in Vietnam was deescalating in much of South Vietnam, pockets of fierce fighting still existed in 1970.

The Screaming Eagles first arrived in Vietnam in 1965 as the First

Brigade was introduced. As the war escalated and Gen. William Westmoreland pushed for more boots on the ground, Second and Third Brigades touched down in December 1967. It was the same year the Pentagon approved the fourth rifle company to each battalion, allowing commanders to have a company provide perimeter security for a firebase with three companies in the field. For those at Ripcord, numbers associated with troop strength meant little, as you'll come to understand later.

Another key contributing factor to the ferocity of fighting at Ripcord stemmed from the fact that President Richard Nixon's Vietnamization had pulled troops from the rest of the country. To the north of Ripcord, all the way to the Demilitarized Zone, divisions of Marines for years had butted heads with the North Vietnamese inflicting heavy losses on the North and sustaining heavy casualty numbers themselves. Those Marines were no longer there by 1970 and that made the North's advances south that much easier.

Born in 1971 at Fort Carson, Colo., my ties to Vietnam come from my father, who served in the Ripcord Area of Operation. Through him and members of the Ripcord Association, this book took shape. It is imperative to note that as a journalist and writer, it is my job to tell the story of these men - as told by these men. Every effort was made to corroborate every man's story, though it has to be noted that as so many of the men who spoke to me for this project correctly stated, two men could stand three feet apart in the jungles of South Vietnam battling in the same firefight and remember completely different versions. That is not due to the fact that one is not being completely honest, it is due to the fact that war is chaotic and confusing. It is widely referred to as the "fog of war." Those two men most likely did see completely different versions and that, too, speaks to the incredibly difficult task of recounting a single firefight, much less an entire battle.

"I was in so damn much combat it's hard to remember if this combat came before that combat," said Lt. James Noll, who led a platoon from Alpha Company longer than the six months officers were supposed to be in the field, and was pulled only after earning a second Purple Heart and a familiar stubborn willingness to limp back into the field to be with his men.

Noll arrived in South Vietnam in October 1969. A teacher in Minnesota, Noll enlisted because, as he noted, he knew he'd get drafted. In Vietnam, he flew to Phu Bai, where he was assigned to the 101st Airborne, a well-respected unit with a rich history. The 101st was also fresh in the news having gone through the Battle of Hamburger Hill in May 1969 and Noll was well-versed in his division's history, past and present.

"We were very aware of what was going on with the Hamburger Hill thing," said Noll. "There was a lot of fighting going on in the A Shau Valley, not just Hamburger Hill. My company was the only company in the battalion to get the assignment to attack Hamburger Hill. Alpha Company came in fresh, full up with people. When they attacked, of course they were rested. They ended up being the first unit on top of Hamburger Hill."

In the wake of the brutal combat at Dong Ap Bia, Americans stateside saw what was fought for, and won, by the men of the 101st Airborne, only to have it abandoned and the North Vietnamese return within weeks. It was a showcase of two clear overreaching problems Americans saw with the United States' involvement in Vietnam: A lack of objectives and body count over territory. Americans never saw, or heard, what an end result may look like in Vietnam.

So much goes into recounting this important piece of American history and what shouldn't be lost in these stories is the fact these men either enlisted or answered the call of their country via the draft and, as young men, served honorably without all the typical trappings associated with

American soldiers in Vietnam. They deserved our respect then, and got little, and deserve our respect today, and continue – for the most part – to be an afterthought to the average American.

Thankfully, through the Department of Defense's effort to recognize the 50th anniversary of troop combat in Vietnam, more attention is being paid to the role of the American soldier in Vietnam and what was accomplished. Through this effort, some of the truths from Vietnam are being explained so that future generations don't further perpetuate falsehoods that took root in American culture during and in the months and years following the war.

America was rife with change in the early 1960s and early 1970s. Civil rights issues plagued those living stateside while men of every color and creed fought alongside one another a world away, fighting to keep one another alive. It's an amazing juxtaposition. Drugs were prevalent in Vietnam, though not nearly to the extent portrayed by the media. More accurate accounts put the drug usage on par with the same demographic stateside. The men of the 101st associated with the Ripcord Battle overwhelmingly testify that their experiences were largely void of drug use. It's easy to see why given their constant battle to simply stay alive to see the next day. Staying sharp was instrumental in that attempt and officers, to their credit, instilled discipline in the young men of the 101st to ensure these young men had every opportunity to fulfill the mission and return home.

Did drug use exist in Vietnam? Of course, and it's no different than any other war at any other time in American history. Drug usage by Americans in Vietnam was largely relegated to rear areas as it was simply too dangerous in the field, especially in I Corps in 1970.

The Screaming Eagles were also puzzled by another popular American misconception: That troops were committing atrocities against the Vietnamese people. Nothing could have been further from the truth for the men of the 101st Airborne Division working the Ripcord AO in 1970. Any villagers that may have been in the area were long gone and pacification and relocation programs had already been enacted.

"In Vietnam, the people live – the Vietnamese people – live along the coastal plains," explained the late Gen. Sidney Berry in a post-dinner speech at the 1987 Ripcord Association reunion. "Very few people more than 20 miles from the coast – particularly in Thua Thien Province, the one in which the 101st conducted most of its operations. When you went even 10 miles from the coast, you started getting into the piedmont, jungle land. And then as you went in another – maybe it was one mile, it may have been 10 miles – you started getting into mountains, mountains that would make the Blue Ridge (stateside) look like foothills. Mountains, strangely enough, that have jungle growing all over them - triple canopy, as we called – three levels of vegetation.

"It was in that non-populated area – which was up against… ultimately against the Laotian border – that's where the North Vietnamese Army – regular army troops of the North Vietnamese Army – established its bases. They brought down their supplies from the north, through the trails of Laos, hooked onto South Vietnam and into our province, established caches (as we called them) of weapons, ammunition, put in their hospitals, their base camps. And then, at their own good time, they would strike out."

Tens of thousands of American soldiers never saw villagers, never saw anyone other than an enemy soldier focused only on inflicting death and demoralization against the Americans. Adding to the complexity of the situation was the preparedness of the North Vietnamese troops in the area, numbers of North Vietnamese troops, which remained largely unknown, or unsure at best, throughout the Ripcord campaign.

Then there was the reality of what was happening stateside, much of which would prove baffling to those fighting for their lives in South Vietnam.

Tet of 1968 was an overwhelming loss for the North Vietnamese. Tens of thousands of troops were killed and it all but ended the north's efforts in the south. Yes, several small towns succumbed to the sudden ambushes and Hue was a site of tremendous loss for the Americans, however the Allies beat back the Northern advances made during Tet. One must remember also that in areas south of I Corps, military Rules of Engagement existed, which hindered American troops' advantages over the North and Viet Cong.

The invasion of Cambodia and Laos also ruffled feathers stateside and threw into question the expenditure of money and young American bloodshed.

Media played its role as well. CBS' Walter Cronkite, who arrived in Saigon in 1968 to see for himself what was happening in the wake of Tet, famously told the American public that the war was at a stalemate and likely "unwinnable." His words provided grave misinformation to Americans watching the war unfold on their televisions and in the living rooms. President Lyndon Johnson even saw the broadcast and admitted that if he'd lost Cronkite then he'd likely lost middle America. In the wake of Cronkite's cataclysmic forecast, Johnson did not seek re-election.

Misinformation such as that provided by the television media was prevalent throughout the war. In defense of the media, how do you accurately report a war like that in Vietnam? Being on the ground in Loc Ninh or Con Thien was not like being on the ground in Saigon or Da Nang, or even Hue.

Media reports proved to be just another rallying cry for antiwar sentiment that continued to build stateside in 1970.

Politics weighed the matter down even further. Gen. William Westmoreland wanted additional troops. Congress and the Pentagon didn't want to give them to him and he was soon pushed out, replaced by Creighton Abrams, who served as general during the Ripcord battle. While men from the 101st battled in the Ripcord Area of Operations, military brass met and debated whether or not the area could be held. Casualty counts were to be kept low in an area where death was a day-to-day reality.

Add it all up, advance to spring of 1970 and the insertion of the 101st Airborne at Firebase Ripcord and you effectively have a situation that was seemingly unwinnable. Support for the war was practically non-existent stateside. Washington was pulling troops out of the country and there was but one division left to stem the tide of North Vietnamese advances south.

By 1970, the Vietnam War was an albatross around the neck of politicians in Washington, increasingly unpopular to average Americans and deadly for those still serving on the ground, especially those in I Corps, south of the Demilitarized Zone and into the vast jungle and mountainous terrain of the A Shau Valley.

Stationed in I Corps, the men of the 101st manned an expanded AO (Area of Operations) that once included full Marine divisions, all of which were long gone. As American troops were decreasing, violence in I Corps remained steady and, at times, increased.

"What was U.S. policy? U.S. policy was to withdraw all of the American armed forces from Vietnam," said Berry in his speech at the Ripcord Association reunion. "That policy had begun at least as early, I think, as March of 1968, when then-President Lyndon B. Johnson announced that he was not going to run for re-election as president. He decided that, I believe – and it has been well documented – because he knew that he could not be re-elected because of the divisiveness of Vietnam as an issue. So he withdrew himself.

"President Nixon – barely elected in November of 1968 – took office in January of 1969. In June of 1969 – June 8th – on Midway Island in the Pacific, President Thieu of the Republic of Vietnam and President Dick Nixon of the United States of America met. And they announced in a press release or communique – which obviously had been written before then – that the United States was going to start withdrawal of its forces from Vietnam, which began in July of 1969. The first increment was 25,000 soldiers, or armed forces personnel.

"At the same time it was announced that what was called – and I think this is a suspect term – Vietnamization was to begin. That is, that Vietnamese armed forces were to take the place of American forces in the combat operations in Vietnam. So, a full year before our experience of Ripcord – which was really from March of '70 until the 23rd of July of '70 – a full year before then, the American policy was announced: withdrawal of American forces; turn the war over to the Vietnamese. That's the overall context in which you and I were serving around Ripcord."

While troops were being pulled out elsewhere, replacement troops, mostly young men ages 19 and 20, kept funneling north to replace casualties few knew of from the 101st. The replacement troops never truly replaced troop strength in the AO, though. Units constantly dealing with an influx of new blood – commonly referred to as FNGs (Fucking New Guys) or cherries did little to better the combat troops' effectiveness in the field. Coupled with the six-month rotation (from the field to the rear) for officers, and the influx of fresh troops in the field, no one in uniform ever really became comfortable with one another.

The confluence of events is enough to make most heads spin, and still does. It's not something that didn't happen in World War II or Korea, however it was profoundly exaggerated in Vietnam, especially by 1970.

To turn the war over to the South Vietnamese and the Army of the

Republic of Vietnam (ARVN), U.S. troops had to at least thwart the north's push southward, a push that did not wane simply because the U.S. troops were on their way out. Left to take on the challenge: The Screaming Eagles.

"Why did we establish Ripcord?" asked Berry. "Let me put you into the frame – the thinking of the people of the higher command. That is, down in Saigon, at MACV (Military Assistance Command, Vietnam), and even above there. This is the last full American division in Vietnam. The withdrawal is steadily going on. It's not long before American forces are going to be out. And the higher command wants those of us in the 101st to conduct offensive operations against the North Vietnamese Army. Why? So that, when our division leaves; we can have given the best chance possible to the Vietnamese to survive as a noncommunist state.

"And that's why you establish Ripcord and you operate around it. Really because that's the westernmost of our firebases and operating bases as again, we are trying to move out – leapfrog out from our firebase to another, using helicopters as our mobility, going back out toward the Laotian border, through which all those North Vietnamese Army supplies and reinforcements are coming.

"The whole focus, then, is on Ripcord as a stepping stone back out toward the Laotian border, and toward the A Shau Valley."

Berry went on to note that offensive operations included attacks against the enemy, while keeping casualties low, at least as far as Washington was concerned.

"This is usually unspoken," he said, "but it's very clearly communicated – because in this withdrawal phase, Americans can't stand, can't stomach a lot of casualties. They'll raise questions that we who are at the civil level of government cannot adequately answer.

"That's what you have to live with when you're at the division level. How do you attack without taking casualties? But there's a more basic question for those of us in the 101st Airborne Division. How do you protect yourself without attacking? If we sit passively on that coastal strip, and if we sit in our Camp Evans, and Camp Eagle, and Phu Bai – if we just sit there passively, what the hell is going to happen?"

The answer to that question is clear. Given that, the reality is that in order for troops to continue to exist and serve, they must attack. That is how to best minimize casualties.

"So – withdraw American forces, attack while you're still there, but don't take many casualties," said Berry. "You hear all this, but on our level at the 101st Airborne Division, we do what we think we have to do - which simply for our survival and preservation of life, is to go out and continue to operate as soldiers must do when they're in a combat zone."

So Operation Texas Star began in April under the guidance of Maj. Gen. John Wright, commanding general of the 101st. Taking part: The 3rd Brigade of the 101st and the ARVN 1st Infantry Division. The job: Find the enemy, scattered among 800 square miles, and prevent the push to the populated areas south of the A Shau Valley.

Little did anyone know that the 101st was about to become part of the longest battle of the Vietnam War, the Battle of Firebase Ripcord. It's a battle that was basically hidden from the civilian population and proved a mystery to even military men who served elsewhere in the country during that period of 1970. From March 12, through July 23, 1970, the 101st took part in the final mass offensive of the war. It was a four-month period that proved bloody to both the Americans and the North Vietnamese Army.

Look at the numbers. President Harry Truman first sent advisers into Vietnam in 1950. By 1959, four Americans had been killed in Vietnam.

In 1960, that number grew to nine. Mission creep, escalation and the draft drew more Americans to Southeast Asia, and more and more went home in body bags. The Battle of Ia Drang Valley (1965), Con Thien (1967-68) the battle of Hue (1968), the Batttle of Khe Sahn (1968), the Tet Offensive (1968) and the Battle of Dong Ap Bia or "Hamburger Hill" (1969), which also featured members of the 101st Airborne Division, remain well known to those familiar with Vietnam while Ripcord remains rarely reported and even less often remembered. Americans were dying by the thousands in 1968 and 1969, the deadliest years of the war. By 1970, numbers of dead dipped, however troops were being withdrawn and fighting was mostly concentrated in northern South Vietnam.

President Lyndon Johnson sent the Marines to the area in March 1965 to stem the tide of North Vietnamese regulars from filtering south with troops and supplies along the Ho Chi Minh Trail and through the A Shau. From the Central Highlands north to the Demilitarized Zone, two Marine divisions and seven Army divisions went to work.

America's military entering Vietnam was its most educated, well-trained and best equipped in history, according to the Department of Defense. The 101st performed well, as you will read.

I Corps became synonymous with horrific combat over the next several years with Marines battling in coastal villages and along the Demilitarized Zone, which left much of the A Shau ignored.

Hamburger Hill was at the mouth of the A Shau. A beautiful valley, it was originally inhabited by the Christian Montagnards, who throughout the war proved to be the Americans' most consistent and cooperative allies.

While few troops found their way into the triple-canopied jungles and soaring peaks of the A Shau, the North Vietnamese took advantage of the Montagnard footpaths to build tunnels, bunkers, and ammunition caches. It became a massive fortress of sorts, hidden from view.

After the Tet Offensive, Gen. Westmoreland set out to cut off the North Vietnamese supply routes stemming from the A Shau and fighting from Hue, north and east, erupted in March 1968.

By April, the 1st Cavalry Division, which had beaten back an entire North Vietnamese regiment in the Battle of the Ia Drang Valley nearly three years earlier, was tasked with Operation Delaware, which soon fell victim to a news blackout when 10 choppers were shot down en route to the A Shau. Nearly two dozen were damaged.

On the ground, there was little resistance and soon victory was declared, but the Americans, working with the 1st ARVN (Army of the Republic of Vietnam) Division, did not secure the area.

The 1st Cavalry Division, then stationed at Camp Evans, was relocated throughout the country and the 101st Airborne Division, headquartered at Camp Eagle, south and east of Hue, began manning firebases spreading north and west of Hue throughout the valley. It was during this time that Camp Evans was turned over to the 3rd Brigade of the 101st Airborne Division.

In March 1969, the 2nd Brigade was mired in fighting with the North Vietnamese Army at Bloody Ridge as the 101st attempted to push the enemy from the valley. The NVA retreated westward toward Laos. Operation Apache Snow, spearheaded by the 3rd Brigade, combat assaulted from the air and found the 29th NVA Regiment entrenched along the western-most mountains of the A Shau, which included Dong Ap Bia, Hill 937 to American troops.

From May 11-20, the battle to become known as Hamburger Hill claimed 56 American lives and more than 400 American casualties. The 101st, a unit that prided itself on its ability and ferocity, was suddenly under a microscope, having endured so many casualties.

Hamburger Hill has often been cited as a pivotal moment in the war as

Americans witnessed much of the carnage on the television sets in their living rooms, then became confused when the Screaming Eagles took the hill, only to evacuate the hard-fought-for hilltop days later.

Of the 58,220 American troop deaths attributed to the Vietnam War, more than 40,000 of those deaths came between 1967 and 1969. The impact of Hamburger Hill cannot be overstated as it took place just months before the offensive that became the Battle of Firebase Ripcord.

The 101st pulled out of the A Shau in August 1969, after Dong Ap Bia and before an all-weather airstrip was to be built on the valley floor.

President Richard Nixon's Vietnamization Program – the reduction of American forces in South Vietnam – began in July 1969, just as the 101st Airborne Division saw its Area of Operation expand. That fall and winter, during the monsoons, the north refurbished its supplies along the trails snaking through the valley.

Once the weather broke, the 101st sought to attack in the valley to thwart the North's attempts to flow through to the south in what would be known as Operation Chicago Peak.

Ripcord was an abandoned firebase about 11 miles north and west of Dong Ap Bia, along the western fringe of the A Shau Valley.

The bloodshed from Dong Ap Bia, coupled with the reality of reactions following Hamburger Hill, led to the decision by the 101st to prohibit any media coverage of what was happening in the area of Ripcord. It wasn't until Keith Nolan's "Ripcord: Screaming Eagles Under Siege" was published in 2000 that Americans first got a glimpse of the horrors that played out for hundreds of Screaming Eagles battling an NVA division intent on keeping its flow southward uninterrupted.

To that point, the NVA rarely engaged American troops in sustained battles. The North Vietnamese historically relied on ambush, hit-and-run tactics and the element of surprise to keep the Americans on edge, to suppress morale. By the time the 101st set up shop atop Firebase Ripcord, the North Vietnamese shifted strategy, opting to stay and fight. It created the longest battle of the war and proved horrific for both sides.

The last full American division left in Vietnam, the Screaming Eagles were tasked with manning the two northernmost provinces of the Republic of Vietnam. Those provinces were obviously easy for the North Vietnamese Army to supply and patrol.

"That is where – during the spring and summer of 1970 – the fiercest, most prolonged ground fighting was going on in Vietnam," said Berry. "It is also, by the way, where the greatest American casualties continued to be taken."

Everyone in the world knew the United States was withdrawing from Vietnam in 1970. The only ones who didn't know? The Screaming Eagles. The young men of the 101st fought valiantly and did so for one another. Even today, the bonds that exist between these men remain incredibly strong.

Unlike their brothers in arms from World War I, World War II or Korea, men who fought in Vietnam did not travel to the battlefield as a unit. By the time Ripcord began, it was a matter of flying small groups of replacements to the battlefield, often a single man on a chopper or groups of two to three men. They were flown in to stem the tide of casualties that mounted along the trails surrounding the firebases. Already understrength, companies dwindled well below the normal figures typically associated with company and platoon sizes within the larger battalion.

"We were going through soldiers so fast it was almost hard to write their names down before you lost them," said Jim Noll, who went on to enjoy a 33-year military career. "What I did was I would team up a new soldier with an experienced soldier and the policy there was you stay together, do everything together so you're never alone. That way, you could always count on one another. You really bonded. If someone got hurt, you always knew someone had your back. If you had to walk point that day, you knew your buddy would be walking slack. If you had to put a claymore out at night, your buddy would have to guard you."

"My thing there, my idea was to do your job as best you could. You had missions to accomplish but I always looked at it and prayed I'd make the right decisions with God's help. I put it in God's hands. I'd make the decisions, no bull-shitting around. We'd accomplish the mission with as few casualties as humanly possible. We always tried to keep the unit and the soldiers safe. It was taking care of people in extreme circumstances."

For the Americans, returning home after the battle was tough enough on its own, but to add insult to injury, they returned to an apathetic, if not downright hostile American public, a tough pill to swallow given the sacrifices they made, and saw, in the jungles of a foreign land.

Veterans returning from Vietnam were ignored, chastised and shunned when they returned to the United States. As hard as it may be for subsequent generations to understand, given the overwhelming support today's troops receive from average Americans, those returning from Vietnam weren't welcomed home. In fact, many returned home to have superiors tell them upon landing stateside to shed their military fatigues for civilian clothes for fear of attack – by their fellow Americans.

Even that did little as sun-tanned skin and fresh haircuts made those returning from Southeast Asia easy targets for those waiting in protest.

1

A Not-So Welcome Home

Tim Newman lived through a hell few can comprehend as part of the famed 101st Airborne Division, a member of Alpha Company, Second Battalion/506th Regiment. A draftee who had to learn to fight, or die quickly in an unforgiving jungle, Newman and the rest of Alpha Company choppered in under fire on the first day of the campaign, March 12, 1970, and was among the last to be choppered out more than four months later, battered and bloodied following a month-long siege that ended July 23 with a heroic rescue by Delta Company.

Tim's story is not unlike many of his fellow Ripcord veterans in that he endured so much, witnessing the loss of brothers in arms and enduring conditions few can even imagine – heat, humidity, earthworms the size of snakes and torrential rains. He did what his country asked of him and when his time was up, he returned home pleased to be intact and headed home to the welcoming shores of the United States.

Finally stateside, he boarded a commercial airliner traveling from Seattle to his home in Buffalo. He sat alongside a middle-aged woman, a seemingly kind woman who he estimated to be in her 50s or 60s. His mistake, as he would find out, was simply that he was dressed in an American uniform as he quietly took his seat.

REMEMBERING FIREBASE RIPCORD

"I'm sitting with her in coach," said Newman. "There's three seats and there's just the two of us in the row. She started up a conversation and said, 'I see you are in the Army,' and she said, 'You weren't just over there in Vietnam were you?' She got up and made a big stink. She went over to the stewardesses and demanded to have her seat changed. She didn't want to sit next to me and began making all this commotion. They ended up putting her in first class and for the rest of the trip home, I was sitting all by myself wondering what the hell I did, what did I do wrong? No one on that plane came up to me to apologize for her. That was my welcome home from Vietnam, getting greeted like that and then someone getting better treatment than you. No one even came over to offer a drink or condolences."

The image Americans had of the Vietnam War was contrary to the reality of the men who fought and died at Ripcord. For the Ripcord veteran, there were no Viet Cong soldiers. There were no villages, no women, no children. There were only North Vietnamese regulars, men who served seven years or until death. There was only a well-trained, disciplined army that had but one order – exterminate American soldiers. Quite simply, the men who fought at Ripcord fought a battle no one knew about, then returned home to have to combat the popular misconceptions that existed about the war.

The North Vietnamese Army used the mountains in the A Shau as a staging area for weapons and troops heading south. Battalions of North Vietnamese would amass against the Americans, intent on holding what they saw as their ground in an attempt to win over the South Vietnamese.

Nick Fotias was a pathfinder at Ripcord, charged with directing helicopter traffic and communication on and off the firebase and other firebases in the I Corps area of service. He, like most pathfinders, was wounded, nearly killed. He was witness to unspeakable trauma in service of his country, yet upon returning home, he, like many, kept it all inside.

A NOT-SO WELCOME HOME

"We all went through that," said Fotias, of Delaware. "It was just a crazy time. The American people weren't too supportive at that time."

Edward Carnes served in the Special Forces, then arrived in the Ripcord Area of Operations over the final month of the battle, opting to serve as a medic. He lost 13 fellow crew members and saw unspeakable horror as a member of a medevac crew.

"I just never thought I was going home," he said.

When he did, he was confronted as he walked through Chicago's O'Hare Airport in uniform.

"I was called a baby killer," said Carnes. "A guy wanted to fight me."

Americans had no idea just how heroic and brave these young men were in the face of almost unfathomable odds. If they had only known that these young men had lived much of the previous year in holes, trekking through triple-canopy jungles and fending off monsoon rains, jungle rot and leeches while battling a fierce, determined enemy.

Floyd Alexander lived through his own personal hell on July 22 and 23 with Alpha Company. He earned three Bronze Stars, saved numerous lives and thought repeatedly that he'd never see American soil again.

When he finally earned his trip home, it included a welcome from three strangers at three in the morning in a Texas airport.

"I didn't want to get a hotel room so I just stayed at the airport," said Alexander. "These three hippies, two guys and a girl come by. She called me a baby killer. I had already been told I wouldn't be treated well so I knew it was going to happen. I didn't say anything. She said, 'Did you hear what I said? I said you're a baby killer.' I got ready to fight because I knew one of them was either going to spit on me or hit me. I still didn't answer, though. If they spit on me they would have had to kill me because I wasn't going to put up with that. She was trying to provoke me into a fight. It wasn't going to happen."

By 1970, the Marines had been pulled out of the I Corps region. President Richard Nixon was pulling troops out of Vietnam, hoping his Vietnamization Program would leave soldiers in the south fighting for their own cause. Not all plans go as expected.

It's a story Americans know little of as a media blackout prevented the press from covering the happenings in the Ripcord AO (Area of Operation). Too far north of Saigon, the few journalists that made it north to Camp Evans, the support base for the Ripcord AO, were always turned away. It was just months after the carnage of Hamburger Hill, just a few kilometers south and west of Ripcord, which created gory headlines stateside and raised questions about the tactics of the 101st Airborne.

Months later, when the campaign at Ripcord was to begin, a media blackout was put into effect so as to not raise suspicions over the operation the 101st Airborne would be undertaking. The division could not afford more bad press, hence the blackout. Division was challenged to conduct its operations – thwart the enemy push southward – with low casualty numbers while trekking through the jungle with understrength platoons and companies.

Over the next four-and-a-half months, the Screaming Eagles fought throughout the area against all odds, constantly undermanned, as the number of Americans in Vietnam continued to shrink.

Veterans of Ripcord were never afforded a welcome home, a sympathetic shoulder or even a congratulatory slap on the back. They were simply ignored. They buried their memories and turned to one another years later, the only ones who would listen, the only ones who could understand. Reunions proved to be incredibly therapeutic for these veterans in years to come.

A NOT-SO WELCOME HOME

"When Ripcord veterans came home, they knew they were coming home from a serious battle," said Frank Marshall, a draftee from north Philadelphia. "When (Ripcord veterans) talked to other Vietnam veterans, they would say they hadn't even heard of Ripcord. It was like it didn't exist. They would talk about Hamburger Hill or about movies like 'Platoon,' where the soldiers didn't like each other."

That wasn't the reality for the Ripcord veteran. He served his country, but he fought for his brother beside him, and the soldier next to him. The bond these men share to this day is unlike any other amongst veterans because in 1970, they had only each other, something most combat veterans can relate to. Unique to the Ripcord veteran was the brutality of war they witnessed, experiences most just buried as they came home and realized the public didn't want them. The hell these men endured, the pain, the memories, it was all stashed away, for decades in many cases.

"When we came back from Vietnam no one really wanted to know," remembered Newman. "The reputation we had, no one really wanted us."

"The story's not told," said Marshall. "It still hurts."

2

Kill or Be Killed

A Chinook bearing the Screaming Eagle approaches Firebase Ripcord with a slingload in early July 1970. Photo provided by James Saller.

The 101st Airborne Division carries with it a rich history. First activated in 1942, the Screaming Eagles were the first to parachute into occupied France in World War II and cleared the way for the 4th Infantry Division's landing on Utah Beach. The first boots hit the ground in Vietnam in July 1965 and the Screaming Eagles fought from Saigon to the Central Highlands and into the A Shau Valley to the Demilitarized Zone throughout the war. The men from the 101st famously fought and took "Hamburger Hill" in May 1969, though more than 50 were killed. Among the first combat troops in Vietnam, the 101st was the last full division in country and suffered one of the highest casualty rates among Army divisions over the course of the entire war.

For those who were being sent to the A Shau in late 1969 and early 1970, there was no disillusionment when it came to what they would see. Fighting in the valley was notoriously brutal and the North Vietnamese Army regulars were known for being tough, well-trained, courageous fighters. Underlying the ferocity of life in the jungle was a series of decisions in Washington dating back to President John F. Kennedy (the advancement of an airmobile Army) and cycling through President Lyndon Johnson's escalation of the war and President Richard Nixon's Vietnamization Program.

"In 1970, we'd been involved since 1965," said Capt. Randy House, who flew helicopter missions around Ripcord from March through the end of July and commanded a company on the ground as well. "Ia Drang Valley fight happened in '65 (7th Cavalry's infamous battle made famous with the publication of "We Were Soldiers Once, And Young" and the movie "We Were Soldiers" starring Mel Gibson, Sam Elliott and Greg Kinnear). It was the first time American recruits, other than Special Forces, had fought North Vietnamese regulars, not just VC (Viet-Cong, the guerilla-tactic fighters typically found in South Vietnam and along the Mekong Delta). Five years later in '70 and the American people – remember we'd had My Lai (massacre of hundreds of Vietnamese civilians by American troops), we'd had Tet (Offensive) of '68, which we now know we won, but that's not how it came out. By the time I got to Vietnam, people were down on the Vietnam War and it wasn't just that they were down on the war, they were down on soldiers, sailors, airmen and Marines. They were down on the people that were doing the fighting that hadn't voted to go to war. These kids were in high school when those decisions were made."

Now those kids were in Vietnam, and in a place where it was kill or be killed.

"It don't mean nothin'" meant survival to the American infantryman, commonly known as grunts. These 18-, 19- and 20-year-old young men, many of whom were draftees, went into combat labeled by their comrades as cherries or FNGs (fucking new guys). They were plucked from their lives stateside – girlfriends, wives, newborn children, jobs, cars – to serve in a war that at that point in time was considered by many a lost cause. President Richard Nixon's doomed Vietnamization Program, intended to turn the battle over to the South Vietnamese, was in effect and American troops were coming home in larger numbers.

Fewer and fewer that left were being replaced.

For those who ended up near the A Shau Valley in 1970, just months after the carnage at Hamburger Hill, it was a matter of survive and move on, "It don't mean nothin'" was code for "block it out and move on." Ignore the pain. Put the horror out of your mind. It meant stepping up when the buddy you'd relied on the last six weeks in the jungle had just had his arm or leg shorn off by an RPG, it meant stepping over the dead and wounded in order to avoid becoming one of the same. It was survive today and live to see tomorrow - day by day, month by month until it was time to go home. They served their time, fought heroically for each other and did what they were supposed to do. They were a tremendous thorn in the side of the North Vietnamese plan.

They paid a heavy cost, though.

Grunts at Ripcord saw action daily, bumping into the enemy early in the morning, in the heat of the day, in the dead of night. Ambushes, Sapper attacks, mortar rounds, RPGs ripping through Night Defensive Positions, it was all part of the process. While Americans back home thought the war was winding down, the young men at Ripcord saw carnage the average person can't imagine. The pain lives with these men to this day.

Contrary to the claims of protestors of the day, the men of the 101st never saw villages, women or children, just NVA regulars, a group of soldiers trained to kill.

As Frank Marshall, a draftee from North Philadelphia said of his time in I Corps, "Everyone I saw was enemy. It was cut and dry." The confusion of guerilla warfare further south was distant past by 1970. Men like Marshall arrived home unable to fit in, often unable to sleep and at times, unable to cope with what they witnessed as kids barely out of high school in the dense jungles and hilltops a world away.

"You can live to be 150 years old, you'll never, ever forget the first ambush you walk into," said Floyd Alexander, a member of Alpha Company. "It was just like hell opened up on you – machine gun fire, trees falling around you, shooting everywhere. I didn't think I'd ever live through it."

"When you are in the middle of a battle, or a war, there is little if any time to reflect on the correctness of what you are doing," said Marc Aronson, artillery. "As has been said before, it is a game played by old men at the expense of young men."

The bonds formed by the Screaming Eagles over those four-and-a-half months live to this day. For those who made it home, the memories of that time in that far-away place prove to be something that only they can truly understand. Even now they rely on one another, just as they did in those days in jungle warfare. It's how they made it home. Battered, bruised and mentally scarred, they made it home.

"It don't mean nothin.'"

3

Frustrations Mount

Exhausted, Marc Aronson gets some sleep on the firebase alongside spent artillery shells. Sleep is something few men achieved on near-constant alert in the Ripcord Area of Operation. Photo provided by Chris Jensen.

By the time President Lyndon Johnson had taken office, he wanted the financial costs of war curtailed. His decision not to declare a state of emergency, therefore not permitting the Army to extend enlistments of the country's best and brightest, and most experienced soldiers, drew criticism from the nation's military chiefs. The decision also meant there would be no mobilization of reserves or National

FRUSTRATIONS MOUNT

Guard, rather a stream of draftees, numbering about 20,000 each month, would be trained to do the fighting, and ultimately end up among the casualties.

Those who fought at Ripcord delayed North Vietnamese Army (NVA) advances by more than a year, ultimately saving lives, tens of thousands of lives, by some estimates, hundreds of thousands of lives. They did their jobs and they did it against incredible odds.

The A Shau Valley was a pipeline and staging area for the NVA. For those in the area prior to April, there was little in the way of contact. Bob Worrall was 1st Platoon leader, Bravo Company, 2nd/501st. "My four months in the field were during the rainy season in northern I Corps and the NVA were more interested in stockpiling ammo and supplies in caves and bunkers by the A Shau Valley than in attacking U.S. troops in the field. During four full months in the field from the first week of December 1969 through the last week of March 1970, 1st Platoon had one enemy contact – a trail watcher keeping an eye on a ridgeline close to a downed U.S. helicopter in late February '70."

By contrast, Worrall's successor, Bob Layton, lost four men in his first day in the field. "April 1970, the NVA wanted to fight," said Worrall.

American brass didn't grasp just how many NVA troops were in those jungles, just how many NVA were entrenched as the choppers carrying the Screaming Eagles began flowing into the area in March 1970. Also known as "The Valley Of Death" A Shau's reputation preceded it with those who fought in its jungles, on its hilltops and along its flowing waterways.

Capt. Randy House was 25 when he first rose above the A Shau in an American chopper. A Texas A&M graduate, House thought he would one day be a horse doctor. Little did he know his desire to fight in Vietnam would end up leading to a decades-long distinguished career in the military. "I did what the Army told me to do," he humbly acknowledged. By 1970, House was flying Hueys in and out of Ripcord, was there from day one and was among those that planned the evacuation July 23. He was the lead ship into the valley to deliver Delta Company on its rescue mission of Alpha Company. It later included commanding the 2nd Brigade of the 1st Cavalry Division during Operations Desert Shield and Desert Storm.

"The year before, Hamburger Hill was a military disaster and a worse political disaster for the administration," said House. "A year later we get this other huge battle, Ripcord. I'm convinced it wasn't covered up. We were pulling out and the press and others were focused other places. Because of the situation, the soldiers that fought there, when you have a battalion commander (Lt. Col. Andre Lucas) that gets a Medal of Honor posthumously, that's a hell of a fight. You go back in history, go back to World War II, Korea and research how few battalion commanders get the Medal of Honor period. So when Andre Lucas gets the Medal of Honor that is a heck of a fight. Nothing was covered up, the story was just never told. It was the end, we were pulling out, this was' 70 we'd been fighting five years, those last five years we were getting out and trying not to have fights like Ripcord."

What the American public didn't know was just how much blood was shed in the Ripcord Area of Operation over those four-and-a-half months

Truth is, more than half of the American casualties from the Vietnam War came from I Corps, an area just south of the Demilitarized Zone in northern South Vietnam, far from the villages and cities, where news reports often originated, and the Mekong Delta, where the Viet Cong conducted guerilla tactics against American troops and the Army of the Republic of Vietnam (ARVN).

Marc Aronson served on Firebase Ripcord as an artillery gunner. He summed up what life in the A Shau Valley area, nestled in the heart of

FRUSTRATIONS MOUNT

I Corps, was like rather simply when he wrote, "I was shipped north to the 101st Airborne. I still remember landing on my first firebase, although I do not remember the name. When I was down south I thought I was in the war. When I got to the 101st, I found out I had been in Disneyland instead. These guys up north were in the war! I remember insulting them about how dirty their gun was; they thought it was clean."

A 20-year-old draftee from Winston-Salem, N.C., Bruce Brady landed in I Corps in March 1970 and saw first-hand the toll fighting took on soldiers in a short amount of time.

"Being new and considered cherries, you weren't accepted right away," said Brady (Alpha Company, 2nd/506th). "A lot of your fellow soldiers kept their distance because they felt you were a liability."

For the experienced trooper, it was a matter of survival. Replacements had to earn their respect. Such was the life of a hardened soldier tasked with tracking troops from the North Vietnamese Army.

The A Shau Valley and the four northwestern most provinces in South Vietnam were home to the bloodiest of battles in the Vietnam War. In the wake of the Battle of Firebase Ripcord, the four-and-half month troop on troop clash left the jungle scarred, cratered and shaken with the remnants of a vicious confrontation. The human toll was worse, as the jungle has an incredible ability to recover, with new growth popping up within days. Records showed 269 Americans killed, more than 1,300 wounded, 18 missing in action. Enemy losses reported by American brass included 1,273 killed in action, 73 killed by artillery, 377 killed by helicopter.

The Screaming Eagles were sent in to find the enemy, kill the enemy and destroy his supplies, supply routes and safe havens. They did so while being incredibly undermanned.

A division in the Army typically consisted of three brigades or between 10,000 and 18,000 soldiers. A brigade is three or more divisions made up of 3,000 to 5,000 soldiers. A battalion is comprised of three to five companies, or 500 to 600 soldiers. A company would typically include three to four platoons and consist of 100 to 200 soldiers. A platoon is three to four squads, or sixteen to forty soldiers and a squad is typically four to ten soldiers.

The last full fighting division left in Vietnam at the time, a time when President Richard Nixon's Vietnamization Program was being implemented, the 101st lacked full power, routinely hitting the jungles with undersized squads and platoons. Companies trekked through the jungle, making contact, engaging the enemy and taking casualties in ambushes and firefights. More than 1,103 enemy contacts were reported in the valley during Ripcord operations.

Fred Spaulding, who rose from the rank of captain to S-3 Air during his time at Ripcord noted the challenges operating with smaller numbers.

"There were 160 men in a rifle company," said Spaulding. "By '70 we might have had 95 to 100. We were already almost at fifty percent strength. By March, we were operating with roughly 75 to 95 men in a rifle company."

Its area of operations tripled and two Marine Divisions gone from the I Corps area, the men of the 101st Airborne were placed in a hornet's nest of activity, completely unaware the extent to which the NVA had entrenched itself in the various trails, bunker systems and safe havens established throughout the area in the days and months leading up to the decision to establish Firebase Ripcord.

Just as with the Battle of Ia Drang years earlier, the first battle with American regulars going toe to toe with NVA regulars, American brass simply had no idea just how many NVA were in the mountains.

FRUSTRATIONS MOUNT

The NVA proved to be well-trained, well-supplied and extremely committed. The NVA soldier committed to seven years, or death, while the American draftee served one year. Casualties and death didn't deter NVA troops intent on defending what they perceived as their turf. Wave after wave of troops infiltrated the hills, ridgelines and trails of the A Shau Valley. More worked underground.

Twenty six different Army units were in combat or supporting roles during those four months in the A Shau. The 2nd Battalion, 506th Infantry, famously known as the "Currahees", was the primary unit called to battle. It wasn't enough. Three American divisions had now been trimmed to one and there were plenty more NVA in the hills with more constantly flowing in.

Credible intelligence about the North Vietnamese troop strength in the area was scarce. For Col. Benjamin Harrison, the lack of intelligence was a source of frustration, something he made clear in his book, "Hell On A Hilltop" and in subsequent interviews.

"The poor and limited intelligence proved to the 3rd Brigade commander at this critical time (late June) is somewhere between disappointing and disgusting," wrote Harrison, in his book, "Hell On A Hilltop."

Communication in the field was, at times, poor as well, Harrison later said.

"That was very frustrating. You have a firebase and there would be a central command there with radio contact with other companies and they would want information and they wouldn't pass it on to the people on the hill because they weren't part of their intelligence net and I found that very frustrating."

When it came time to establish Ripcord, frustrations would only mount.

4

The Initial Assault

From left, Dan Biggs and Rodger "Chip" Collins, both members of Bravo Company. Photo provided by Dan Biggs.

"Everybody in the world started shooting at us." – Dan Biggs, Bravo Company

The A Shau Valley has been explained by many of the men who trekked through it as simply beautiful - snaking, thickly canopied trails winding from mountain ridges that soar over valleys anchored by winding creeks at the base of massive mountains. Soaring trees, rushing creeks with warm, flowing water and picturesque waterfalls provided a gorgeous natural landscape against the horrors of war being fought in the maze of jungle that stretched as far as the eye could see.

"Walking through the jungle I enjoyed when you weren't getting shot at," said Lee Widjeskog, a lieutenant in Alpha Company. Armed with a Bachelor of Science degree in wildlife biology and newly married, Widjeskog was a product of ROTC (Reserve Officer Training Corps). "Where I thought it was really hot was on the firebases."

Firebases were quickly erected mobile war centers that housed anywhere from a few to a few hundred American troops and equipment. Mountaintops were pummeled, then leveled and turned into dusty operations centers for the Americans. While there was safety in numbers atop the firebases, there was also danger as the North Vietnamese often knew the mountaintops and routinely had coordinates mapped for mortar rounds once the Americans set up shop.

"In the jungle, it was shaded," said Widjeskog." It was humid, but it was shaded. I didn't have the direct sun (like the firebases would). I also felt a lot safer in the jungle. I felt that we had more control. I was wrong. When you are on the firebase, you know they know where you are, you're just sitting there waiting for them to do something. Because there was no vegetation, the sun just beats back on you. In the jungle, it's hot and it was hard to climb up the hills."

Veterans of jungle warfare learned to listen to the sounds provided by nature and absorb the information she provided. Widjeskog was among those who took notice.

"If you had monkeys in the trees and fish and snails in the river - that was a good sign, because that meant the NVA hadn't been there in a while," he said. "They would scour the streams in the river for the fish and snails."

Dan Biggs arrived in late June as a replacement member of Bravo

Company. After getting his assignment at Camp Evans, he along with several other new GIs boarded a transport chopper headed to Firebase Ripcord, completely unaware of the danger just minutes away via chopper.

"We loaded up into this slick, three on one side, three on another. There were two pilots. We lifted up and we started flying out toward the A Shau Valley. We started following this stream. I thought 'Man how beautiful it is out here? It's green, there are rivers are flowing below me. We flew for about 20 minutes and up ahead we could see this waterfall, and then when we turned that corner, all hell broke loose. Everybody in the world started shooting at us, that's what it felt like. One shot would have been too many to me. Everybody on that chopper was looking at each other. We realized we were in deep shit."

While it may have been beautiful from above, it was hell on the ground. Relentless heat and humidity created deplorable conditions for those making the daily treks, weighed down by rucksacks, through the jungle. Young men from the 101st searched for North Vietnamese and their supplies, on the lookout for trails and bunkers. The wet conditions made jungle rot common and men would often have to pick leeches off one another at the end of the day.

The triple-canopy jungle was also tough for the chopper pilots to navigate in and out of. The lifelines for men in the jungle, they made their way through wind, rain and uncertainty to those on the ground. Choppers were the only way in or out of the jungle and in order to get supplies, men had to hump to landing zones (LZs) or blow their own, knocking down trees that soared to 150 feet above the jungle floor.

"It was a beautiful area," said Capt. Randy House, remembering his bird's-eye views from the Hueys he flew in the area. "It was hard, we were landing at times on a little ridge where only the back of your skids were on the ground and your front skids were just over the air and you

THE INITIAL ASSAULT

were looking straight down into a valley 1,000 feet below, right through the chin bubble of the helicopter. These pick-up zones and landing zones were really small. If they were down in the valley, (pilots) would hover down, where the trees were so high, come in, make your approach, come to a hover and sit down very carefully just missing tree limbs - sometimes even hitting them with your main rotor blades or tail rotor. When a crew chief tells you coming down, (as) you're coming down through the trees, 'OK sir move your tail four inches to the left, five inches to the right' and you know next to it is a tree the size of a sequoia."

Lt. Chuck Hawkins had arrived in Vietnam on Feb. 22 and joined the 2nd/506th in early March when he took over 2nd Platoon of Charlie Company under Capt. Isabelino Vazquez. Within a week, the self-described green lieutenant was green no more.

"As that first week unfolded the company found itself in a series of night-time firefights against the K-12 Sapper Battalion, which was sending small teams to attack U.S. positions in the field," said Hawkins. "Turned out the firebases were easier; troops in the field are more alert. Toward the end of that first week I took out my first night-time ambush patrol. Did it the Ranger way by having a larger element leave the NDP (Night Defensive Position), dropping off a four-man ambush team, and later the larger group returned to the NDP. Unless the enemy counted carefully all he should know is that a patrol went out and then returned.

"It rained that night. The ambush was a miserable event and we got nothing for our efforts.

"The next morning, back in the NDP (two of the company's four platoons had secured an old outpost on a hilltop on Rocket Ridge) we set about cleaning weapons. I noticed that the machine gunner who had been on the ambush with us the night before had his gas cylinder plug in backward. So, if we had made contact with the enemy our main firepower source would have been a single-shot machine gun. Not the gunner's fault, though he should have noticed the error by the sound the plug makes when turning the weapon up and down. The company armorer in the rear was responsible for making sure weapons are assembled correctly. It's the next level of maintenance above operator maintenance.

"I pitched a bitch through the company CP (Command Post) and the issue never recurred.

"Bottom line: The green lieutenant wasn't green any longer, and knew a lot more about some things from what the troops knew, but should have known. I started to become a teacher as well as a leader."

And so began a violent, deadly military campaign.

"How they were ready for us I'll never know, but they were ready for us."
– Lt. James Noll, Alpha Company, 2/506.

Attempts to secure a firebase began March 12 when choppers flew Alpha Company to Hill 902, south and west of Ripcord. Capt. Carmelito "Sonny" Arkangel and Bravo Company were inserted along a ridge south and east of the hill while a pair of ARVN companies landed on the west ridge.

The site was to be the 101st Airborne's key forward operating firebase in an effort to ultimately push into the A Shau. It was known the area was being used as a warehousing area for the North Vietnamese Army (NVA). North and west of Ripcord, near Firebase O'Reilly, NVA headquarters for its 324B Division had been established. Base camp was at the base of Hill 902, located about two-and-half kilometers south and slightly west of Ripcord. No one seemed to know how many NVA were in the hills, on the trails or underground, though. Ripcord was centrally located with 902 to the south, Hill 1,000 about a kilometer to the west and Hills 805 and 605 two and three kilometers east, respectively. Ripcord was lower in elevation than Hill 1,000, and that would prove to be a considerable issue as the campaign wore on.

Lt. James Noll, a platoon leader with Alpha Company, was twice wounded in Vietnam. His second Purple Heart came in mid-July when he and Bruce Brady, his RTO, were hit with shrapnel from a grenade. Photo provided by Bruce Brady.

Ripcord was originally slated to be an alternate landing zone for insertion plans at Hill 902. Battalion command was transitioning to Lt. Col. Andre Lucas by this time and the plan was to open a firebase along a ridgeline west of a series of already-established firebases in the valley. Lucas had assumed control as the day approached to send troops in.

Bill Heath, already in country five months, was part of Alpha Company, third platoon. On March 11, he was among a group that knew they would be heading into an area to secure a firebase. The men were given Coca-Colas during a re-supply, something that was a rarity, Heath noted.

"They knew what we'd be doing the next day," he said.

Alpha Company, under the command of Capt. Albert Burckard, choppered into the valley with the intent to land on Hill 902, which had been prepped for months to become the new firebase. That plan was short-lived as approaches revealed a hot landing zone and less-than-ideal conditions for landing troops. Only two of the landing zones were big enough. Dense vegetation forced a decision to be made as four platoons from Alpha Company were en route. Lucas and then-Brigade Commander William Bradley diverted the flights.

Burckard graduated from Virginia Military Institute (VMI) a second lieutenant in 1967, having attended Frederick Military Academy, Portsmouth, Va., during secondary school. His father served in the Army Air Corps in 1936 and his great-grandfather fought with the 11th New York Cavalry dating back to 1863.

"I had always wanted to be a soldier, before I can even remember," said Burckard. "About 1955 I was given a German helmet by a cousin who brought it back as a souvenir from World War II and I guess I was hooked on the Army after listening to stories about his combat (he was wounded in 1944 while crewing an anti-aircraft gun) experience.

THE INITIAL ASSAULT

Upon his graduation from VMI and his first tour of duty as an obligated volunteer in the Army Active Reserve, he extended indefinitely and volunteered for Vietnam. At 24 years old, he landed in Vietnam in 1969 an infantry captain and was assigned to the 101st Airborne, an assignment he embraced knowing the history of the division dating back to World War II.

By March, his Alpha Company was in the thick of it near the A Shau Valley.

"I learned of the LZ (Landing Zone) switch to Ripcord after our 14:20 (2:20 p.m.) pickup and were already in the air," wrote Burckard. "We had watched the Air Force prep Hill 902 the day before so I guess there was not time for much prep on Ripcord, if any, before we touched down there after about 40 minutes in the air. The LZ situation (hot or cold) really doesn't matter as long as the trees are cleared because you do the same thing as soon as the skids touch down – get your feet on the ground and get the hell away from the noisy and dangerous helicopter as quick as you can! You run for the first cover and concealment you see, get down and report the situation to higher up."

Adding to the confusion, ARVN (Army of the Republic of Vietnam) soldiers inserted north of the site had intelligence that indicated a large NVA presence in and around 902. Ray Hines, Artillery LNO (liaison officer) with the 2nd Battalion, 506th Infantry recalled enemy radar transmissions at the time.

"Lucas was the incoming commander," said Hines. "An insertion was planned just to the west of Ripcord at the time. If you were on Ripcord and looked to the west, the terrain dropped steeply into the valley, with a healthy stream flying from right (north) to left (generally south). West of the stream was a ridge that rose from the junction of the two streams and climbed to the tallest mountain around (Coc Muen, west of 902). Three company-sized insertions were planned, however there were only two landing zones large enough. The middle insertion site selected had an opening that was not big enough. Lt. Col. Howard Crowell sat in the right door on the bench (in the chopper), Lt. Col. Lucas was in the middle on this trip, Maj. Koenigsbauser was in the right jump seat and I sat on the bench in the left door. Lt. Col. Crowell's solution was to 'have the Air Force bomb the LZ to make it bigger.' When we came back for the insertions within the next couple of days, Lt. Col. Crowell was gone and Lt. Col. Lucas was in charge. The middle LZ did not get bombed, so the insertion was made on Ripcord. The LZ was hot."

"I told whoever was in charge, 'you know 902 is socked in,'" said Capt. Randy House. "These mountains, you're flying in terrible weather, December, January, February, March, April into May, it's the worst weather you've seen for mountain flying. We had an alternate LZ, because we always had one. I make a run, I try to get in and it's just socked in. I remember calling whoever was in charge and saying, 'we aren't going to get in anytime soon and if we want to put boots on the ground, we better go to the alternate.' The alternate ended up becoming (Ripcord)."

Ripcord, established by the 101st in 1969 was originally established in 1968 by the 1st Cavalry. Bunkers remained on the hill, some of which were used by the NVA, which controlled the hilltop as the Americans arrived.

Hueys carrying Alpha Company soared in as Burckard and second platoon got in and fourth platoon, under Lt. Dudley Davis, was moved north as the men took fire from the west. A half hour later, Davis and his radio telephone operator were dead in a hail of mortar rounds. First platoon arrived and moved west as third platoon stayed at the crest. Small arms fire continued from the north and west and would continue until air support was called in.

THE INITIAL ASSAULT

"My lead element, second platoon under Lt. Gary Kelly, landed with no incoming fire because, I suspect, the landing on Ripcord was as much a surprise to the NVA as to us," remembered Burckard. "We started taking fire as soon as my second unit, fourth platoon under Lt. Dudley Davis, touched down. My CP (Command Post) element was with the fourth platoon. I moved quickly up to the top of Ripcord to make a better assessment of the situation. That was when a Spec4 (specialist 4) next to me, was shot as well as the door gunner on the next UH-1 (Huey) and this NVA fire also brought down that helicopter. We later took the two door guns, M60s, off the chopper and used them against the NVA until the ammo ran out."

Third platoon, under Lt. Jim Noll was next to land, just as the mortar rounds started coming in more rapidly and with greater accuracy, Burckard noted.

Noll was a combat veteran, having served with the 101st in the A Shau since November. He had seen brutal combat in the months leading up to the March assault on Ripcord. He brought a sense of experience to the company and applied lessons learned to situations his platoon would experience.

Not even in the area when the assault began, Noll and his platoon had been working alone along a ridgeline, clearing a landing zone when the call came to move.

"We got a call on the radio, 'Get up to the LZ,'" remembered Noll. "We had to literally run. In come the helicopters and we could hear on the radio that part of our company had been picked up and dropped on Ripcord. It was unbelievable. We went from this real rough, piedmont area into the Annamite Mountains, which ranged from about 5,000 to 10,000 feet in elevation. We go into what was to become Ripcord and there's a helicopter on the pad, shot down. We look down and see the ground coming up at us. You could see the ridge of the mountain we're going to land on coming up. We had a couple of North Vietnamese pop up and shoot at us. They hit the helicopter and wounded a couple of the soldiers and door gunner. We did a shitty landing and I rolled out of there.

"(Burckard) grabbed me and said to get my unit and get over to the other ridgeline. He pointed and I thought, 'Oh crap!' He had another lieutenant come in and he grabbed that lieutenant, a West Pointer in his very first combat mission, and told him to go to another ridgeline. This lieutenant (Dudley Davis), and his unit, got outside our makeshift perimeter and was killed – seconds into his first combat."

"We were told later that it was suspected that Ripcord had been used by the NVA as an impact area for mortar practice and they were already well zeroed in," wrote Burckard. "Third platoon was last in and by that time incoming NVA small-arms fire was fairly continuous as well as mortars. Lt. Davis and Specialist Fourth Class Heater were killed in one of the early incoming mortar barrages."

"We were the last or second to last platoon to hit Ripcord. When I got there, the fourth platoon had already been sent out and got trashed," remembered Tim Joliet, a lieutenant from Ohio in charge of Alpha one. "By the time I landed, the firebase was under incredible fire, mortars, small arms and heavy weapons. No one was returning effective fire, just wasting ammunition."

Frank Marshall, a 20-year-old draftee from Philadelphia, was on the first several choppers in that day, part of Alpha Four.

"Our company (had) been in the field for 56 days and after getting supplies on the helicopter pad, we were flying right back out," wrote Marshall in his journal. "Every one of us knew this was a big mission and all the big brass who planned this mission knew we would be in contact and we all felt this tension that we would, especially with all the Cobra gunships circling overhead that were to fly beside us."

THE INITIAL ASSAULT

James "Tiny" Aanonsen was a machine gunner in Alpha Four, a towering figure from Staten Island, N.Y.

"I was an M-60 machine gunner," he said. "They told us we were going to land on top of Ripcord so we could secure it. We were going to set up a firebase. We flew in and the rounds were already coming in on top of us. It was RPGs, mortar rounds. They told us to duck for cover because we didn't know where it was coming from."

"Our platoon was third or fourth to land on the unsecured firebase," added Marshall. "The first helicopter landed on the bare hill and Sgt. Orvel Koger, his RTO (Radio Telephone Operator) and the lieutenant got off. Everything was quiet and the second helicopter landed. (Gary) McCoy, (George) Westerfeldt and I were coming in. There were Cobra gunships flying all over the hill and the tension was rising. We were all very quiet, just looking at each other in fear, knowing that something was about to happen. As our helicopter was landing, a red smoke grenade was thrown and right then we knew it was a hot LZ."

Red smoke means a landing zone is under attack.

"The door gunners were yelling to get off and stay low," said Marshall. "McCoy, Westerfelt and I got off one side as Sgt. Koger was on the ground telling us which way to go. As the rest of the company was landing, mortars and gunfire were hitting all over the hill. McCoy and Westerfelt ran into a split between two big rocks and I ran to a smaller one in front. Bullets were flying all around me and it looked a lot safer where McCoy and Westerfelt were."

McCoy and Westerfelt then got hit and Marshall called for a medic. The two were soon on a chopper headed out. Meanwhile, Koger and the gunships had zeroed in on an enemy position, but no one seemed to be able to get close enough to take it out. The order came from Koger to take the position.

"We dropped our rucksacks and just grabbed our weapons and ammunition and started down the hill, taking cover as we could," said Marshall. "All of a sudden I remembered I left my extra rounds of grenades for my M-79 by my rucksack because my vest tore as we landed and I took it off. I had to run back up the hill while my squad covered for me, then back down. I was never so scared as bullets were flying all around me. When we found the enemy position, I kept firing grenades at the position to keep them from shooting at the gunships. Between my grenades and the firepower from the gunships, we knocked out the position."

Joliet recounted the confusion and chaotic moments surrounding the insertion.

"When I landed on Ripcord, the place was just, it was hell," he said. "You couldn't stand anywhere on that hill and not have the ground popping up with puffs of smoke from rounds and artillery. I remember saying to myself,' Shit this is like standing in a rainstorm wondering if you should run away from the raindrops or staying and hoping they don't hit you.' It was that bad. "

Heath remembered the scene atop the hill from Alpha Three's point of view.

"You had a chopper down and three or four groups on the ground," he said. "The call was to bring in the rest of the guys. The first sortie is on the ground engaging the enemy and the birds are coming back to get us. We could tell that Ripcord had been a firebase before. There were remnants of bunkers, remnants of wire. As we come in we're all sitting on the edge. I look down and I can see the ground is pinging with bullets, but you've gotta get out of the chopper, so here we go. I was top heavy and when I landed, I was doing somersaults. We crawled up into our area and we're engaging the enemy. Eventually we pushed everything back and everyone calmed down."

THE INITIAL ASSAULT

Joliet had his hands full, and not just with the North Vietnamese.

"The hill was infested with poisonous centipedes, just millions of them. We took our bayonets and cut them in half and the two halves would run around, it was just awful," said Joliet. "We poured gun oil on our boots hoping that would keep them from crawling up and then we'd put ponchos on but it was hotter than hell so that didn't work. We spent the day calling in air support and killing centipedes. Jesus (Chewy) Lopez spotted an NVA 81mm mortar position on a hill about a mile away. I called in the position and requested a fire mission. Not long after a Cobra (Sweet Griffin Niner Fox) was on site and made contact with me. I gave him the position and with his profile blocked by the sun he laid two rockets about 50 meters from the tubes. I adjusted his aim and told him to unload on it. He put about 28 rockets and mini-guns on the area and it was quiet until the next day. We spent the night waiting to get attacked by a force of NVA estimated to be in the thousands."

Joliet wasn't alone in worried about getting attacked. The company as a whole was down in numbers and his platoon was down to 19 men.

"When we set up the perimeter I told everyone to locate a good position and a better position and to set up at the good position," remembered Joliet. "After dark and on my command, everyone moved to the alternate position. Our back was to a very steep hill that we had walked up from Ripcord. There were two large trails leading up to our position to our front and I placed a machine gun on each. We stayed on full alert all day and that night. We had cold C-rations and I did not allow anyone to smoke, talk or move unnecessarily from the time we got there until we left. We heard movement all night around us but were never probed."

Fear ran through each of the men that day. It lingered through the night as well.

"We were under constant mortar fire," said Noll. "When my platoon secured the hilltop I had the rest of the company come to me. I don't know how many airstrikes we called in the next day trying to knock out the mortar positions. The mortar fire was coming from Hill 902. The enemy had that pretty well established. How they were ready for us I'll never know, but they were ready for us."

Back at Evans, Lt. Earlston Andrews was acting executive officer of Echo Company. Andrews was the lone black lieutenant in the battalion.

At the Tactical Operations Center (TOC), the battalion sergeant major is seeking volunteers to re-supply Alpha Company, which is under heavy fire around Ripcord.

"I was flabbergasted by his reply," Andrews wrote. "People listening to transmissions of what is taking place at Ripcord, willing to let it happen, without making an attempt to prevent it. I briefly – in milliseconds – scan and observe every face at each duty station in the TOC in disbelief. There are people looking at me with expressions of indifference, guilt and maybe shame. A few eyes cease looking in my direction, focusing on the floor."

Radio transmissions, the sound of warfare, continued in the background.

"It's difficult processing what I'm hearing and witnessing," said Andrews. "A company of American troops is running out of ammunition and in need of medical supplies. The only volunteer is a battalion sergeant major, between 45 to 50 years old, who already wears a Combat Infantry Badge with a star."

Andrews, without hesitation, volunteered. "'Sergeant major, give me time to have my driver take me back to Echo Company to retrieve my helmet, M-16 and ammunition,'" he wrote. "I... grab my helmet, M-16, drape two bandoliers of ammunition (400 rounds) across my chess. Hurriedly leaving the orderly room, I inform Echo Company's first sergeant that I am going on a supply mission to Ripcord."

THE INITIAL ASSAULT

Andrews is surprised to see the sergeant major in a pressed uniform, with no weapon and no helmet, waiting. The chopper is ready for departure, its bay loaded with tactical supplies, including light infantry ammunition – hand grenades, M-79 grenades, M-60 ammo, M-16 ammo, flares and medical supplies.

"My first thought was, 'Where am I going to sit?" Andrews wrote. "The only p lace to sit is on ammunition containers stacked almost to the ceiling of the chopper. Sitting on stacked ammunition, slightly bowed at my waist, my helmet is rubbing against the chopper's bay ceiling."

Within 15 minutes, the chopper and Andrews are in a warzone, far from the relative safety of Evans.

"The chopper executes a wide circle around Ripcord," Andrews wrote. "Below is a bird's-eye view of a tropical rainforest of various hues of green. Located in that green is an anomaly, a small, light-brown spot. Erupting from that brown spot are multiple mushroom-shaped dust clouds rising from the ground at numerous locations, resulting from barrages of incoming 82mm mortars, 120mm recoilless rifles and 51-caliber anti-aircraft machine guns. Mortar and recoilless rifle rounds are raining down, crisscrossing (Ripcord). Mortar rounds are impacting at will and some appear to be walking across the hilltop. The NVA concentration of firepower is intense."

Shelling continued, coming from numerous well-camouflaged locations surrounding Ripcord. As he gazed downward, Andrews remembered the calming feeling that came over him.

"One side of my brain tells the other, 'You got yourself in a pickle this time Andrews. One well-placed hit by an enemy round and we will go out like a Fourth of July celebration,'" he wrote. "Then, I totally comprehend the seriousness of the situation and didn't have goddamned time to be nervous or worried. The chopper is going into Ripcord like an eagle with wings flared and talons extended diving for salmon in a stream, nose up and tail down. At that instant, an extraordinary feeling of inner calmness streams throughout my being, which I've never experienced before."

As the chopper floated down near Impact Rock, the sergeant major leapt from the bay with a crate of ammunition. Dust and debris were unavoidable and mortar rounds continued to hit the hill. The noise described by Andrews was deafening with mortar rounds, rotor blades from the chopper and Alpha Company's fire.

Andrews, now in his first combat under fire, asked himself what it was that he was supposed to do. The sergeant major calmly returned and assumed control. Andrews began passing crates of supplies out of the chopper bay, which the veteran soldier placed near Impact Rock. On one of his return trips, the sergeant major is carried a wounded soldier over his shoulder.

"I position the body in the bay. As ammunition is being unloaded, looking out the opposite side of the chopper's bay, I observe, totally exposed, having left his fighting position attempting to crest the hilltop, a sergeant limping toward the chopper. He has a leg wound and is attempting to use his M-16 as a crutch. Gaining eye contact with the chopper's co-pilot, he gives me a nod."

Andrews dashed from the chopper and sprinted toward the wounded soldier with mortar fire and small-arms fire crisscrossing the hilltop.

"Running, time feels as if it is suspended and distant," wrote Andrews. "My brain focuses on the rattling sound of an M-60 machine gun. The gunner is firing in short bursts, as if on a live-fire training range. My world becomes silent. For some unknown reason, spring across that hilltop, I have an intense, uncontrollable urge to glance up and out searching for the horizon. It is a crystal-clear, pale blue day, not a cloud, and visibility to the South China Sea. Upon reaching the sergeant, interlocking my arm under his shoulder, we hobble to the chopper. When we arrive, the

THE INITIAL ASSAULT

battalion sergeant major enters the opposite side with a wounded troop draped across his shoulders. At lift-off, impacting mortar rounds are approaching. The pilot banks the Huey down toward the valley floor, nose down and tail up, increasing speed in a dive."

Several wounded troops are aboard. One has a head wound and Andrews described him as being in a semi-conscious state, but not critical. The sergeant major was comforting the soldier as he moaned. Two troops appear to be sleeping. Soon they are on the ground at the 326th medical facility at Evans.

"I walk into my quarters, sit on my bunk with my M-16 laying across my lap, ammunition draped across my chest and reflect a few seconds on what I witnessed," wrote Andrews. "I recline into a deep sleep. The last thought on my mind is the sleeping soldiers. What began as an emergency resupply of tactical and medical supplies transformed into an emergency medevac for WIA(Wounded In Action)s."

One of the "sleeping" soldiers was Lt. Dudley Davis, who had been killed. His RTO (Radio Telephone Operator) died en route to the hospital.

Andrews earned a Bronze Star for his actions that day.

"A medal was not my priority," he wrote. "I did not consider it heroic, only service rendered; just something that needed to be done."

By the time Paul Buhr had landed on Ripcord Davis was dead. It was late afternoon.

"When the chopper landed I was in the middle," said Buhr, a member of Alpha One. "There were five guys in the chopper. Four had their feet hanging out. I was supposed to follow the machine gunner out the right side. I was the assistant gunner. The helicopter landed on one skid. It was tilted, like crawling uphill. I didn't have the strength and just rolled out the left side. The helicopter took off and then I got up and looked around. I couldn't see anyone anywhere. I couldn't even see Impact Rock. You had to go up a little hill before you could see the rock. I started walking off to the right and suddenly there were 20 people yelling at me to get down. I ended up crawling up to Impact Rock. The captain was there. I hooked up with the rest of my platoon."

After being hunkered down on Ripcord all day, Buhr, Joliet, and Alpha One went down in a valley to the northwest, which was shaded by Hill 1,000 to the west.

"It was dark down there, plus there was jungle," said Buhr. "We started up Hill 1,000 and didn't go to the top, we went into a saddle. It was just a narrow spot, where we started to set up an NDP (night defensive position). We threw grenades down the hill in case the North Vietnamese were following us. On the way up the hill they were bombing the suspected positions where the mortars were being fired. Shrapnel from the bombs would hit the side of the mountain and go up, hit the top of the trees and fall, making a tinkling sound. You could hear it falling. It was real steep. I got hit in the shoulder with a piece of shrapnel. It started bleeding and the medic bandaged it. It was right where my rucksack was on my shoulder. We went up the hill. It was about a half hour before dark and all of a sudden the captain called the lieutenant and told him to come back. We went down the valley up to Ripcord. As we were getting there, the rest of the company was leaving and going south, southeast to the next ridgeline, which leads over to 805. The whole company went over there and we stayed on top of Ripcord that night. Right after dark the fog came in and you couldn't see your hand in front of your face. We were scared. It was spooky. We wouldn't have been able to see them coming."

Heath was part of a four-man team sent to serve as a Listening Post (LP) from Noll's third platoon. He wasn't confident he'd live to see the next morning.

THE INITIAL ASSAULT

"We thought that would be a one-way mission," he said. "We're going to have to pick four guys to go to this LP and we're wondering how they are going to select them. We cut cards. I got a Jack and I was like, 'Yeah!' All these guys beat it. Myself and Dale Lane and two other guys went. Dale had the radio. We had a machine gun and we set up claymores on the perimeter. For us to retreat it was going to be up a hill. I said in the dark, there would be no way to get back. If we got into something we're going to have to fight it out. We had a starlight scope. There were so many bad guys in those hills. They were using white flashlights. It looked like someone was opening a bunker, then there'd be light, dark, light, then dark. We knew there were a lot of bad guys out there. I didn't sleep. I just envisioned 800,000 guys rushing at me. Fortunately, they didn't attack us."

Casualties were safely medevacked out on the 13th, but the company had been crippled. Four platoons now became three as the remainder of fourth platoon was divvied up between the rest of the company.

"We combat assaulted onto Ripcord on 12 March with 92 men, but three days later we were down to 75 men," said Burckard. "So I disbanded fourth platoon and reassigned the men among the other three platoons."

"Because of the casualties we suffered, the company was left short of men," said Marshall. "We went back to three platoons. My squad went to the first platoon. The only two men my squad lost were McCoy and Westerfelt. The rest of the night heavy artillery and flares continued over the area from nearby firebases for our safety."

The next day, Alpha Three and Lt. Noll started patrolling around Ripcord.

"At first light, we broke our little area and went back inside the perimeter," said Heath, who had been set up as part of a four-man listening post. "Lt. Noll came to me and said, 'I want you to walk point off the hill and go to the adjacent hill. Ken Lilly was behind me, Noll not far back. We left there, going down the hill and I spot a bunker. I called back to Noll and someone brought a LAW (light anti-tank weapon) up. Lt. Noll was on one side as I fired the LAW into the bunker. He ran in with his M-16 and 45. We started running in after him. There was no one in it. We started going up the face of this hill and I'm cutting my own way. There was no way I was taking a trail."

Joliet and Alpha One had returned to Ripcord March 13.

"Worried that there might be an ambush at the bottom of the hill, I put the platoon on line and on my command, we all threw a grenade and charged the trees as fast as we could," said Joliet. "We did not stop until we reached the perimeter at Ripcord. I didn't get Capt. Burckard's permission to do the recon by fire because I was pretty sure he would have denied the request. We made it back without incident but the unexplained explosions freaked out everyone on the firebase. Capt. Burckard handed my head to me for scaring everyone and not requesting permission first."

Joliet's men were to remain on the firebase as the rest of the company left Ripcord to move to a ridgeline several klicks away, Joliet wrote. It was something Joliet didn't like, or understand given the depletion in numbers, and the fact that Joliet's men were already carrying several KIAs on litters.

"Worse yet, my platoon was left to cover the entire firebase that day and night," he said. "About noon, we started receiving incoming 81s from the same site as the previous day. I call in air support and again Sweet Griffin came on site. The new position was about 100 meters above the previous site. I gave him the adjustment and told him to fire for effect. He put a full pod of rockets on it and again a mini-gun. We didn't receive any more incoming after that."

That afternoon, Joliet again ordered the platoon to surround the hilltop

THE INITIAL ASSAULT

in two-man positions high enough to maintain visual contact with the positions on either side.

"The firebase was a great rock and it was next to impossible to do more than scratch holes on the surface," said Joliet. "It was far bigger than my platoon could possibly cover. My instructions to the squad leaders were simple and absolute: Until dusk, look like you were preparing to set up for the night to deceive observers, move to an alternate position after dusk, deploy claymores and do not move, smoke or talk until dawn. If movement is observed, throw a grenade, if assaulted, throw more grenades and use the claymores. Don't fire unless and until your position has been found and you are receiving direct fire."

The resupply chopper had provided water and enough Korean War-era walkie talkies for each position, Joliet noted. The platoon checked status by breaking squelch on the walkie talkies a certain number of times for each position and again for each position's status. Sit-reps were conducted every 15 minutes. It kept everyone awake and alert, Joliet said.

What happened later that night showed exactly how important communication proved to be among squad and platoon members. It also illustrated the stress that came with being in combat.

"We had two nine-man positions except I had three at mine, an RTO, grenadier and myself," said Joliet. "About 2 a.m. I saw movement to my left. I attempted to make radio contact, but to no avail. Charlie Steffler was the grenadier and was deadly with the M-79. He could put a round exactly where he aimed, every time. At first we thought it was one of our guys, but they didn't respond to radio calls, was too short to be an American and his movement was stealthy. I finally decided that the position had been taken and ordered Charlie to fire a round at him. An instant before he pulled the trigger, the figure stood upright and turned to present a profile. We both realized too late that he was a friendly."

"Lt. Joliet thought he saw movement in the fog," said Buhr. "Billy Rose got hit with shrapnel. He got hit pretty bad in the back and neck.

As the trigger had been pulled, Charlie tried to swing the barrel away, according to Joliet. The round landed short and detonated a few feet away from Rose.

"I wouldn't let anyone go to him until dawn," said Joliet. "We spent the next four hours alternately listening to him moan in pain and fearing the worst when he didn't. At first light the medic and I moved to him. His right side was a mess and he had a partially severed artery in his arm pit. When he fell, he landed on the arm and his weight kept the wound closed. We could not reach the damaged part of the artery and when we tried to move him he bled profusely. We needed to get him stable in order to get him evacuated. We were finally able to stop the bleeding by stuffing a filthy towel into his armpit and tying his arm tightly to his side. He had other injuries, but none appeared to be life-threatening. We had no morphine or any other pain killer other than aspirin."

"The guys took turns keeping him awake all night. The next morning, it was pretty late, about 9, before the fog cleared enough to get him out," said Buhr.

"We became enveloped in ground fog and the medevac was not able to land until mid-morning," added Joliet. "That was the last I saw of (Rose) until I saw him a few years ago when he reached out to me."

Joliet said he and Rose met at a Ripcord reunion where Rose explained that his squad leader, his night defensive position partner, did not follow Joliet's instructions and set up claymores during the day and the clackers were left when positions changed. The squad leader ordered Rose to find the clackers and move them, however they were gray and invisible at night and his search caught the attention of Joliet.

THE INITIAL ASSAULT

"After he was medevacked his squad leader told me that the man had gotten up to relieve himself," said Joliet. "I did not know the truth for all of those years. I was shocked and stunned to find out what really happened."

Once the medevac left, Joliet's platoon departed Ripcord to rejoin the company. The conditions and realities of heavy fighting were setting in with the soldiers.

"We occupied the part of the perimeter where the dead had been placed," remembered Joliet. "They were stacked on top of each other because there was very little flat ground. They were covered in ponchos and the wind kept blowing the ponchos off, exposing them to the unrelenting rain. We took turns recovering them. A day or so later we got some body bags and my platoon had to put the bodies in the bags. Ghastly is the only word to describe that process. That experience fills my dreams to this day."

Soon, a recon platoon was headed back to the firebase after having been ambushed. Their lieutenant had been killed and the rest of the squad-sized element (less than ten men) took turns carrying his body.

"I was sent out to link up with them and take them to our position," said Joliet. "I took a squad and set up an ambush about 1,000 meters from the company. There was heavy fog and misting rain all morning and it was hard to see in the distance. Eventually we spotted the point man and made contact. For reasons I could not fathom, the medic was walking point. The lieutenant was tied to his back and he was carrying, or dragging him. The medic had a .45 in each hand and was not wearing a shirt or helmet. He lost his medic bag and rucksack. His bare skin stuck out light a spotlight. He was clearly in shock when we linked up. He would not release his weapons or let anyone help carry the body. I forcibly took the weapons away but let him carry his lieutenant to the company perimeter."

Buhr volunteered with some other members of Alpha Company to take the lieutenant's body to the landing zone.

"That was my first experience with a dead body," said Buhr. "He was a very handsome young man. The only wound you could see was that a piece of his nose was gone."

On March 14, Noll's third platoon was continuing movement in the area surrounding Ripcord. The platoon took small arms fire that day, then on the 15th, went back up Ripcord where it met with Bravo Company, which had Scout dogs with it. Everyone was socked in on the 16th and there would be no re-supply.

Fighting continued for three consecutive days and Ripcord could not be secured. B52s were called in to bomb the area so the firebase could soon be established. Burckard was awarded the Silver Star for his efforts in leading his company throughout the day and night of the 12th.

"There was not a lot of 'thinking' going on but just ingrained reactions to the situation as it changed and developed," said Burckard. "Wherever we could identify the direction of incoming fire, we fired in that direction and when we could see the source of enemy fire in that direction and when we could see the source of enemy fire we would bring Army ARA (aerial rocket artillery), artillery or Air Force-Navy air strikes on the target. That sort of thing lasted pretty much the rest of the day and partly into the night. Our 'thoughts' were really just trained responses to the immediate situation.

"My thoughts since then have been almost exclusively about the men killed who never had the opportunity to live their lives to a reasonable age, as I have. I know it sounds strange, and maybe it's normal, but when I find myself involved in a pleasurable experience, like playing with my grandchildren, watching a beautiful sunset or even just working in my yard, I find myself thinking about those guys and how they

THE INITIAL ASSAULT

never lived long enough to experience some of the wonderful things in life that I have. I even catch myself trying to maybe 'channel' some of them so they can see or feel what I do. I know that sounds weird, but that's the way it is."

Various troops saw contact daily throughout the four-and-a-half-month period. March was marked by skirmishes in the hills surrounding Ripcord as companies humped through the jungle in search of the NVA, their ammunition caches and anything that may have helped sustain the enemy as it entrenched itself in the mountainous terrain throughout the valley.

"I was a machine gunner, so I had to protect myself and my squad," said James "Tiny" Aanonsen. "We got hit every once in a while. We'd set up on top of a mountain every night. Every so often we'd run into something or mortar rounds would come in on top of us. It was very quiet at night. Over there the enemy was all around."

Tim Newman, a draftee from Buffalo, joined Marshall's platoon and Alpha Company mid-March. Like many new infantryman, nothing could prepare him for the realities of warfare in the jungle.

"I came into Alpha Company as a replacement," said Newman, who remembered flying into the jungle and being rather green. "The (door) gunner was telling us it was hot. Being a cherry, I'm thinking, 'yeah, it's hot, speaking of the obvious. It's 90 degrees and the sun's out.' Little did I know what he meant by hot, but it was the LZ (landing zone) was under fire. As I was getting off, I was standing around hearing popping sounds all around me. One individual, I don't know who, directed me down and asked me if I wanted to get myself killed, but in not so many words. 'You frickin' cherry we're under attack.' That was my first realization that I was in Vietnam and in a hostile situation."

Newman was picked by Marshall and other members of Alpha's first platoon. With Marshall, a Philly boy, and Aanonsen, from Staten

Island, N.Y. already in place, the men quickly became known as the "Yankee Squad," Newman remembered.

Newman was tapped to be Tiny's assistant machine gunner and the Buffalo native found it tough keeping up with the legs of the 6-foot, 6-inch Aanonsen. "He was quite vocal in the field," said Newman. "He was respected in the field because of his experience and his size. A week after I was inserted, we were in contact coming off another LZ and Tiny was coming down a hill. We got hit and the next thing I know he's yelling, 'On line!" and I'm thinking, 'On line, what do you mean on line?' We ended up on line charging toward where we were being fired on. He's got the machine gun on his hip and I'm trying to keep up with him as he's striding over everything, trying to keep up while holding onto the rounds as we were on an assault going toward the enemy position. He took care of me while I was a cherry out there."

Bruce Brady was also inserted with Alpha Company, in March, assigned to Noll and Alpha Three. He, like most draftees, didn't understand the mission and landed in the jungle with one goal – to survive to see another day and get one day closer to getting home. He didn't have to wait long for his first firefight. It found him within hours of landing and getting his assignment.

"I was assigned to carry a radio for the platoon sergeant, Dick Ames," he said." That night we had to dig in, you dig in two-man positions. We were told the next night we'd hump out. We were on a ridge. The next morning at daybreak we got hit with some RPG (rocket propelled grenade) rounds. They'd harass you, a lot of times you'd hit and run. That's what they did. They hit and ran. Being a cherry, I was no doubt very, very scared. I just got here and I've got a year to go. I was opposite the side that got hit. A lot of the guys were calm, they knew it was a hit and run.

"At that particular time I didn't realize they were pulling people out. In the field, you weren't privy to a lot of information. I lived with a radio

THE INITIAL ASSAULT

glued to my ear, but we weren't privy to a lot of information. Going in I didn't realize it. After talking to some guys I realized we were in it hot and heavy. Being assigned to it, we didn't know any different. We realized we had to stay out months on end and that was normal operations. Later on, some of the guys started talking about the war winding down, but for us it didn't register because something was going on all the time.

"We never stayed in same location two nights in a row. We were always on the move. You were triple canopy. It would have been impossible to get supplies from the air. You had to go to a clearing. One of our objectives at the time was to blow LZs (landing zones). We get dynamite and C4. Chain saws would be brought in. Our objective was to make LZs to get men in and out and supplies in and out. We were constantly giving our positions up because we'd constantly blow LZs."

Troops would hump through the jungle in platoon-sized elements, occasionally meeting up, but for the most part taking on assignments in smaller groups. Companies would spend days in the jungle, routinely running out of food or water while waiting for a chopper to provide resupply or transport them to a firebase for the rare stand-down. Men would capture rainwater, which was plentiful, or refill their canteens in nearby rivers for water.

"One time we got socked in for four days, didn't have food, ammo, but you could hear people talking up on Ripcord," remembered Brady. "You could hear them building Ripcord, even at night you'd hear sounds coming from Ripcord. It got built pretty darn quick. Being in the field, you wondered if you would be safer being up on Ripcord. In the field you always had the worries of being hit at night. It was somewhat comforting hearing the activity on Ripcord, but you'd hear them taking mortar rounds. One night we were close enough to hear them sliding the mortars into the tube. We called in some gunships and you didn't hear any more mortars."

Pulling the Trigger

While platoon elements were humping in the jungles surrounding the hill that would become Firebase Ripcord, soldiers from Headquarters Company were on the hill working to make it a firebase.

"Lt. John Darling was my (commanding officer) in commo," said Peter McSwain (HHC, 2/506th). "He came to me and said Mac get your hard hat, your flak jacket, rifle and some ammo and go to the helicopter pad. A bunch of us went there, we took off and landed on a hill that was all cratered and de-vegetated and had pieces of broken equipment scattered everywhere. Here and there you'd see a blown-up helmet or something like that.

"We went out on a Chinook at that time. As soon as I got a few yards away from the Chinook, these guys with me, Lt. Darling was one of them, yelled at me and they jumped into a shell crater. I jumped in too, the same crater. They had been around long enough that the force of gravity worked better for them, I'll never understand how they beat me into that shell crater, but I jumped on top of them. They told me we were getting mortar fire. I had gotten sand blasted against me and I heard a thud - that was the first time I'd heard that.

"The hill was just a bare, bombed out hill at that time, there was no wire or anything. After a while, there was a rifle company on the perimeter. I went down and I was in a foxhole with some of the most depressed guys I'd ever seen. It was foggy and raining."

Troops were inserted rather often, as is the case when casualties start taking their toll on platoons. Phil Tolson was a sergeant when he landed in the Ripcord area as a replacement for Bravo Company.

"I got on a helicopter and I think I was the only one on there," said Tolson, a draftee from Northeastern Pennsylvania. "It was a logbird and they were taking supplies out to somebody. They took me out by myself in a clearing in the middle of nowhere. There was no one anywhere. I got out and it was on a pretty good hillside. I was almost 6-3 at the time and rucksack had to weigh about 80 to 90 pounds. It was awkward, plus I'm on a hill. When the (chopper pilot) hammered the throttle, the downdraft knocked me right off my feet and I fell backwards. My rucksack didn't have quick-release straps. It flipped me backward and my rucksack came to rest against a big tree stump. I couldn't get back on my feet for nothing. I'm thinking, 'I'm done, it's over. I made it here and I can't go anywhere. If a gook comes I'm done.' I'm frantically trying to get up off that stump and I can't. I'm standing on my head like a dummy.

"Then I hear voices. I couldn't tell if they were American or Vietnamese. Finally this little guy comes up and he's laughing and harassing me. He said something about a stupid, cherry shake-and-bake, then takes me back in the jungle to catch up with the rest of the guys."

Back at the Command Post, night settles in and Tolson prepared for his first night in the jungle.

"We're digging in and I'm digging and the guy next to me says, 'Oh shit.' I said, 'What's the matter with you?' and I smell this horrible smell. He had uncovered a dead North Vietnamese soldier. He called Capt. (Bill) Williams and we had to dig the guy up and check him out. They finish uncovering this guy."

Troops would routinely check dead North Vietnamese soldiers for intelligence, whether it was mapping, notes or personal effects.

For those in the field, coming face to face with the enemy was quick and rather routine, especially as the days and months wore on. Getting used to pulling the trigger was something you had to learn, or face the prospect of not going home alive.

"One day we were pinned down all day, we'd lost our point man and had several wounded on a ridgeline. Below us, you could see several Vietnamese," said Brady, Alpha Company. "There were six or seven of us that opened up on them. We had a good range on them. We were on top looking down. At the time, they were hitting Delta Company. We had one killed and four wounded that day."

Firing on another man for the first time wasn't difficult for many. Training had been intense, but being in the A Shau Valley and seeing the North Vietnamese troops in action made it easier to pull the trigger.

"You don't think about it mentally," said Brady. " It just comes to you. You have to react mentally. I think you do it more in self-defense. If you can lay down some fire, you feel like you make a difference."

For those with rank, it was a matter of responsibility.

"I got to thinking about this - this is crazy, this is for real," Tolson remembered. "Prior to the time I went to Vietnam I knew it was real. Until the first time someone shoots at you, at least for me, it was like, 'Yeah, OK.' After the first firefight it's like 'Holy shit, if I screw this up, I get some people killed here.'"

5

April Fool's Day

Bill Williams took over as captain of Bravo Company March 26, relieving Carmelito Arkangel. His first days in the Ripcord Area of Operations were a whirlwind of combat, confusion and death.

March 31 was marked by the death of three men who, while on patrol, stumbled upon a small group of North Vietnamese crouched in spider holes camouflaged on the floor of the jungle. Springing up from their holes, the North Vietnamese took out a scout dog, his handler and West Pointer, Lt. Harry Hayes.

Capt. Williams and two platoons from Bravo Company air assaulted onto Ripcord in the late morning hours of April 1 under intense mortar, recoilless rifle and small arms fire in what would come to be known as the April Fool's Day Assault. Capt. Rembert Rollison and Delta Company arrived on the northeast side of Ripcord while Alpha Company set up shop east. A recon squad from Echo Company was also in the area and a three-man pathfinder team was on hand.

Capt. Dave Rich's B Battery/2-319th Field Artillery unit set up atop Firebase Gladiator to provide artillery support to those around Ripcord.

Capt. Dave Rich was one of many heroes at Firebase Ripcord. Rich, the most decorated soldier to emerge from the Ripcord battle, received the Distinguished Service Cross, Silver Star, Bronze Stars and seven Purple Hearts. He died in November 2011. Photo provided by James Saller.

APRIL FOOL'S DAY

Craig Van Hout had been in country since December 1969 and had seen his Bravo Company shrink from four to three platoons prior to the combat assault onto Ripcord. As his chopper made its way toward the hilltop, he sensed something about this mission was different.

"I was carrying an M-60 (machine gun) that day and I had a new guy, Chip Collins, as my assistant gunner," he said. "I was riding in the doorway of the Huey and had the sensation that something was a little bit unusual. The door gunner was more tense than usual. I thought it was a regular, routine assault, but there was more electricity in the air. I was ready to stand on the skids and looked down to see puffs of dirt coming up. You could see where mortars were landing. The gunner's yelling at me to get out and we're about 20 feet off the ground and like, no."

Van Hout and Bravo One disembarked and were greeted by Sgt. Terry Radcliff.

"He met us and told us (the landing zone) was hot and gave me an area to go for a position to secure. We were to dig in and stay down. We're getting mortared and that's the first inclination that something was amiss.

"Collins and I went off to an area and, a new guy, he's kind of doing this prairie dog imitation with his head going up to see what's going on and I'm saying 'Get down.' We tried to dig a hole, but the area was hard. We hit barbed wire that was buried and just hugged the earth. We had one round that came in relatively close and when it exploded a bunch of debris hit me in the face and body. Much of it was dirt and pellets. I had a piece of shrapnel lodged in my jaw and I pulled that out. It wasn't much more than a sliver. We just stayed down. I didn't fire the machine gun because there was nothing I could see to shoot at."

Collins died April 9, 2002, at his home in Virginia at the age of 51. He was instrumental in the founding of the Ripcord Association and was the initial editor of the association's newsletter, "The Ripcord Report."

He detailed his experiences from April 1 in the May 1986 edition of "On Ripcord" in a retrospective entitled simply, "The April Fools."

"As we prepared for the C.A. (combat assault) I began to sense an uneasiness from some of the guys. Old-timers could be extremely superstitious. It was April Fool's Day and they didn't like that a bit. Not in the Nam. Van Hout and I finally boarded a bird. From the air the huge mound of dirt that was Ripcord looked harmless. When we finally landed we were pointed in the direction of what was eventually to be the TOC (tactical operations center). Within seconds I could hear popping sounds in the valley around us. Then came the sssh-crump. I had landed in a shallow depression on the wrong side of Van Hout. He had already taken te-te shrapnel in his face. Had I been on the side I was supposed to be I would have caught more of that shrapnel. The rounds were extremely close, within a few feet and the depression was the only thing saving us.

"I flooded Van Hout with questions. I didn't know what that stuff was. What the fuck is that noise Van Hout? 'Mortars. God Damn, get down!' I was flabbergasted I didn't have anything to shoot back at. The mortars continued indiscriminately. People were falling all around. I looked behind and slightly above us and saw that Terry Radcliff was down. A widening pool of blood was flowing out from under him."

Van Hout estimated that Radcliff was hit within a half hour of landing.

"He was up top somewhere and came down to check on his men," said Van Hout. "He went to the two guys in the position next to us, John Edwards and Slim Williams (Spencer). When he checked on them there was an explosion. He was flat on his back and dead already."

Collins continued to describe the scene as the medic ran to Radcliff.

"Radcliff's helmet had been knocked off. His blond hair rifled in the breeze. He looked serene, like a child that had finally drifted off to sleep. Raw-boned Doc Kellogg scrambled over and felt for a pulse and shook his head at Van Hout. Van Hout replied, 'Fuck.' Kellogg laid Terry's helmet gently across his face. The wind kept on fluttering (his) golden hair."

"It killed him instantaneously," said Van Hout. "He was the first guy I saw get killed in Vietnam. It sucked the wind right out of you. It was pretty devastating when that occurred because he was a good guy. We looked up to him as our leader. He was coming down to make sure everyone was secure. That was just the way that he was – making sure his guys were where they were supposed to be."

Williams had been making the rounds with Radcliff when he turned one way and Radcliff stayed put. That was the difference in life and death for the Bravo Company captain.

Maj. Laurence Law, battalion executive officer, flew in to establish a command post and soon began coordinating medevacs from a boulder on a slope leading to Ripcord. The North Vietnamese relentlessly shelled Ripcord, noted Williams, who explained that the enemy had clearly mapped the area, freely walking mortars to and fro on the hill.

Soon, a mortar slammed into the boulder, knocking Williams to the ground and killed Lt. William Wall, a forward observer for Williams. The blast also claimed the life of a pathfinder and peppered Law with shrapnel in his back. Williams came to the aid of Law, turning him over to medics before a chopper could fly him out. Lt. John Darling, a West Pointer, took over the command post and began directing suppressive fire and the medevac traffic.

Burckard, in charge of Alpha Company, had flown to the rear the day before for a briefing with the colonel. During that flight, he listened to the radio as Bravo got ambushed.

"Lt. Col. Lucas had his hands full with this contact, so I just scrounged up some Cokes for my men and made it back out to the field," Burckard wrote in his journal. "Official word is that the operation into the AO (Area of Operation) around Ripcord is a go tomorrow – hope it's April Fool…"

Alpha Company landed at 9 a.m. on Ripcord and started receiving small arms fire some 30 minutes later. Mortar rounds started coming in as well, Burckard noted in his journal.

"My company went into the LZ (Landing Zone) 600 meters east of Ripcord that we had cut on 15 March," noted Burckard. "No problems. We had a ringside seat watching Bravo Company on Ripcord and really felt helpless not being able to do anything. We found a bunker that the NVA (North Vietnamese Army) had built since we left two weeks ago. I used it as my company command post. All of Bravo Company, the recon platoon and the battalion advance party consisting of personnel from artillery, engineers, battalion Tactical Operations Center and pathfinders got into Ripcord. Every helicopter to approach the LZ drew about three-to-four rounds of 82mm mortar fire. Bravo started taking casualties fast. About 10 air strikes went into the north, 200-to-400 meters away and also to the east. Phantoms and Skyhawks were dropping 250- and 500-pound bombs and napalm. We adjusted five seconds, two ships each, of ARA (Aerial Rocket Artillery) to the east and southeast. A short ARA round landed near my location wounding one of my men."

After loading the man onto a medevac, the chopper's blade struck a tree on the LZ and had to land on Ripcord. Attempts by the NVA to take out the chopper failed.

"The medevac ships got into Ripcord by flying low to the north and then popping up – not giving the enemy time enough to hit it with a mortar," noted Burckard. "A direct hit on the Bravo Comapany

APRIL FOOL'S DAY

command post killed the forward observer and two others, wounding six more, including the XO (Executive Officer), Maj. Law."

Fighting continued throughout the day, finally subsiding as night fell.

"We were there all day," remembered Van Hout. "In hindsight, the NVA probably ran out of ammunition or rounds to shoot at us. Eventually things calmed down and we were walking around. We didn't have the wherewithal to defend ourselves. At dusk we walked off Ripcord to the saddle on the next hill and hooked up with another company. It was like an elephant walk in the circus with the whole company in a line – you grabbing the rucksack of the guy in front of you, walking along this trail. They were firing illumination rounds, it could have been artillery, over top of us. Every time a round went off and lit up the area, we got up and walked. It was the only way we could see to walk down the trail. The thought to me was if they had one guy on the trail with a machine gun, he could have taken the whole company out. It countered the training we had received, but out of necessity, that's the way we walked out."

The total casualties for the day were six dead, 26 wounded. Bravo left Ripcord on foot around 7 p.m. and linked with Burckard and Alpha Company, leaving three dead behind and some equipment, according to Burckard. The remaining dead and wounded had been evacked by air prior to nightfall. Burckard's position had been secured, "having low ground on all four sides," he wrote.

Bill Heath and Dale Lane were the members of Alpha Three charged with finding Bravo, in the dark, and getting them to safety.

"Bravo Company's numbers were down to the point where they knew they couldn't hold the hill if they were attacked," said Heath. "They were in a very tight position. Dale Lane and I were to go off our hill and get Bravo linked up. When we left it was just getting dark. We got down into the saddle and the jungle thinned out a little. We called up to Bravo, 'Send your guys down.' We saw movement in front of us and we think it's the enemy. 'Has anyone from Bravo left? Negative, negative.' It's almost completely dark and we see a silhouette of a human. The guy in front stopped, turned and said something and I could tell it wasn't Vietnamese. We didn't know recon had been inserted. We almost fired on the recon guys. We linked up and they were carrying some dead, some wounded, so we helped them carry them up to our area."

The following day, Bravo was ordered north. Burckard knew their supplies had been depleted, so he gave them three cases of LRRP rations, which amounted to one meal per man.

John Schnarr was a member of the recon team working in the Ripcord area under Lt. John Wilson on April 1. Schnarr's father served in World War II and having tried college at Indiana University, Bloomington, he watched a friend volunteer for the Marines and felt he should volunteer for the draft. He did so, opting for a two-year enlistment. He was assigned to the 101st, just like his father had been, and upon landing in Vietnam, chatted with some veterans who happened to be recon soldiers. They told Schnarr of the six months in the field, six months in the rear, warm showers in the rear, good food.

The Vietnam Schnarr had landed in was a completely different Vietnam. Still, the young soldier volunteered for recon at the age of 20 and was assigned to the 2nd of the 506th. His rear job? It came less than two weeks before he was scheduled to DEROS (date expected to return from overseas).

Echo Company and recon had been in the Ripcord AO (Area of Operation) for months by the time April had rolled around. It was recon that reported large numbers of North Vietnamese in the area, trails and bunkers in the area.

Recon operated in five- to seven-man teams and when Schnarr and his squad landed on Ripcord April 1, there were four recon teams. By the end of July, there were but two left.

Echo had been flown to the rear for a three-day break after being socked in for weeks in March due to weather. The team could not be re-supplied and was looking forward to the break. It last less than two days.

"We were pretty damn hungry and needed a break," said Schnarr. "It was supposed to be a three-day thing. The second day they gathered us up and told us what was happening at Ripcord and they wanted recon teams there. We geared up and went to the helipad and listened to the radios and said, 'Shit this don't sound good at all.' We went with full strength. It was (John) Wilson's first time as platoon leader. It was in the afternoon when they finally took us out there. Alpha Company was on the hill. We circled for a while because there was a lot of incoming. The pilot looked back and told us we were going to make a pass before getting in. Ten feet off the ground the crew chief told us to jump. I threw the rucksack down and jumped out behind it. There were about 10 of us that got in, the rest flew back under fire. Wilson got in. We jumped in and rolled into a shell crater there, not very well oriented to what was going on. We figured out who made it in, who didn't."

A chopper had been shot down on the hill and Schnarr and recon were set up along the perimeter of the hill. He was facing north.

"There wasn't much to do but look down the hill," said Schnarr. "I remember watching the artillery strikes come in. We hung around there until it got dark then they decided they were going to evacuate the hill. Wilson came over and said we'd head to a saddle there to the east. The idea was we were going to lead the way down the hill in the dark. There was a trail. We did that, went over there that night and left a couple bodies buried up in a bunker, then they tried to blow the helicopter in place. We tried to hook up with Bravo that night. The next morning we got up and they wanted us to go up and check Ripcord out again and recover a couple bodies Alpha Company had left up there. We did that. We didn't run into anything going up. We got up there and dug up the bodies, recovered them. They were in ponchos so we carried them down the hill and turned them over to the guys from Alpha Company. Then they wanted us to go back up the hill and secure the hill, which we did. At some point in time the direction came down to leave one group. Lt. Wilson, myself, Van Walker, Neil Whitler, Charles (Domey) Donning, Red Baron, Scotty, Wilson stayed on top of the hill to secure the hill."

Burckard received the three dead bodies around 6 p.m. The day was nasty with rain and fog. Visibility was just 50 meters. The mission, which included a squad from Alpha Company, along with the Echo recon team, took four hours, Burckard would write.

The captain's group included eight engineers, a pathfinder, three artillerymen and three additional officers, all that was left of the battalion advance team. Burckard's first and second platoons were settled 400 meters to the southeast while third platoon settled with the captain. The weather, he wrote, was bad.

"It was very rough going," Burckard wrote. "It was slippery, wet and uphill. Recon platoon never got to their objective. They ran into some NVA and got one man wounded. Medevac is impossible in this weather."

Following their work on Ripcord, the men of Echo Company, the recon squad, were given another assignment. Lucas wanted the team to probe Hill 1,000 to more accurately pinpoint mortar positions at the top. Artillery and airstrikes had yet to eliminate the positions.

"We split off and did that," said Schnarr. "It was another one of those days where we were pretty well socked in. There was a little knoll down there in the saddle and it was very, very foggy. We started that direction

APRIL FOOL'S DAY

and that's where we got ambushed - RPGs, machine guns and AKs, the initial ambush they fired RPG and the RPD (Russian) machine guns. Everybody hit the ground, the young kid Charles was walking slack and he got hit in the leg pretty sizeable piece of shrapnel through his leg. I had an RPG hit a tree or limb over me, nothing serious, just got peppered."

The men knew if they returned fire, they'd give up their positions via the muzzle blasts. They had no idea where the enemy was firing from.

"We were pinned down and got on the radio and talked to Wilson and told him what we were in," said Schnarr. "They decided they would come down and help us break contact and they did."

Wilson led the men away, skirting off the hill, going around 1,000 meters toward the night defensive positions of Alpha and Bravo companies. With darkness setting in and Domey slowing the team, an NDP (Night Defensive Position) was established. Wilson realized he had lost his radio frequency code book and wanted to return the next morning to see if he could find it. He needed volunteers, got none and appointed three men to go with him.

"Recon platoon sent a patrol up to Ripcord to try to recover some of the lost equipment," Burckard wrote. "About 100 meters from the top they were fired on with small arms and RPGs from the top. Apparently Ripcord was occupied by the NVA during the night. I brought my first platoon over to my location in case recon needed fire support. Recon platoon shot three NVA dead and possibly wounded more."

"The rest of us kind of argued against that," said Schnarr, of the mission back up Ripcord. "He needed about three or four volunteers to go with him, and he didn't get any so he appointed them. He took Scotty, I was behind slack. Neil Whitler was behind me. We went up the side, it another one of those socked- in days. The side of the hill was barren for the last 75 yards up the hill, no brush, no cover, nothing.

We worked up and Scotty got up to the first line of bunkers. We were spread out about 15 feet. He jumped down and gave us the signal to get down and we did. He's telling us that there are two of them up there. Wilson went over there and peeked over the side. Wilson had an M-16 with a silencer on it, which doesn't do much by the way. He went over the edge and emptied a magazine in the hole and said, 'I got 'em, I got two.' About that time return fire started and he and Scotty started coming our way. An RPG came and Wilson got hit. We got down again. They didn't come down over the edge to fire at us. We grabbed Wilson, who was unconscious, and we drug our way down the woodline. We called for artillery, but they couldn't get anything to us. TOC (Tactical Operations Center) had come on and said they'd have to call naval guns on us, big guns. We gave them our location and they said that was danger close. They fired a marker round first, and of course, we couldn't see anything. They fired then, and they were pretty well on target."

Burckard noted that as recon pulled off Ripcord, artillery blasted 105mm rounds for two hours – a total of 472 rounds.

"Things were quiet after whatever they unleashed on them. In the meantime, we're talking to medevacs trying to get Wilson out," remembered Schnarr. "He was semi-conscious, moaning. He had some pretty bad chest wounds, head wounds and other things. We eventually got a medevac on station and the pilot thought he could follow a blue line up, which is a stream, and he did, but we could never direct him in."

The weather proved too dangerous even for a litter drop. The team could never pinpoint the chopper's location.

"We could never get a visual on him," remembered Schnarr. "As much as he dared, (the pilot) eventually said he was running low on fuel and headed back. That was about the time Wilson gave up his last breath. We decided the best thing to do would be our original plan, go around the south side of Ripcord. Alpha was going to meet us over there. We tried to make a litter out of ponchos to carry Wilson, but that slowed us down quite a bit. They ended up deciding Neil and Van were big, strong guys and they ended up lashing his hands together and hung him over Whitler's neck and he carried him on his back. He'd trade off with Van Walker until we got over and got hooked up. Then we went back to the NDP on the east side."

"The weather prevented the medevac from getting into them and Lt. Wilson died," said Burckard. "I instructed recon to discard all non-essential equipment and move to my hill. I sent a squad to meet them halfway. We put Lt. Wilson with the other three KIAs. When recon was safely at my location, my forward observer, Lt. Brennan, called in ninety-six 105mm cofram 'firecracker' rounds and a batter three (18 rounds) of WP (white phosphorous). We heard loud screams from the top of Ripcord. We dug all day into my location and some of the fighting positions are becoming quite elaborate."

The morning of April 4 it had finally cleared enough to get choppers out to the men. Alpha was prepared for NVA fire from Ripcord, but it never came.

"The fog lifted long enough for three log birds, one medevac and the command and control ship with Lt. Col. Lucas to get in," wrote Burckard. "My count now is Alpha Company, 91; recon, 17, engineers, seven; artillery, one (Capt. King) and pathfinders, one (Lt. Anderson). The NVA tried to hit us with mortars as the log birds came in, firing about six rounds, but none came closer than 100 meters."

Schnarr was in the hospital when Gen. Sid Berry arrived and wanted to know what had happened. The general also distributed Purple Hearts to the wounded.

Fighting was tough and seven men were killed, 21 wounded. The hill was vacated late in the evening as fire slackened.

REMEMBERING FIREBASE RIPCORD

The significance of Hill 1,000 can't be underestimated. It held high ground over Firebase Ripcord and would prove to be one of many thorns to the 101st during the campaign.

Burckard praised the efforts of his men and noted each man in his company gave up a LRRP ration meal so that 15 men from other units had four to five meals apiece.

On April 5, a blue team consisting of infantrymen, hitched a ride on a slick to Ripcord to rig the downed Huey for extraction, according to Burckard. The team began to take 82mm mortar fire, heard by Alpha Company, second platoon, coming from near Hill 805 to the east.

"They would call 'shot' over the radio and I would pass it on to the team on Ripcord – about twenty men – so they could take cover from the incoming fire," said Burckard. "(The team) took four wounded while on Ripcord. We called in air strikes on the suspected NVA mortar location. As long as a strike was in progress, the mortars would not fire. As soon as the jets went off station the mortars would begin again. While the jets were bombing, Charlie Company was inserted into my landing zone. They took no incoming rounds. All told, we adjusted 13 airstrikes."

Burckard moved out with his command post to second platoon's location, then moved first platoon forward with third platoon following as rear security. The group slid up to a hill just ahead of the valley that separated the group from Hill 805. The company set up a night defensive position, with everyone digging in completely, he noted, the first time the company had dug in completely together since leaving Firebase Jack in the lowlands since Feb. 14.

Burckard's notes spell out the complexity of movement in the triple canopy jungle surrounding Ripcord. Alpha, and other line companies, could be somewhat close to one another, yet feel like a world away due to the thick growth in the jungle.

APRIL FOOL'S DAY

"We all just took things one day at a time," Burckard would write. "Because we operated relatively independently in company- and platoon-size elements, we rarely had an opportunity to talk directly to, or at length, with any 'higher ups' about what the heck was going on around us. Our battalion commanders, either Lt. Col. Crowell or Andre Lucas were sometimes above us in a command and control ship but rarely made an appearance on the ground where we were."

Williams, Law and Darling each received the Silver Star for their actions April 1.

6

Sporadic Contact

Through April 10 the 2/506th and 2nd and 4th Battalions, 1st Regiment Army of the Republic of Vietnam (ARVN) took part in reconnaissance operations in and around firebases Ripcord and O'Reilly in an attempt to locate and destroy NVA (North Vietnamese Army) mortar and recoilless rifle positions. Meanwhile, attempts to secure Ripcord continued as various platoon- and squad-sized elements worked the hills, ridgelines and trails throughout the Ripcord area.

Isabelino Vazquez-Rodriguez was born Dec. 22, 1930, in Puerto Rico, and drafted into the U.S. Army Nov. 6, 1950. After training in Puerto Rico, and a stop in Japan, he ended up in Korea in April 1951 and reported to the 3rd Infantry Division, then assigned to Company G, 15th Infantry Regiment, where he served a year as a sniper and later, squad leader due to the high number of casualties. He would eventually serve as platoon sergeant and platoon leader, again because of the high number of casualties.

He stayed in Korea for another couple of months and would eventually join the Special Forces in 1960. In November 1965 he landed in South Vietnam, where he built a floating camp in the Mekong Delta - a snaking waterways that served as the water equivalent of the Ho Chi Minh

SPORADIC CONTACT

Trail of South Vietnam, a passageway for North Vietnamese and Viet Cong troops, supplies and assaults.

Vazquez-Rodriguez suffered a serious injury that forced him to spend five months in a hospital in Yokohama, Japan. In 1968, he returned to Panama to join the 7th Special Forces at Fort Gulick, where he received a direct commission as captain, then assigned to the 75th Ranger Regiment in 1969 in Vietnam. From there, he met Lt. Col. Howard Crowell, who transferred him to the 2nd of the 506th.

"He's the most intimidating 5-foot, 6-inch guy you're ever going to meet," said Pete Meloro, clerk for Charlie Company at Camp Evans. "He had a presence. When he came in he was in charge. There was no doubt in your mind that he was in charge. And you knew that if you were going to question something he said you damn well better have your shit together. This man was not wrong about military. He was a stern task master. He kept people alive. He was a great man."

"He took care of his guys," said Howie Colbert, a Charlie Company veteran who had arrived in country in May 1969. Colbert had set mechanical ambushes at Hamburger Hill with the 101st. "He trained more like Special Forces than regular ground pounders. To keep continuity in all the platoons, which at that time we were broken down into squads, we were running the hub. The CP (command post) was in the middle and you had all these satellites moving the same way. Vazquez was brilliant. He pretty much organized us into a fighting force."

On April 2 Vazquez arrived at Firebase Gladiator as commander of Charlie Company, charged with preparing defensive positions so that the firebase could serve in place of Firebase Granite, which had been attacked and destroyed by NVA units a month prior. Charlie Company built that firebase up within a couple of days, noted Sgt. John Fowler, a veteran member of Charlie.

"We sent a platoon to Gladiator and re-erected it for more support for

Ripcord," said Colbert. "We were getting probed left and right. We distinguished ourselves when we killed every member of a K10 Sapper Company. "They got a lot of us, too. We were supposed to be up on 805 for some kind of support thing and were in a big firefight that night. (Lt. Jim) Campbell had tied claymores in the trees for some reason, so when he blew the ambush, which was mostly sappers, there was nothing left but feet laying in the kill zone. These guys, I don't know how they rolled over, but they policed their dead really well."

"Our mission changed quickly and our unit was ordered to attack and seize Hill 927, better known as Ripcord," said Vazquez-Rodriquez. "The company moved on the ground from Firebase Gladiator instead of using the routine air assault. Some of the battalion units have suffered severe casualties while executing air assaults simply because the enemy was waiting for three or more helicopters to land before initiating their attacks. My policy was to never land on top of the objective using one landing zone. I use three different landing zones and approach the objectives on three axis."

Lt. Chuck Hawkins was a 23-year-old West Point graduate (1968) who had, since the age of 4, grown up in the wilds of Alaska, where he hunted, roamed the forest and enjoyed life as a child in the wilderness. In 1964, he received an appointment to West Point from Sen. Ernest Gruening, one of only two senators who voted against the Gulf of Tonkin Resolution, which landed the United States in the Vietnam War.

Fresh out of West Point, Hawkins headed to Infantry Officers' Basic Course and Ranger School, then earned his first assignment with the 4th Armored Division, 1st/51st Infantry in Crailsheim, Germany. Within a year, he had two reassignment orders, flight school and Vietnam. He requested assignment to the 101st Airborne and on March 6, 1970, reported to Lt. Col. Andre Lucas and the 2nd/506th rear headquarters.

SPORADIC CONTACT

Two days later he was in the field under Capt. Vazquez with Charlie Company. He was leading Second Platoon. By May 30, he'd received his captain's bars.

Hawkins is well-versed in the battle and has insight only those who lived it and studied the aftermath can elaborate on. Activities in early April around Ripcord were very much guarded as Hawkins explained.

"During this period enemy activity in the AO (Area of Operation) did not seem to exceed or fall below expectations," said Hawkins, who was given charge of Alpha Company as captain after serving under Isabelino Vazquez-Rodriguez. "I reviewed the brigade and battalion TOC (Tactical Operation Center) journals extensively when I was doing some primary research on fratricide for DOD (Department of Defense). There was enemy contact sporadically throughout the battalion AO but it did not seem to have focus or building toward the eventual siege of the firebase. We were probed on Ripcord several times, but only once was this substantial. We figured the enemy was taking a 'wait and see' approach, and the more we kept improving the firebase the longer they would watch to learn what was going on.

"We did anticipate being hit by a ground attack at some point, but there were no signs of a major build up. Hindsight, of course, shows how much we missed or how good the enemy was at infiltration. We were spread very thinly. It would have been easy for the enemy to avoid contact with our units operating around the base."

Taking the Hill

Delta Company (2nd/506th) was moving through the jungles near Ripcord in early March under the command of Capt. Rembert Rollison, a hard-charging combat veteran from Hinesville, Ga. Rollison, who carried a shotgun along with his southern accent, replaced a commander Lt. Col. Andre Lucas had dispatched on March 6. His impact on the company was felt almost immediately.

"Rollison was a fine, fine fellow," said Lt. Jim McCall, himself from Louisiana, who went to Officer Candidate School after entering the Army at age 18. "It was his second tour in Vietnam. He had been an instructor at Ranger School. He was a tough, tough taskmaster. I attribute his leadership to the fact that we didn't lose more people than we lost and we had so much success in the jungle. A lot of the men complained about shaving and wearing the uniform properly, carrying the right amount of stuff we needed. The platoon leaders and senior NCOs (Non-Commissioned Officers) knew exactly what he was doing and why he was doing it. The respected him quite a bit. The fact that he was an instructor at the Ranger School made him tougher and it made us tougher. We took a lot of pride in that."

McCall explained how Rollison would train the company to move stealth-like through the jungle, maintaining light and noise discipline at night.

"Some units would move through the jungle with recon by fire, just firing everything up, just to make sure the enemy knew they were there and maybe tried to get out of the way," said McCall. "With Rollison, he had us move quietly through the jungle and nobody's going to even know we're there until we make contact and we're going to have the advantage. It was a unique concept and I think everybody in our company bought into it.

"We moved every night when we were in the jungle. We would move and set up a temporary position at dusk and send out a recon team and then the recon team would come back and say, 'We've got a position.' When we moved, light and noise discipline was max. We didn't want the enemy, if they were watching, to even know we moved."

Delta Company was moving along a ridgeline, within eyesight of Ripcord, when McCall came into his first firefight.

"Jack Flaherty had the point element," he remembered. "We were in a

SPORADIC CONTACT

line. The formation looked sort of like a big question mark. The top of the question mark was moving along the ridge and got hit. Rollison trained us whenever we made contact to drop into the hasty ambush; drop, drop our rucksacks and get behind anything we can get behind to get ready for action. The North Vietnamese element thought the point element was the only element out there and tried to circle. One of the enemy soldiers came around my side and tried to flank the point element. My medic, Steve Gunn, was out in the open. We went into the hasty ambush he just dropped into this clearing. This North Vietnamese soldier came over this log and saw Gunn. He grabbed his AK-47 and swung around. I took aim and popped him, killed him right there on the spot. That's the first person I ever killed. Of course, there was a lot of emotion and adrenaline pumping. That night, we moved into a Night Defensive Position and we were getting set up and the radio operator came over and said I had a message from the rear. The message was from the Red Cross; it said my wife had given birth to my second child that day. So you can imagine the emotion going through my mind at that time. I had taken a life that day and gotten word that I was instrumental in giving a life."

Rollison and his men had discovered a bunker complex at the base of Ripcord, southeast, while during this same time, Hawkins reported hearing hand-cranked generators atop Ripcord and to the south of the soon-to-be firebase. Rollison's men cut down an NVA squad leader who had intelligence on him indicating enemy morale was high. The dead soldier was also well-equipped, and was carrying an AK-47, three magazines and documents that indicated the squad had two RPG (Rocket-Propelled Grenade) launchers.

Rollison's group later walked up on an enemy site that included uniforms hanging on a line. Artillery and air attacks peppered the hill and soon, contact became less and less with the enemy.

For a month, the area around Ripcord had proven deadly, however

REMEMBERING FIREBASE RIPCORD

Ripcord itself had yet to be secured. That all changed at 4:30 the morning of April 11 when Hawkins and Charlie Company began their assault on Hill 927 (Ripcord) and within two-and-a-half hours, the soon-to-be firebase was secured, which allowed two engineering dozers to be dropped in by Chinook.

"My company was lead company," said Sgt. John Fowler, Charlie One. "We didn't encounter any resistance. We secured the perimeter and dug positions. Capt. Vazquez organized defensive positions and the kind of combat positions we'd build. He organized fields of fire, bunkers. He was so good and so fair, so clear about what he wanted you to do. He was so confident and so competent and we had no problem following. He was a good man to have at that point in time."

Lt. Bob "Gypsy" Wallace, Charlie One, was nearing the completion of his six months in the field when he learned Charlie Company would be assaulting Ripcord.

"I thought I was going to have a rear job," he said. "They told us we were going to walk up Ripcord. I was so scared when we went up."

Lt. Jim Campbell was a grizzled combat veteran as well and had also been trained by Capt. Isabellino Vazquez-Rodriguez.

"Charlie Company had been working up and down the ridgelines east of Ripcord, so they sent us to open Gladiator," remembered Campbell. "When I landed on Gladiator it was just a hilltop with an LZ (Landing Zone) on it. The reason to put a 105 (artillery) battery on it was for support. You've gotta have a 105 support that can get in there close, to support the assault of Ripcord. We landed on an LZ just east of it, on the hill going to 805. Hawkins was acting company commander. Me and Bob Wallace and a third lieutenant, we assaulted in there and one of the units got in a firefight down there, then we assaulted the hill, took the hill and started building a firebase."

From left, Charles Hawkins and Jim Campbell are pictured at the 2014 Ripcord Association reunion. Photo provided by Chris Brady.

Howie Colbert was with newly appointed Capt. Hawkins on the assault up Ripcord.

"We decide we're going to walk up instead of trying to CA (combat assault) in," said Colbert. "Chuck Hawkins had taken over the company as Vazquez left for R&R (rest and recuperation). He had his shit together. As we started to go, one of the gunships accidentally ejected one of his pods. He didn't know who was down there. Next thing you know we're being buzzed by our own choppers. It was pretty early in the morning when we made the siege up Ripcord. I was walking point for the CP (command post). Hawkins was like third behind me. Everyone else was online. As we were going up, we stuck out like a sore thumb. They were dropping 82s in front of us and all this crap was coming down on top of us. Next thing I know Hawkins grabbed me by the shoulder and said slow down. I was trying to keep up with (Sgt. Paul) Burkey. My eyes are big, Hawkins' eyes were big and I'm trying to scope this thing out. It was just a barren piece of shit, no place to hide. You could see the crater marks all over the place. We were going to slide off to the treeline, go up and make our positions."

"We assaulted it and there was literally nothing there," said Campbell.

"That's when we started building it."

Once the firebase was secured, work quickly began.

"We brought in dozers, knocked off the top and made it into a firebase, called it Ripcord. It was lower than the hills around it, which was a lot of the problem," remembered chopper pilot Randy House. "The enemy had the high ground and had critical observers and some critical firepower above this big firebase."

"We moved bulldozers with tracks and blades to begin the preparations," remembered Vazquez-Rodriguez, who was charged with building the firebase. "The plan to prepare the firebase was in my head and it was based on the base camp I built in the Mekong Delta in South Vietnam. I knew that the first days were critical because it was to their advantage to hit our unit before good defensive positions were available. We requested and got two defoliation missions and moved the 81mm mortars and recoilless rifles from Company E into our position. We also moved Battery B, 319th Field Artillery into position with the 155mm howitzers and also one engineer squad to help build defensive plans. I also placed Lt. Hawkins' platoon outside the proposed (fire) base real estate on the most likely avenue of approach for an enemy attack."

Under Vazquez-Rodriguez' keen supervision, an apron of barbed wire tanglefoot, at least six feet in width and secured with triple concertina wire and hog wire compressed beneath the tanglefoot, was laid. The idea was to keep Sappers from crawling underneath to access the firebase. Tanglefoot is set low to the ground as Sappers were trained to crawl, clothed often in only a loincloth, or less, underneath the wire and dismantle any explosives that may be set to deter enemy advances.

"We had one of the best concertina wire setups I had ever seen on any firebase," said Ernie Claxon, Headquarters Company, and a veteran of the Korean War.

SPORADIC CONTACT

"During the day we'd clear, with axes, brush from the fighting position and start to put in concertina wire," said Peter McSwain, Headquarters Company. "During the night, we would sit there and take shifts staying awake. I remember when it rained, every 45 minutes it would pool up on a half shelter above and spill over and soak me. I also remember, the M-16s wouldn't take a bayonet, but some of the guys had them anyway. They'd strap them to their boots. The first night I was going to be awake for an hour, then wake someone else up and trade off. A guy put his bayonet to my throat and said, 'I'm going to sleep now and if you're asleep when I get up, you won't.' That helped me to concentrate."

"One of the most important stories with Ripcord is Vazquez and the way he built that firebase," said Campbell. "It was built different than any other firebase. He knew how to do it. The positions were different. It was damn near invincible. That's the remarkable part of the Ripcord story. We stayed there a month building it. It was awful work. It was back-breaking work from daylight to dark to get those defenses in. It was brutal work but he's a superstar in my view – the best there ever was. Everyone in Charlie Company will tell you that about Vazquez."

Colbert remembered Vazquez saying there would be no relying on previous positions.

"'We're digging L-shaped positions,'" Colbert remembered Vazquez saying. "It was really smart. They were dropping 82mm rounds on us every day. They knew exactly where everything was. Poor Lt. Campbell. He was in charge of putting all the tanglefoot out. He was really good."

"The aprons of wire were reinforced with M49A1 static trip flares to let our fighters know when the enemy was in the wire," said Vazquez-Rodriguez. "We also placed M2A3 personnel mines connected with detonated cord and capable of detonating in sequence. Our inner perimeter and last line of defense consisted of rolls of reinforcing wire, also known as hog wire, unwound and placed on vertical positions and secured by six-foot engineer's stakes. This wire is difficult to cut and easy to check during daylight hours to determine any type of breach by the enemy.

"We registered the 81mm mortars real close to our wire defenses; the recoilless rifles were located to deliver fire support directly onto the wire obstacles. Our 155mm howitzers were registered to hit specific locations within the overall fire plan. Our fire plan included air support to be controlled by our artillery forward observer and platoon leaders if necessary. The construction of the firebase was not an easy task. We were hit constantly by enemy artillery and lost several soldiers. The enemy launched several attacks with small units, but we never flinched. Every solider in Ripcord was committed to defense of the firebase to the last man. The same feeling and commitment was adopted by Lt. Hawkins' troops; they were the first to probably be hit, but retreating was not in their dictionary."

Ripcord itself has been described as about the size of four football fields, however Vazquez-Rodriguez explained there were many ridges and trails coming into and out of Ripcord.

"The Tactical Operation Center (TOC) was embedded on the southern slopes of the hill in such a way as to minimize or camouflage the position and size," said Vazquez-Rodriguez. "It was constructed of Conex Containers buried side by side to accommodate the TOC of the 2nd Battalion, 506th, the 2nd Battalion, 17th Cavalry, 501st Signal Battalion, the 1st Regiment of the Army Republic of South Vietnam and a Special Forces Detachment of the ARVN. These tactical operation centers are known as the 'forward' meaning that they are not the main centers for these units.

"An additional TOC was built to accommodate Battery B, 2nd/319th Artillery and a Battery of Army Republic of South Vietnam. Th(is) number of units at that location indicate that Ripcord was fairly large in size. The fighting positions around the perimeter of the hill were placed in such a way to allow the defender to defend themselves by firing on different enemy possible approaches and defend each other's positions if the enemy was successful to breach the main perimeter."

Positions were channeled deep and the overhead low to ensure the enemy would have difficulty locating positions on the firebase, according to Vazquez-Rodriguez.

"Our goal was also to engage the enemy at close range and let the artillery and our mortars to engage the enemy at medium and long range," he said.

Ripcord featured three helicopter pads, one at the northeast end of the base, close to artillery ammunition bunkers, ideal for unloading artillery rounds. The second helipad was along the southern slope, the pad of choice for Vazquez-Rodriguez anytime he approached so that an eye could be kept on Hills 1,000 and 902. Another was located at the opposite end of the firebase.

"The main enemy resupplies came from the trails at these locations (south)," he said.

The enemy would pepper Ripcord routinely over the next 90 days from those locations, though the real assault on Ripcord wouldn't begin until July. In the valley, around Ripcord, American soldiers would notice an uptick in contact with the North Vietnamese throughout the area of operation (AO).

Ripcord itself took incoming, but was never breached by land, a credit to Vazquez and his attention to detail, according to Meloro.

"People would always come back from the hill cursing about how hard he worked them," said Meloro. "Now they see him at reunions and they thank him. He built it so that there was no way the NVA would take that hill by physical force."

One member of Charlie Company was killed in the construction when he dug into a live grenade.

Work was hard as the days were hot. Combat engineers constructed fortifications in the rear and those fortifications were flown to the firebase for installation and reinforced with sandbags.

"We did a lot of work in the rear preparing for Ripcord, building bunkers and when we were out in the field we had to blow foxholes, a lot of demo - cutting trees and clearing fields with fire and laying concertina wire, setting claymore mines," said David Kenyon, 326th Engineers. "We were working all the time. The bunkers were made out of twelve by twelve beams. The bulldozers dug all the holes to put them in, they just set them in, covered them sandbagged them.

"After the bunkers, command post and artillery were set up. We combat engineers were fortunate enough to leave Firebase Ripcord. I cannot imagine what other service men went through in and around Firebase Ripcord."

Greg Kiekintveld, also a combat engineer with the 326th, remembered watching Ripcord getting mortared from Firebase Gladiator. Soon he was landing on the hill.

"We'd supervise the ground infantry, putting in tanglefoot, concertina wire, while we have other guys working on fortification," said Kiekintveld. "I was out there before we sent out the wooden bunkers we made back at Evans. When I landed it was roots of trees and stumps of trees that had been blown up by artillery. We kept throwing stuff down the hill.

"I was there a couple days right after they got the dozer in. I remember a lot of fog. You couldn't see twenty-five feet in front of you. Our shelter at night was just a bunch of ponchos stretched out over several stakes. We'd work all day then crawl under there at night and write letters home."

Ripcord, as it may have been suspected by some early, was right in the middle of the North Vietnamese operations aimed at pushing southward.

"We didn't realize we were in their division command area," said Fowler. "We were right in the middle of it. Why they didn't mess with us sooner, I don't know – once they figured out we were going to try to interdict.

"There was just a crushing blanket of harsh reality, and understanding that no action would bring them back, but also the other reality that there was not time for self pity." – Lt. Bob Layton, Bravo Company, 2/501.

Contact was sporadic throughout the month of April.

David Corradetti was a 19-year-old draftee from Gibstown, N.J. that ended up in Vietnam in November 1969. Bob Lemon was drafted out of high school in Florida and qualified as an M-16 expert.

Lemon was assigned to Charlie Company, third platoon Sept. 1. He had seen some heavy combat as a veteran of Charlie Company by the time the Ripcord campaign got underway. He remembered Steve Steward had just earned his sergeant stripes in early April.

"I was talking to him," said Lemon. "I went to see the chaplain. I asked him to go and he wouldn't go. The next day we went up a forced march up these rocky areas leading up to Ripcord."

Assigned to the 101st Airborne, Corradetti ended up in the Ripcord Area of Operations during those early weeks and remembers pulling duty on the firebase, where he and his fellow soldiers from Charlie Company reinforced the hilltop with wire. Then the call came to leave the firebase, as was typical for troop rotations.

"We got the call to go, about 10 o'clock we were humping through the boonies and stopped to take a break," said Corradetti. "All of a sudden RPGs (rocket-propelled grenades) just started shooting. We walked into an ambush."

An RTO (radio telephone operator), Corradetti was standing beside Steward when he was killed. It happened so quickly and right beside the young trooper. Corradetti was also hit.

"We were third platoon back," he remembered. They pulled back and Corradetti was choppered out.

"The NVA (North Vietnamese Army) were up on this hill," remembered Lemon. "RPGs came in and Steward got killed. I got wounded – shrapnel in my arm to the bone. It was like five hours later, we were getting taken care of and they attacked again. I jumped and a round hit this tree. I saw sparks and it hit across my fingers. I dove down the hill, dug a foxhole with my helmet. I hit the hole, had two guys crouch behind me. I opened up with my M-16. I saw something fire back and I went with my (M)60. We got medevacked the next day. We must have had eight wounded."

It was April 6, just days after the April Fool's Day assault and days before Ripcord would be established by American forces.

By late March and early April, the men of Bravo Company saw the North Vietnamese getting more aggressive during contacts in the field.

Lyle Kohmetscher was a platoon sergeant with Bravo Company, 2/501st. He served under Robert Worrall and Lt. Robert Layton.

SPORADIC CONTACT

"March was an uneventful month as we went on squad- and platoon-sized recons in the highlands," said Kohmetscher. "We had many new replacements that arrived in Vietnam in February and March."

Kohmetscher was drafted into the Army in late July 1968 and landed in Vietnam Aug. 8, 1969. Prior to landing in the Ripcord AO, Kohmetscher spent time just north around the Demilitarized Zone.

Layton knew Vietnam was in his future. He had spent the better part of two years thinking about it.

"I was a ROTC (Reserve Officers Training Corp) officer and received my commission upon graduation from Ohio University in mid-March 1969. The way ROTC was then structured, cadets applied for a branch assignment (artillery, transportation, engineering, etc.) at the end of their junior year. I applied for infantry, so from that point I pretty much knew Vietnam was in my future. I thought if I was going to go, I was going to be prepared and wanted to be an officer.

"Following graduation, I reported to Fort Benning, Ga., in early April and began a nine-week Infantry Officers' Basic Course (IOBC). There was little question in our minds that ultimately we were headed for Vietnam. Following IOBC, I volunteered for paratrooper training and Ranger training. Following graduation from Ranger training, I was assigned to Fort Leonard Wood, Mo., where I commanded a Basic Training Company from October 1960 to January 1970. I had a 30-day leave before reporting for Jungle Operations Training at Fort Sherman in Panama and then on to Vietnam."

The weight of what he was about to undertake wasn't lost on Layton, who was 24 at the time. He understood that he would soon be the leader of young men in battle and that is why he took on the additional training.

"While the Army considered IOBC to be adequate training to lead combat troops, I understood that I had an extraordinary obligation to the soldiers I had yet to meet," said Layton. "Throughout my training I was aware that at some point in the future I would meet and lead a platoon that had no voice in choosing its leader. I would be presented as a settled fact and therefore my obligation was to be as well trained as possible.

"In terms of conduct of the war, all my training presented the war in terms of large unit operations on massive search-and-destroy missions. In my mind's eye, the war was conducted in rice paddies in flat terrain. The reality of my war was in the mountains of I Corps, the northernmost part of what was then South Vietnam. The vast majority of my operations were at platoon level."

Layton landed near the A Shau Valley and was immediately hit with the reality of war and its costs.

"Bob Layton took over 1st Platoon in April after I left to be Bravo Company XO (Executive Officer)," remembered Bob Worrall. "Layton couldn't have picked a worse time to come in with several deadly contacts in early/mid-April in an area a couple of kilometers southeast of Ripcord called 'Re-Up Hill,' then relieving Alpha Company after they were hit by a sapper attack on Firebase Granite, just east of Ripcord."

He has been at headquarters for the 2nd Battalion/501st in Phu Bai and had no idea what was happening in I Corps, much less the Ripcord Area of Operations. On April 8, he choppered into a hill a little more than a kilometer from Ripcord. Upon setting foot in the jungle, he had a young GI greet him.

"I remember this kid telling me they'd killed a trailwatcher and did I want to go look at him," said Layton. "I remember thinking that I'm probably going to see more of them and taking a pass. I don't think I was emotionally prepared, but I was certainly prepared. I don't know if anyone is emotionally prepared the first time."

SPORADIC CONTACT

Layton then met the two platoon sergeants, including Kohmetscher, and the company commander, Bob Stanton. Kochmetscher assembled three squad leaders as the company was attempting to get off a landing zone. Layton was given three squads of seven men each, though he had little time to get to know them. They were on the move.

"I lost my squad my first morning in the field," remembered Layton. "When the squad was hit that morning there was a certain air of unreality – how could this happen so quickly? There was no break-in period. I was in combat. When we secured the ambushed squad's position, the priorities were to maintain security, treat the wounded, evacuate them. I was very fortunate because I had a platoon sergeant who directed the nuts and bolts of security and a combat medic who very capably treated the wounded. My contribution was mostly limited to orchestrating the events. The harsh reality was we had dead and wounded and NVA in the vicinity. In retrospect, and I don't mean this to sound cold, I was probably lucky that I didn't know these men. Had I been able to develop a relationship, emotions may have limited my actions.

"Following evacuation of the dead and wounded, I think numbness was probably the most descriptive adjective. There was just a crushing blanket of harsh reality, and understanding that no action would bring them back, but also the other reality that there was no time for self-pity. The remainder of the platoon needed a leader and my job was to step up. Fortunately, the remaining members of the platoon understood that the ambush was not a result of an overt action of mine. There was no sense of recrimination toward the new platoon leader. Indeed, I think some felt sorry for me that I had to begin my tour this way.

"The reality is that the loss of that squad weighs on me more as time passes. In total I lost eight men in Vietnam and six were in the first week. I really didn't know any of them, yet they were my responsibility. I find that as life goes on I have this real emptiness resulting from the fact that

REMEMBERING FIREBASE RIPCORD

I didn't know them. Their anonymity prevented my finding closure."

Kohmetscher remembered those two days, April 8-9, well.

"We air assaulted into an area called Re-Up Hill on April 8," he wrote. "Second and third platoons went to the west to a Night Defensive Position (NDP) on Re-Up Hill. Our platoon, first platoon along with the company command went a short distance to the east. One squad was set up as a defensive position and ambush site while the other two squads set up on a small knoll just to the north in an NDP. This area had an uneasy feeling to all of us as Sgt. (James) Mace had shot and killed an NVA before we had even left the landing zone.

"At around first light on April 9, the forward squad was hit by a surprise attack by a small NVA group. They had overrun their position and were trying to kill them all. We saw this from our position and immediately responded. Dennis Sartin was the first man from the platoon to charge their position and undoubtedly saved some lives. I, along with several men, was right behind him. In this attack, three were killed – Sgt. (James) Mace, PFC George Selman and PFC Leroy Nelson, all of them having arrived in Vietnam on Feb. 12, 1970. In addition, the other five members of the squad were badly wounded. They were Jose Morals, Tom Patchell, Lenard Blackely, a guy whose last name was Bristol and Thomas Gates."

Gates spent the rest of his life as a paraplegic, and passed away Nov. 25, 1986, from complications related to wounds he received at Re-Up Hill.

The battle wasn't finished. After the dead and wounded had been evacuated, Herman Allen Clay Jr. spotted an NVA soldier outside the perimeter near the same spot the squad had been hit earlier in the day.

"He asked me if anyone was in front of us and I said, 'No,'" remembered Kohmetscher. "Before anything else could be said he stood up and took aim at something. He fired his rifle at the same time the NVA he had spotted fired his. They literally killed each other. This was our fourth KIA for the day. Clay had also come in country on Feb. 12, 1970."

Less than two months in Vietnam and these young men had lost their lives. April was tough on Bravo Company.

"Later that day we moved back to the LZ we had landed on the day before," said Kohmetscher. "We set up an NDP there for the night as I recall. Everyone, to say the least, was nervous and full of anxiety. We were also carrying the extra equipment from our wounded and KIAs. Medevacs did not take equipment back."

It was April 10 and Kohmetscher's first platoon was to march to second and third platoons on Re-Up Hill. Just prior to leaving, a meeting was taking place in the middle of the night defensive position when Wayne Sistruck walked up.

"I was telling him to get down when a sniper fired one shot and hit him in the chest, killing him immediately," said Kohmetscher. "This was a fifth KIA in less than 24 hours. Sistruck had arrived in Vietnam on March 2, 1970. We got him out, but still had the extra equipment from 10 men to carry. We joined the other two platoons later that day. Our losses were a shock to everyone."

Layton still carries the grief of that week with him to this day.

"It was very, very clear to me the idea of relaxation or letting your guard down was absurd," he said. "I have told people the toughest job of my life was as an infantry platoon leader in Vietnam. I've never worked as hard, felt so much responsibility. I've never been as involved in a job as I was then. If I have a crappy report at the office, the sun still comes up. The downside of a bad day there was what I saw the first day. There's no way you can let your guard down."

It's difficult to understand the strain these young men must have been under, despite the intense training they received. As Layton, and others, explained, life in the jungle was minute to minute. You never knew when you may encounter contact. It may be days, a week. You still had to be sharp.

"I never knew what day it was," said Layton. "I remember we were out of the Ripcord AO, south and east, and found this nice little stream. We called a halt to movement, established a perimeter and took baths. That's one of the things I think people don't understand. You don't come in out of the field every night and shower, shave or eat. We were just out there, four, five, six weeks at a time. That was normal."

Reflecting on that time as a young officer, Layton explained the grind and the goal of keeping young men alive.

"The job was to keep these guys straight, keep them in line," he said. "The notion that, here I am, I'm down to 15-18 people and I'm responsible for their lives; When you really think about what that means, the grind can get to you. I never assumed that trail was safe, that there were good things around the corner. My whole operating procedure was be prepared. My whole MO was if I can't see it, don't believe it. There were times when if we'd go without a contact for a couple weeks, they would start to lighten up and you'd have to start kicking ass and tighten them up again. It was that mental, emotional grind that was constantly there."

Cheeseburger Hill

Alpha Company, following an eventful March, was around the Hill 805 area April 6-10. Bill Heath remembered the area well, having kept a daily log. Hill 805 was earning quite a reputation.

"We started calling it Cheeseburger Hill," said Heath, a reference to the 101st Airborne's previous involvement at Dong Ap Bia, or Hamburger Hill as it famously came to be known during the May 1969 assault about five kilometers south and west of Ripcord.

SPORADIC CONTACT

April 6-7, the men of Alpha moved around the hill, then moved to the top on the eighth.

"We thought it would be a big fight," he said. "There were plenty of signs of gooks."

As Alpha moved around and up Hill 805, Charlie Company was prepping for an assault of Ripcord.

For those working with artillery units on the firebase, there was a different view of what was happening.

"There was a daily grind to the war, as is common in any war," said Marc Aronson. "Some days we were on offense, we shot fire missions in support of the infantry in the hills and valleys around us, or in support of other firebases who were under attack. Other days, especially after July 1, we were in a defensive mode, firing missions to keep the bad guys at a safe distance… Some of us worked a night shift and tried to sleep during the day, but most of the time you just worked when you had to, sun, rain, light or dark. The bad guys in the hills around us did not give warning when they were going to attack, so we were constantly on our toes for anything unusual. You could be sleeping, eating, taking a rare shower or anything in between and be interrupted by the enemy around us.

"We had a free-fire minute many nights, normally around 3 or 4 a.m. Everyone just fired whatever they had into the jungle around us hoping to kill a bad guy or two, or to at least give them pause for thought. From day one we had the occasional mortar fall in, before July 1 here and there most every day."

Life in the Jungle

Late April saw several companies humping around the firebase. Things were somewhat quiet for Burckard and Alpha. Days were filled with movement through the thick jungle, explained by the captain in his daily log.

"Mountain terrain in double- and triple-canopy jungle is difficult to navigate with very limited visibility and no reference points except other hills, which you can't see anyway."

Troops, placed in the field for days and often weeks on end, would get "kick-out" resupply, which included a chopper arriving on site and "kicking out" the supplies to the troops below.

"Kickout resupply is when you don't have a clear landing zone and the supply items much be 'kicked out' of the helicopter to land, hopefully somewhere near enough to be recovered," said Burckard. "Most resupply is brought directly from Ripcord where it is stockpiled and then taken to field locations by slick. The supply items are brought by CH-47 (Chinook) from Camp Evans to Ripcord."

Lt. James Noll's platoon, Alpha three, received a kick-out of demo on Thursday, April 23, and was to blow a landing zone. Burckard noted there had been little enemy activity in the area west of Ripcord, only several older trails.

"I find myself thinking more and more about going home as I get shorter," he wrote. "Getting short" was a term soldiers would use to describe their final weeks or days in the field. "Should have a little over three months left," he added.

The next day, Burckard and Alpha continued moving toward Coc-A-Bo Mountain. Noll and his men used 18 cases of demo to cut the landing zone. Lt. Jeff Wilcox and Alpha one were dealing with a case of worms.

"We got a couple of cases of bad C-rations the other day," noted Burckard. "I have had diarrhea on and off for about a month."

SPORADIC CONTACT

A one-day platoon standdown at Ripcord had been approved beginning with Alpha three (Noll) slated first. Fog socked in Alpha Company just as Noll's men ran out of food. Ripcord was also socked in so resupply was out of the question.

The next day, Monday, April 27, things moved a bit, with Alpha one and two getting resupplied, however Noll and his men remained socked in and could not be extracted or resupplied. Burckard was picked up in a command and control chopper and flown onto Ripcord, where he was briefed. He learned the 2/501st was in daily contact just three kilometers south of his Alpha troops and that the ARVN were preparing to go into the A-Shau to occupy Firebase Bradley.

More telling was the information he gleaned from Lt. Col. Lucas.

"The president announced a 150,000-man troop cut within a year," Burckard wrote. "Lt. Col. Lucas seems to feel that the U.S. units will be relegated to firebase security and the ARVNs will do the groundwork. It seems the two airmobile divisions will probably remain as the 'fire brigade.'"

Noll and his men finally flew to Ripcord at 10:30 a.m. Wednesday, April 29, where they enjoyed their first full meal in three days, Burckard noted.

Lt. Lee Widjeskog arrived that day to replace Lt. Gary Kelly.

During the standdown at Ripcord, all of Burckard's men got a hot meal, clean clothes and had their ammunition resupplied. Despite the "creature comforts", life on a firebase for a combat infantry soldier was a bit disconcerting.

"It was much more comforting to be out in the jungle by ourselves," wrote Burckard. "At least we could move around and make our own defensive accommodations. On top of a firebase, you felt you were sleeping in the center of a bull's eye for both incoming and outgoing mortar and artillery fire. It was never good to be on a firebase."

Looking up at the firebase, Burckard noted the progress that had been made in a short amount of time.

"Ripcord is now a thriving firebase with two 105mm batteries," he wrote. "One is our old friend B Battery, 2nd Battalion, 319th Artillery, my forward observer's (Lt. Tom Brennan) battery, with M-102 howitzers. The other battery is ARVN with the old split-trail 105mm howitzers. There is also an ARVN regimental CP (command post) with our battalion TOC (Tactical Operations Center). They also have a mess hall and battalion clearing station for the wounded. The 'new' approved type fighting positions are being employed there – two-man positions with overhead cover on the sleeping part."

7

Ahead of the Siege

By May contact was subsiding as the NVA (North Vietnamese Army), still in the valley in large numbers, appeared to be staging for an all-out assault.

Reports of bunker findings were common by troops in the jungle surrounding Ripcord.

Alpha three and Lt. Jim Noll found four six-foot by ten-foot A-frame bunkers with a heating system running from a centrally located kitchen area, according to Capt. Burckard's daily log.

"The bunkers had three feet of overhead (earth) cover," he wrote. "Six fighting positions surrounded the area. It was probably an NVA platoon-size winter camp."

"In May it went quiet," remembered Capt. Randy House. "You could have played golf in that AO (Area of Operations) and you probably wouldn't have seen an NVA soldier. In May it was like they went away but what we know now thanks to Ben Harrison's book ("Hell On A Hilltop") what they were doing they were kind of trying to lull us into a false sense of security. At the end of June it started picking up and we were getting shot at, getting mortared."

REMEMBERING FIREBASE RIPCORD

The jungle is never quiet long.

Burckard, in his daily log, wrote about learning of movement into Cambodia, only that American troops were working with ARVN to attack NVA base camps across the border.

On Thursday, May 7, to the south and east of Ripcord, Firebase Maureen suffered a ground attack which resulted in six killed and 12 wounded. Medic Kenneth Kays, a conscientious objector, earned the Medal Of Honor for his heroism during the battle. Having lost his left leg below the knee due to a satchel charge explosion, Kays continued to crawl to those in need, administering aid while applying a tourniquet to his own injury.

Monday, May 11, Alpha Company first platoon, under the leadership of Lt. Jeff Wilcox, worked atop Hill 465 and found two NVA-built bunkers. Alpha had occupied the hill on March 29. The bunkers were new, noted Burckard.

"Wilcox also reported that the NVA had dug up all of our trash sumps, apparently in search of food," said Burckard. "This is a common occurrence because the NVA are always short on food. If we stay in an area long enough, a good tactic is to ambush a buried trash sump. The battalion has gotten several kills in the past with this tactic."

Lt. Col. Lucas visited with Burckard near Hill 465 late in the evening of Tuesday, May 12.

"He said the move to Firebase Bradley in the A-Shau Valley was off permanently because the brigade had overextended itself as was evidenced by the high number of casualties taken on Firebase Henderson May 6."

Alpha Company combat assaulted into an area south of Hill 465 where the brigade MINICAV (usually two Cobras and a two slicks) ran into

AHEAD OF THE SIEGE

contact. Delta Company was set up about 2,000 meters to the west. At 4:30 p.m., a chopper attempting to land members of Delta took about 10 mortar rounds, remembered Burckard.

"The enemy tube was only about 500 meters to my southeast," he wrote. "My forward observer, Lt. Brennan, and I adjusted artillery, ARA (Aerial Rocket Artillery) and counter mortar fire with my 81mm tube. I don't know if we got them or not but they didn't fire anymore. We found two RPG rounds from B-40 rocket launchers on our landing zone. This hillside is a recent NVA position. We found two 51-caliber anti-aircraft machine gun positions and an eight-foot circular hole with a center pedestal and an adjoining bunker, for crew protection."

Thursday, May 14 proved deadly after more than a week of relative peace. Alpha One began moving at 8 a.m., south up the ridge. No more than 200 meters from the night defensive position, Bob Lowe, the point man, was killed when the NVA opened fire.

"The platoon returned fire with a tremendous volume of firepower," said Burckard. "The NVA responded with grenades, which wounded five of my men, including Lt. Wilcox."

Machine gunner Tiny Aanonsen and Wilcox had been hit in the ambush. The platoon had been ambushed. Aanonsen sprang forward with his M-60 machine gun, spraying bullets into the NVA which allowed his fellow soldiers to gather the dead and wounded. In the course of the forward movement, Tiny sustained shrapnel wounds in his arm, shoulder and leg. His time in the field up, he was medevacked out; Wilcox was treated by medics for shrapnel, including a piece in his head. Gerald Mauney was also choppered out and would die two days later, on May 16, from wounds received in the firefight.

Third platoon and Lt. Noll had moved in behind Alpha One to provide covering fire. Noll and Sgt. Arvel Koger went into the kill zone to

REMEMBERING FIREBASE RIPCORD

get Lowe's body, Burckard wrote. They could not get his equipment so they fired a tracer round to destroy it.

"I pulled both platoons back and called in ARA, tube artillery and 81mm mortars at a distance of 200 meters," wrote Burckard. "The ceiling was too low for airstrikes to be effective so I had to send two beautiful Navy A-4 Skyhawks away. After three hours of pounding with everything I could get in, I sent second platoon and Lt. Lee Widjeskog up the hill. They got into the bunker area without receiving fire and destroyed the bunker with a 90mm recoilless rifle. I left half of second platoon there overnight and put the other half on the far side of our night defensive position, near the landing zone.

"We expected to get hit because Delta Company to our west spotted several NVA moving around our western flank just after the contact. They night was quiet except that the first platoon's Kit Carson scout, a former Viet Cong, got very sick and went into semi-consciousness with spasms."

Lt. Darling lost his life May 18 when his chopper was shot down as it flew from Ripcord to Camp Evans. A favorite amongst his men, his death still weighs on many.

"Basically the chopper got shot down," said Ernie Claxon, who served under Darling." They were taking a new radio to Alpha Company. Jeff Winters and I were going to go out and do it. For some reason, Larry Stone (Harry) he went out instead of Jeff and of course it got shot down. We heard that recon finally found it.

"We called him the Duke. He acted like John Wayne. He was a good man, straight-up honest good guy. He led by leading."

"When I was around him, he was a very cool head," remembered McSwain, also of Headquarters Company. "Darling was a soldier's soldier. He was an Airborne Ranger, he was a West Point graduate. I

AHEAD OF THE SIEGE

thought he was an outstanding officer and soldier. It was many, many days later they found the burned wreckage of the chopper."

Still patrolling in the area, Alpha Company listened as Delta Company, a kilometer to the west, took 10 rounds of 82mm mortar on their landing zone, Burckard would write. There were no casualties. Later that afternoon, men from Alpha found a fresh .51-caliber machine gun position with an attached bunker.

"In it were some expended brass (shell casings) from a Soviet sniper rifle," Burckard noted. "The NVA had probably used the position to snipe at U.S. aircraft. Farther up, at the top, we found a 60mm mortar position with attached bunker, a half dozen fuse cans, fuse plugs and discarded (powder) charges – probably used a few days ago."

Burckard kept notes as to how the NVA were building and fortifying positions. He also took note as to how meticulously crafted the positions were.

"Examined the bunker here more closely," he wrote. "Standard 'A' frame-type with two exits. Very solidly built, about eight-feet long, four-feet high and three-feet wide at the base. Usually two logs make up the roof with earth on top."

The captain explained the first indication of bunkers in a specific area would be the presence of tree stumps, sawed off around a foot above the ground. The trees were typically four- to six-inches in diameter and several would be cut over a large area to ensure the natural concealment of the area would not be too disturbed.

It was May 20, and it rained all day. Still in the same general area, near Hill 460, Alpha Company came upon a trailwatcher coming up as the troopers went down the trail. The North Vietnamese soldier jumped off the trail to the left and let about five men go by.

REMEMBERING FIREBASE RIPCORD

"He must have gotten scared," Burckard wrote. "He popped up in front of the M-79 gunner, in front of my RTO, and sprayed the column with his AK-47 and then bounded down the hill before we could get a shot at him. I leveled my M-16 at him, the only clear shot I had an enemy soldier in my 18 months in Vietnam, and my rifle jammed! The man in front of the M-79 grenandier, SP4 Michaels, got an AK round in his rear end. We had to medevac him by jungle penetrator.

8

Meeting of the Minds

On May 19, officers from the Army and ARVN (Army of the Republic of Vietnam) met at Camp Evans to discuss what was happening at Firebase Ripcord.

The biggest known in Vietnam was perhaps the consistency of the unknown. Those operating south of Ripcord and the A Shau saw more Viet Cong and constantly questioned who to trust. When it came to the North Vietnamese, the question was always how many and where. At Ripcord, when it came to finding the North Vietnamese, there was never any difficulty. The only question was how many there were, however it became clear rather early there were many, many enemy troops in the jungles surrounding the firebase.

Peter Senft enlisted in the Army in 1969.

"I just had a feeling that if I waited for the lottery, I'd be a single-digit, pop-up target," he said. "I enlisted and chose what to do. I volunteered to be part of the shake and bakes."

Following basic training at Fort Dix, he was assigned to Fort Hollabird for an additional 16 weeks of training, then NCO (Non-Commissioned

Officer) school for another 12 weeks. It was May 1970 when he received his orders for Vietnam.

"There were 20-some in my class and all went to Vietnam," he said. "I was assigned to the 101st and assigned to Camp Evans, to S2 shop. One of my first responsibilities, within a day or two, was to give an analysis."

Startled by the findings, he reported them to his superior, the S2. Clearly, it never went any farther.

"I spent two days going over prisoner interrogations, intercepted radio communications, captured documents and all the reports that had come in. After two days, I said, 'Holy shit, you gotta be kidding me.' We had two fresh NVA (North Vietnamese Army) divisions, plus support, surrounding Ripcord - 20 to 30,000 around Ripcord. The response was, 'You're a cherry, you don't know.'

"I don't know that it ever went past the S2. I believed in the chain of command. Throughout the entire battle, I'm wondering where the rest of the division is and why we aren't committing more men. E5s don't go to colonels and tell them, 'You're fucking up.' I did my job and told people what I was supposed to tell them."

Senft's belief was supported by others, who clearly had an idea the numbers of NVA in the area were immense.

Staff Sgt. Kemett Messenger, discussing Ripcord activities in Doug Bonnot's book, "The Sentinel and the Shooter," noted, "I was greatly surprised by the lack of information that the brigade S2 had regarding the size of the enemy force confronting us in the area of Fire Support Base Ripcord, until I learned that the captain was not yet cleared for the sensitive and compartmented information we provided. It was difficult to sanitize the information and still provide a comprehensive picture of the scenario around Ripcord. It was apparent to me that the size of the enemy force around Ripcord was far greater than he understood."

Messenger was with the 265th RRC (ABN) at Camp Eagle. He had previously been chief of NVA Low Level Tactical Exploitation at the 8th RRFS. Messenger noted he was "fully" aware of the size of the enemy force deployed around Ripcord and that the intelligence was being reported through normal channels.

Part of the Operation Texas Star mission, Senft said, was to interdict the supply lines that came off the northern end of the Ho Chi Minh Trail southeast.

"In many ways Texas Star was a success because it delayed that advance," said Senft. "There's no question about it in my opinion. I watched what unfolded."

That success came at great human loss as activity in Ripcord escalated.

As activity escalated, there were concerns over the costs of the war. Those concerns came from the very top, all the way back in Washington. Lt. Robin Graham detailed some of these concerns in "An Annotated History of the 2nd Battalion (Airmobile), 506th Infantry (1 March 1970- 1 August 1970)".

Graham reported that he was to provide Lt. Col. Andre Lucas with a detailed list of munitions spent. That concern, and the idea that anyone above was concerned with how much artillery was being used to keep troops in the field concerned many.

Dealing with Death

In late May, a medevac chopper was shot down in the Triple Hill Area, west of Ripcord, as a recon team from Echo Company was attempting to evacuate two troopers injured in a Cobra fire mishap. It was the morning of May 28, a morning that proved to be rather rough for Ralph Motta, a member of the recon team, and all involved.

"I remember watching as another team was trying to extract some wounded individuals," remembered Bob Romig, a lieutenant with Delta Company. "The medevac took a hit. When you are an officer and you stand up, they call you as an individual and take you to that unit. I was taken to that unit and told to link up with that recon team. Our objective was to carry those individuals that were shot down back to an LZ (landing zone) so that they could be extracted."

Romig had heard about Vietnam while drilling as a member of ROTC (Reserve Officer Training Corps) at Ohio State University. After two years in ROTC, he stayed on, having been given the option, and was commissioned as a first lieutenant in 1967.

"I assumed this was my war, my time," said Romig. "Standing up at graduation and taking the oath as a first lieutenant, there were catcalls. It was intense."

He didn't want anything to do with artillery or armor, so he signed up with infantry. Following training, he got orders for Vietnam, landing in country in November 1969. He was assigned to Delta Company, where he took over first platoon.

Little can prepare one for the horrors of war. Romig, like most young officers, had to deal with the reality of war while balancing the need, and strong desire, to keep his men safe all while ensuring they do their jobs.

"They were charred and in bad shape," he said of the bodies. "We were given body bags, which had been dropped in. We carried them on poles. There some members of that team that refused to carry those individuals and that was a very difficult time for me to deal with. It took two of us to carry one. We got back to an LZ."

MEETING OF THE MINDS

Another Delta team linked up with Romig's men and provided security as the dead were choppered out.

"We were in a little NDP (Night Defensive Position) when Robert Romig saw a gook and shot him," remembered Motta. "That's when all hell broke loose. I caught a lot of bullets coming at me."

When two members of the recon team were injured from Cobra fire, a medevac was called in and a jungle penetrator dropped.

"Richard Titus, I think he lost a foot to a booby trap," said Motta." They were hauling him up and the NVA shot him up with an RPG. We had to go over and try to get him out. We encountered a few Vietnamese, engaged them."

The medevac team had no soon than dropped the penetrator when the bird went down in a ball of fire. The crew of four was killed. Members of the recon team were shocked and intent on finding those responsible. Delta Company was called in for support.

"We initiated contact," Motta said of the mission. "We killed the guys. They (Delta Company) finished the job."

The NVA soldier responsible for taking down the chopper was one of two killed. Another was taken prisoner and flown out.

Another Painful Loss

On June 2, the men of Alpha Company landed on Ripcord for a quick re-supply. Hawkins had taken over Alpha Company from Burckard.

The next day, Alpha was again on the move, trekking toward Hill 1,000 with Lt. Lee Widjeskog's second platoon in the lead.

"We were going up Hill 1,000, our point man was John Conrad," remembered Widjeskog. "Little was the slack man for John. Apparently they came upon some NVA sitting on the trail, having some lunch I guess.

Suddenly Conrad caught a glimpse of NVA along the trail and fired off a round, then fell back when he turned and Little was no longer there.

"John fired one shot," said Wikjeskog. "Basically the slack man is supposed to be doing the firing, the point man is supposed to spot it, step aside and let the slack man shoot. Slack man was gone. The guy was deathly afraid to be out there. They dropped back and we called in artillery."

Widjeskog then directed the two to head back down the trail. It wasn't happening.

"Conrad said 'I'm not going back, get someone else to walk point.'" Widjeskog said. "Wieland Norris volunteered. He was basically a machine gunner. He grabbed an M-16 and went up. We started forward. Wieland had only been out with us a short time. All of a sudden his squad leader hustled past me and said 'I've got to get Wieland off point,' and he pulled away from me."

With the commotion behind him, Norris suddenly said he thought he heard something ahead of him. Sgt. John Koozer, who had assumed slack duty, had turned to check on the commotion from the rear.

"The NVA fired and killed Wieland, shot him in the heart," said Widjeskog. "They hit Koozer, one bullet went through his cheek , one went through his shoulder. If he hadn't turned, he probably would have been hit in the heart. Then all hell broke loose. We called in artillery. We called in gunships. We didn't hit anybody, they skedaddled. One of my gunships happened to get one of my guys slightly wounded. Not a good day."

MEETING OF THE MINDS

Norris was the younger brother of action star Chuck Norris. He was also a husband and a father. Chuck, a veteran of the Air Force, had started making a name for himself in southern California, having opened several martial arts studios.

Leigh Freeman was with Charlie Company, along with his buddy Rick Thomas. The two had gone through basic training and AIT (Advanced Infantry Training) with Wieland, or Willie as they knew him.

"Rick and I knew him very well," remembered Freeman. "He was like my big brother. He was older than a lot of us. He was 26. Most of us were 19 or 20. He told us about his life and how his brother Chuck owned a string of karate schools in California. He and his brothers Aaron and Chuck were in a Dean Martin movie. That was one of their first forays into Hollywood. He told us about how he had a third-degree black belt, but he never had any bravado, never bragged about it.

"When we were in basic training Willie was our platoon leader," said Freeman. "When we went to AIT, Willie and stuck together. He had the top bunk. We all met up again to fly to Vietnam."

Prior to heading to Southeast Asia, the three would often go out drinking together, enjoying big parties in Monterrey and Salinas. Wieland would often rent motel rooms and buy the beer.

Amazingly, the three men ended up in the 101st Airborne together, with Rick and Leigh headed to Charlie Company while Wieland drew an assignment with Alpha Company. While entire companies trained together and were shipped off together to battle in wars dating back to World War I, the same couldn't be said for men drafted into the Vietnam War. The one-year abroad cycles coupled with six-month in, six-month out cycles for officers all but ensured high turnover rates, especially by the time 1970 and Nixon's Vietnamization Program had begun.

REMEMBERING FIREBASE RIPCORD

The assignments at Camp Evans were a surprise to the young infantryman as the Army seemingly does everything alphabetically, which would have placed Freeman in Alpha and Norris and Thomas in Charlie, Freeman remarked. The separation was tough, Freeman said, and he and Thomas thought often of Willie and how he was making out with Alpha.

Once they landed in country, Wieland changed, according to Freeman. That change concerned Freeman and Thomas as well.

"At Phu Bai, I looked over and saw Willie reading a book - it was the Bible," said Freeman. "I'd never seen Willie with a Bible. His mother gave it to him. He said, 'I'm not going to make it.' I told him, 'You have to think positive.'

"That first night (at Camp Evans) we met later for supper at the mess hall and that was the last time Willie Norris and Rick and I had a sit-down meal together," said Freeman. "That night we did bunker guard together. The next morning we had breakfast, then Rick and I never saw him again. He got on a chopper to go meet up with Alpha Company and we went with Charlie Company. Thirty days later Willie got killed, June 3."

Charlie ended up going on standdown June 8, at which time Freeman and Thomas began asking about their buddy Willie. They ended up in a chow line with some members of Alpha Company and asked if they knew Wieland.

"They said 'yeah, he's dead,'" remembered Freeman. "They said his body was already en route to California."

Widjeskog reflected on that day and the burden that comes with leading and issuing orders, orders that sometimes send men to their deaths.

"People die when you don't know enough," he said. "It's really hard to get to the point where you can say you did it exactly right. There probably is no exactly right. Nine times out of 10 you go back up the trail and there's nobody there. It's that 10th time when people get hurt. I look back, when you lose people you wonder what you could have done differently. I wouldn't have stopped Norris from going up there. I didn't know that he'd only been there about a week. I thought everyone had been there as long as I had, or longer. His squad leader was concerned and he did the right thing. He was just too slow."

Unconfirmed Sightings of Caucasians

Bravo Company choppered into the Triple Hill area just north and west of Ripcord on June 21 and it didn't take long to find NVA soldiers. Capt. Bill Williams' troops discovered NVA and what appeared to be a Caucasian wearing a U.S. uniform. Bunker complexes uncovered by the men in Bravo yielded little. Three days later, another small group of NVA appearing to wear U.S. uniforms was found but contact was never made and Bravo Company was ordered off the Triple Hill area and onto Hill 805 by Lt. Col. Andre Lucas.

"When we took Ripcord, the other units were out operating in the field somewhere around Ripcord," said Lt. James Campbell (Charlie Company, 2nd/506th). "During the period before the siege, there was contact here and there, they weren't sustained. There was a standdown in the middle of June, we came in for a week, which you got once every six months, that's when you could tell everything had changed. You started running into enemy here and there and wherever. It didn't make a difference where you went, east, west, north, south, these contacts were heavy contacts."

When Metal Was Metal

Dan Biggs, a replacement for Bravo Company, was 21 with college experience when he arrived at Camp Evans in late June. From North Carolina, his arrival on Firebase Ripcord June 23 was a memorable, and nearly deadly, one.

"I didn't think anything about how bad it was because I didn't have a clue," said Biggs, who was joined on the chopper with five other cherries headed toward the firebase. "The helicopter came in on the lower pad at Ripcord, hovering at about six feet. We had our rucksacks on, with everything in them they said we'd need and our trenching tools on our rucksacks. The pilot's telling us to jump and I yelled back, 'We can't jump with these rucksacks on, we're going to break our legs and be casualties before we get here.'"

The chopper lifted off the firebase and headed back toward Evans. "We were dripping with fear," said Biggs.

Touching down, the chopper was immediately greeted by the sergeant major. "What the hell are y'all doing back here?' I said they wouldn't touch down, they were six feet off the ground," Biggs remembered. "Why the hell didn't you tell us it was a hot landing zone?" Briggs quizzed the sergeant, who told the men to get something to eat and be back on the helipad for departure for Ripcord at 5 that afternoon.

Biggs was the lone member of the group to return. He got onto the chopper with another group of men, and this time, was prepared.

"This time the helicopter went in much quicker and he dropped down. I got off facing the downhill side of Ripcord and had to go around the front of the helicopter. When I did I saw a guy running down the hill holding his guts and bleeding profusely. I raised my M-16 up in the air and pointed to this guy, because I figured they needed to get this guy out of here because he was bad off. I caught him around the waist and loaded him in the helicopter. During this time, you're hearing the helicopter, that's all I could hear, hell I thought I was safe. When the helicopter lifted off I started hearing the clack, clack, clack of bullets going by."

Biggs began running up the hill, his boots sinking in the clay with the weight of his rucksack weighing down his slim, 6-foot, 3-inch frame.

MEETING OF THE MINDS

"Bam, bam, bam, I got nailed to the ground," said Biggs. "I thought, 'Holy shit, that's gotta be a sniper; he's already sending my ass home and I've been here five minutes.' I laid there on the ground, afraid to move, because if I move he's going to know I'm alive and finish me off. I could feel wetness and dampness on my right side, but I don't feel a sting or anything."

A medic appeared atop the hill and asked Biggs if he was OK. Still lying face down, Biggs told the medic he was OK and that there was a sniper in the distance. He moved his right hand toward his midsection to check himself for injuries. Slowly moving, so as not to alarm the sniper, he noticed blood on his hand, but was still puzzled as to why he felt no pain.

"I'm thinking he hit me somewhere," said Biggs. "I let another 20-30 minutes go by and made my move because it was getting dark. I said, 'I'm coming in, don't shoot me!' I reached to balance myself because I still had my rucksack on. I started to run and when I did, I lost my balance and grabbed this poncho laying there loose on the hill. Underneath it were three dead American soldiers and it scared the living hell out of me. I thought, 'Oh my God, that's close to death.' I start running and hear the clack, clack, clack of the bullets going by me. I ran to a bunker and I dove in head first. I gathered myself a little bit there."

The empty bunker had a bloodied M-60, numerous claymore switches and detonators and thousands of rounds of M-60 ammo. There were also cases of grenades and anti-tank LAWs (Light Anti-Tank Weapons). It was dark and he soon got a call from the command post. It was Capt. Ben Peters, who had recently taken over Bravo. He was directed where to go to meet Peters.

"I go to the command post bunker and it was well-fortified. You walked in about four feet, turn right, then you go three to four feet and you're underground. They were built with those L shapes for direct hits on the doorways," said Biggs, who testified to the brilliance of Vazquez and the design of the overall firebase.

In the command post, Biggs met Peters and the sergeant. "Peters said, 'Soldier, I thought you were dead' and I said, 'Capt. Peters I thought I was dead.' He saw the blood on me and he said, 'Where did you get hit?' I told him I wasn't hit that I knew of. He said, 'Turn around,' and I turn around with that rucksack on and he said 'Shit soldier, you're not going to believe this.' The sniper had hit me four times in the trenching tool on my back. It was folded down. The bullets hit the shovel - now, remember metal was metal back then, and when it hit, it knocked me to the ground. The bullets ricocheted off and some of the bullets stopped in my canteen. The water spilling onto my leg came from the canteen and the blood came from the guy I had helped onto the helicopter."

From there, Biggs was briefed by Peters on the status of Ripcord and told to go back to the bunker from which he had come. He was to throw grenades down the hill every 15 minutes.

Delta on Duty

Delta Company (2/506) was pulling guard duty on Ripcord in late June. Soon they would be humping up Hill 1,000 where they would meet fierce resistance from NVA troops.

Sgt. Mark Skinner was sent to the rear during that period in late June after developing a severe case of jungle rot, something many of the soldiers dealt with thanks to the hot and humid conditions during that time of the year. When it wasn't steaming hot, heavy rains would soak men in the field.

"Both of my legs up to the knees were just festered," said Skinner, a draftee from Richmond, Ind. "You pick that shit up anywhere and the sanitation in the field is just horrible. There just wasn't anything you could do with it. You just lived with it. It was itchy, stinky and gross."

Skinner didn't complain and it wasn't until his case was noticed by a medic that action was taken.

"(The medic) said, 'Get on the chopper, we're heading back,'" remembered Skinner. "I wasn't able to go down to my foxhole and say goodbye. I couldn't pick up my ruck or anything. When I left, it was that quick."

'Chieu Hoi'

Alpha Company, having been depleted in near-constant contact over the first three months of the Ripcord operation, was shipped to Firebase O'Reilly, just north and east of Ripcord, to refresh and beef up troop numbers.

It was there, on June 21, that an injured North Vietnamese soldier walked up on Bruce Brady, who had been on the perimeter taking care of nature's call, and surrendered.

Sniper Mike Bodnar, assigned to Echo Company, had the enemy soldier in his view when he surrendered.

"He was in bad shape, outside the wire," said Bodnar.

The soldier, while being interrogated on O'Reilly, testified he belonged to Company D, 19th Sapper Battalion.

Part of a small group of snipers – about seven from Camp Evans – Bodnar would be assigned to line companies or go out in smaller recon squads.

He was drafted at age 19, at a time when he had a good job working in the steel mills near Pittsburgh.

"I had a good job, I was making good money," said Bodnar. "I had a fast car."

After basic and advanced training, he went to NCO (Non-Commissioned Officers) school. About to graduate, he got word his grandfather, a World War II veteran, had passed away and he would have to leave prior to graduation. He lost those final weeks, and his sergeant's stripes. When he returned, he was on his way to Vietnam.

Once in country, he as assigned to the 101st and learned there was a need for someone to go with a sniper team for security. Confident in his abilities, having spent time as a hunter and fisher under the mentorship of his uncle, a Marine Corps veteran who had taught him to shoot and care for his weapons, he volunteered.

In the sniper program, he finished second in the class and ended up with the 2nd of the 506th at Camp Evans.

"We were spread thin," said Bodnar. "There was maybe eight of us, at the highest level. Some were wounded, some were killed. The honors graduate, the guy that finished ahead of me, was killed. We would walk along with a line company at times and at times, we'd operate by ourselves. They'd give us two security guys, one carrying a radio."

On firebases, he operated on his own, setting up in locations where he could best take out enemy positions. He was on Ripcord in April, before it was even established as a firebase.

At times, they'd work in sniper platoons.

"We'd be given specific grid coordinates," said Bodnar. "We'd sneak into those places. We wouldn't move into those areas in daylight. We'd move into those areas as it got dark. Our final position we'd set up in full guard. There were places we'd set up to observe. We'd watch it for movement in the daytime."

MEETING OF THE MINDS

Bodnar was injured on O'Reilly, having taken shrapnel in the buttocks. He could have been medevacked out, but chose to have a medic tend the wounds and returned to duty.

"The 1st ARVNs were (at O'Reilly) and there weren't even foxholes there yet," said Bodnar. "We had some action there and there were some guys coming back and forth from Ripcord. A company would come in and land at O'Reilly and march off. We had an artillery observer saying it was getting bad at Ripcord and they needed replacements."

Flying into Ripcord, the chopper Bodnar was riding in was spiraling down and taking fire.

"We went in on the lower pad," he said. "We were corkscrewing in. We jumped off the bird and looked for cover and we got into a foxhole as the next bird was coming in. Just as he's setting down he got stitched. It shut the slick down and it couldn't take off. One of the guys was wounded pretty bad. I wasn't too far from the pad. When it quieted down they came in and lifted the Huey out."

Bodnar started scouting locations immediately. He would remain on Ripcord until late July.

"When it wasn't terrible, I would move around to different areas and find a spot," he said. "There were a few of the hills that were within range for me. I was trying to pick out the places they were watching us from. When I'd get a bead on them, I'd range in and squeeze off three or four rounds. When I didn't see anything else, I'd move to another area. It was just like I was hunting."

9

Hill 902

Charlie Company stands on the helipad used by Lt. Col. Andre Lucas on the southern portion of Firebase Ripcord. Over their left shoulders is Hill 902, where Charlie Company was engaged in a furious battle July 2, 1970. From left, Dale Cooper, Bob Tarbuck, Steve Manthei and Doc Powell. Photo provided by Steve Manthei.

By late June, word had spread that an attack on Firebase Ripcord should be expected in the first few days of July. An intercepted communication indicated such an attack was forthcoming.

Practice alerts were conducted in the late-night hours of June 30 and early morning hours of July 1 at firebases Ripcord and O'Reilly.

Shortly after 7 a.m., a North Vietnamese 60mm mortar crew, overlooking Firebase Ripcord from Hill 1,000, launched an assault on the lower-lying firebase. Fire was also reported from the Hill 805 area. For the next three hours, around 30 mortar rounds were fired at Ripcord, half of which landed inside the perimeter wire. Artillery response from Ripcord was swift and decisive. The young Screaming Eagles triggering that response may not have realized it at the moment, but the assault on Ripcord was the start of a siege that would last the next three weeks, a siege that would claim many lives and scar many more.

Just two days earlier, Gen. Sid Berry had joined the division. The next four weeks proved to be among the most trying of his military career, he would tell Ripcord veterans more than 15 years later.

"On the first of July and continuing through the 23rd of July, the North Vietnamese Army began a sustained drive to eliminate Ripcord as a very prickly thorn in their flesh," he wrote in a speech to Ripcord veterans in 1985.

There was no avoiding the shift in strategy by the North Vietnamese. It was evident on the firebase and in the field in the days after that first July shot. Casualty counts increased. From July 1 to July 7, daily attacks on Ripcord were reportedly conducted by two NVA regiments. More than 160 rounds of 60mm and 82mm mortar and 75mm recoilless rifle fire landed on the firebase.

Attacks on American troops were becoming more prevalent, more frequent and, in the case of July 1 on Hill 902, more brazen. Attacks to the firebase were near non-stop.

"After July 1 (it was) every day, everywhere on the hill," said Marc Aronson, B 2-319 artillery, of the attacks on Ripcord. "There is an old cliché that says if you can hear them coming, you're OK; it is the one you don't hear that kills you. We also got some CS (chlorobenzalmalononitrile) gas mortar rounds shot at us, generally just a pain in the neck. Our gas masks were not that efficient. Putting them on after an attack just kept the gas closer to you. Washing it off was near impossible and not worth the effort.

"Strangely, in my opinion and experience, you could get used to them coming in and exploding around you. War has its own strange rhythm, predictable some days and just crazy as heck other days. It has its own sounds and smells, its own sense of time and place, its own peace and quiet, its own beauty and hellish experiences, its own 'right' and 'wrong'."

In firefights around Ripcord during those first seven days of July, 18 American troops were killed and 104 wounded while 30 NVA were reported killed, according to the After Action Report.

Also after 7 a.m. the first day in July, five 82mm mortar rounds and small arms fire struck Ripcord from the southeast. Fifteen more 82mm mortar rounds struck the firebase just before 9 a.m. The shelling would continue throughout the day, into the evening. By day's end, 15 artillery soldiers received minor wounds.

Charlie Company (2nd/506th) was charged with seeking out the mortar positions and eliminating them from Hill 902 to the south and west of Ripcord, a task easier said than done.

"We were finding a lot of movement," said Bob Tarbuck, Charlie One. "We found an underground hospital. They had cut steps in a hill (near 902). You could smell them. You could sense they were in the area. The reason they put us on that hill was because Ripcord was getting rocketed. We were to identify the targets. I'm sure they realized we were a thorn in their ass."

HILL 902

"We're over by 902 and found a new bunker complex, freshly dug, commo wire, everything," said Steve Manthei, Charlie One. "We went up the steepest side of 902. I had heard recon had been up and found it clean. They had a read on mortar positions and knew there were a couple in the area. We spread out in a circle with the CP (Command Post) in the middle. Another squad came up the northwest side. The first night there was nothing, it was quiet, pretty eerie though because we had found that bunker complex. It wasn't small. It was pretty big. You know when you can smell them, they were close. Everybody was a little bit higher alert, especially the old guys, the guys who had been there and understood. We had a lot of new guys who didn't realize just how big it was."

After spending the night on 902, the men of Charlie received a pallet of LAWs (Light Anti-tank Weapons) and were told to find the mortar positions from which Ripcord was being shelled and fire on them. Second and third platoons stayed on the hill while third platoon was rotated back onto Ripcord.

"The battalion commander, in his great wisdom, floated his helicopter over our position and dropped off a bunch of LAWs, giving our position away," said Charlie Company veteran Howie Colbert. "From where we were off the trail there, you could see where they'd drop a mortar into their tube. There would be a puff of smoke coming up through the vegetation. It looked like someone smoking a cigarette was blowing smoke rings up through there."

"We could hear it," said Lt. Bob Leibecke of the mortaring. "Some idiot thought it would be good to slingload a load of LAWs in. We were told to shoot down where we thought the sound was coming from. That was like an open invitation for the NVA. Even though they say we had no warning, when you do that you're opening yourself up."

With mortars raining on Ripcord from the position at the base of 902,

REMEMBERING FIREBASE RIPCORD

Charlie Company fired the newly acquired LAWs into an area where smoke had been seen.

"It went right down into where that puff of smoke came," said Manthei. "I know it did some damage. That's why we thought we were getting out of there. We thought we would be getting out. When you drop a LAWs rocket down on an enemy position, you know it's going to piss them off."

Charlie Company had undergone massive turnover in a matter of just days leading up to the days at 902. Capt. Isabelino Vazquez was gone, Lt. Jim Campbell was gone. More were expected to leave.

Capt. Tom Hewitt had days earlier replaced Vazquez, a man loved and respected by those who served under him. Hewitt had very little time to acclimate to his men prior to the events at 902.

"We were sorry to see (Vazquez) go," remembered Sgt. John Fowler. "Capt. Hewitt joined us when we went on a little R&R at Eagle Beach. We appreciated that down time and Hewitt got to know some of us during that down time. After that standdown we regrouped and combat assaulted back into the Ripcord area, near Hill 902.

"There was a long ridgeline that led up to 902. We had inherited a group from The Big Red One. A lot of the things they did in the rice paddies they thought they'd bring to us in the mountains."

A couple of ambushes were set and the company was airlifted out. Late in June, they were reinserted and asked to move down the trail and recover the ambushes. It was about a week prior to the events of July 2, remembered Fowler.

"As we moved down the trail to pick up the ambush, they had been turned on us. The NVA had found them," said Fowler. "They blew the claymores, taking out our point team, wounding them in the legs. As

HILL 902

my RTO (Radio Telephone Operator) moved up to see what that was, they blew another. We both received shrapnel and a blast concussion. We couldn't hear anything. We called for some support and an officer to help us. We had to medevac out."

That meant another veteran combat soldier was lost with the exodus of Fowler. So not only was Charlie operating with a new company commander, but many of its veteran members were cycling out or had been medevacked out of the field.

"He never talked about his family," said Colbert of Hewitt. "He carried a .22 target pistol and a shotgun. He was always doing weird stuff, going through the perimeter and coming back up to check on everyone. I thought he was looking for an early Purple Heart. That was my perception."

Colbert, serving his second tour in Vietnam, was on Hill 902 on July 1 before getting pulled out, his time in the field up.

"On 902, we lost really before the battle," he said. "We had a couple of really key people that went on R&R (Rest and Recuperation). They decided to relieve a platoon for a standdown, which left nothing but a skeleton crew for 902. At that time, Coop (Dale Cooper), Jack Dreher and myself were pretty much at the end of our tours. Jack drew the short straw and had become the senior RTO that night. I left, Coop left."

Cooper was part of Charlie Three, which had, as Colbert alluded to, rotated onto Ripcord for a hot meal, shower and new clothing, leaving just two platoons from Charlie Company in the field.

To address some of the attrition, Lt. Charles Van Cleve, who had spent time with artillery and Delta Company under Capt. Rembert Rollison, was assigned to the company as a forward observer. He, too, was due time away from the jungle.

"We ended up going on standdown on Ripcord, the day I was supposed to go on R&R," remembered Van Cleve. "(Charle Company) had no FOs, so I got the lucky task to go out with them. I was pretty pissed off about that. I had no association with them, I'm an officer, I was field artillery. I was very tight with Capt. (Dave) Rich on Ripcord and finally, I knew no one."

Van Cleve knew the service. His father was a Flying Tiger in World War II. He had started classes at UCLA. His father had bigger plans.

"I was raised duty, honor, country," he remembered. "I was never supposed to go to Vietnam. My father had set me up to go to the Air Force Academy, but I joined because I didn't want to miss the war."

He ended up in Vietnam in January 1970, at the ripe age of 19.

By the time Charlie had arrived at 902, there was clear evidence the NVA were there, or at the very least, weren't far away.

"We found out we'd be staying and that's a no-no, especially after doing something like that," said Manthei. "It was the first time it had happened. We had done other ambushes, used mechanical claymores, we never stuck around after we blew something up though."

"Never had we made enemy contact and stayed a second night," said Don Holthausen. "A couple times during the day they would shoot mortars. We're on 902 and right down in the valley, you'd hear them mortaring Ripcord. We'd fire down on them, fired a couple LAWs down on them. I'm sure they were annoyed."

"We were used to not being in the same place two nights in a row," said Tarbuck. "That night, Manthei and I walked up to the CO (Commanding Officer, Hewitt), and asked if he had coordinates for us. They said, 'We're not going anywhere. We're staying here tonight.' We said, 'We can't do that. They're going to come up and find us.' We went back and fortified our positions. Some of the holes were shallow. As soon as they told us (of the decision to stay), we went and dug our positions deep. I pulled my guard and went to sleep."

Manthei remembered discussing the decision to stay another night with Hewitt.

"He said, 'No, we gotta stay,'" recalled Manthei, "which was kind of disturbing. We thought we should booby trap it and move off the back side. There were hooches built on that hill and a hammock and that was insane. We stayed and the rest is pretty much history."

As night fell, first and second platoons dug in.

"I didn't sleep much that night," remembered Manthei. "It was just one of those deals. I was on guard at 4, maybe a little before."

"My position, with Don Holthausen and Bob Tarbuck, was just down the hill (south) to the east," said Manthei. "The CP was on top of the hill. Sgt. Gillespie was out to the southeast a little bit, in a hole. The next position was Danny Smith and the gun position. Around the corner on top of the hill I could see Bob Smoker, (Thomas) Herndon, (Stephen) Harbor and Steel. I believe the next position was to the north."

With that, Manthei and other members of his platoon readied themselves for what they thought may be a long night.

"We had three claymores and a radio in our position," he said. "I carried eight grenades and I had them out. Trip flares – everyone had everything out. We were prepared. Your weapon was your baby and you kept that as clean as a whistle so it worked when you needed it."

Van Cleve, who was dug in not too far from the command post, said Hewitt did his job, and had the men prepared for the night. He remembered Hewitt personally coming over to his foxhole and requesting it being dug at least chest deep.

"Hewitt saved my life," he remembered. "The ground was harder than shit. We had a foxhole, but when Hewitt walked over he said it wasn't nearly deep enough. He said we needed to dig it deeper. It was hotter than hell that day. That's why it was four-and-a-half feet deep, right up to my chest. If it wasn't for that, I would probably be dead. He did that at every fighting position, too.

"I know that people were questioning his decision to spend two nights on that hill, but I bet you it was not his decision to spend two nights on that landing zone. "

First and second platoons set up a Night Defensive Position atop Hill 902. Capt. Hewitt, asleep in a hammock in the command post, was killed as a rocket-propelled grenade ripped through shortly before 4 a.m. The attack was considered "well organized and well planned" by American brass. Hewitt's decision to sleep in a hammock was bizarre most admitted, especially given the requests he made of his men in digging their bunkers.

The chaos that ensued in the darkness of the night was horrific.

"I was on radio watch," said Van Cleve. "Leibecke was the only other guy on the radio at that time. He calls up command post and he said, 'I think I see movement.' I said, 'Make sure; you are absolutely sure you see movement?' I had been out in the field five-and-a-half months, I'm not green, but I had never been in anything like this before. He gets right back on the radio and said, 'I see movement.' I said, 'Pop your claymores.' He said they didn't work. I said, 'Oh shit.' I called the firebase and asked for light. That's when all hell broke loose. Leibecke and I had five minutes pass where he and I had discussions. No one else was on the radio, period."

HILL 902

The NVA were brisk and brutal under cover of darkness.

"When the first RPG (Rocket-Propelled Grenade)s went off, I was wounded – my hand," said Van Cleve. "The first thing I did (after the initial RPG) was get the (command post) radios to my foxhole, and my M16. It was a little two-man foxhole and it's deep. I turn around and a guy is standing straight up above me and it happened to be (Gerry) Cafferty. He tells me the command post has been wiped out and the captain is dead. I pull him in my foxhole right behind me."

Van Cleve was holding a headset from each radio to each of his ears. His first instinct was to protect the lifelines - the radios.

With his radio telephone operator and himself already crammed into the tight foxhole, Cafferty made it even tighter. Attempting to rally anything in the way of support on the radio, Van Cleve was also trying to fend off the enemy.

"This gook is standing behind a log throwing satchel charges at us," said Van Cleve. "My RTO didn't have a weapon, Cafferty didn't have a weapon. In OCS (Officer Candidate School) we learned in night fighting you don't aim down the scope of the weapon, so you center the butt on your chest and aim that way. I set one radio down and I set the gun on my chest and tried to shoot this guy. I shot in bursts."

Van Cleve also got back on the radio in an attempt to get flareships in. The light that was provided, according to Van Cleve, was "miniscule and lasted a short time." The company set was in his left hand, while the forward observer set was in his right hand, which was wounded.

"We were all facing to the east-northeast from my foxhole, the direction the action was coming from," said Van Cleve. "There were lots of RPGs, but much more satchel charges. AK fire was at a minimum from what I heard and where my placement was."

Cafferty recalled the dire situation members of Charlie Company faced in the minutes after the attack began.

"There was all kinds of confusion, explosions," he said. "We realized the gooks had gotten into the perimeter. One of the positions was taken over and they got in, plus they were outside. It's hard to fire at them without hitting your own men."

"We dug holes, I was set up behind a log," said Leibecke, of first platoon. "That firing position saved my life. All you could do is pop up and duck down. We dug those holes chest deep. You can stand in there and duck down and be completely protected. When they hit at 4 o clock it was RPG after RPG and they threw satchel charges. I was talking to the FO (Van Cleve) and battalion the whole time trying to bring in jets, thinking why not just dump it on top of them?"

By 4:12 a.m., Charlie Company was calling for a flareship. Nine minutes later, a call from Charlie Company requested aerial rocket artillery. Both arrived in support of Charlie Company around 4:30 a.m., according to the After Action Report.

"Lt. Leibecke would periodically try to get direction from me," remembered Van Cleve. "He said I skillfully conveyed to him Capt. Hewitt wasn't with us. I have no recollection how I conveyed this but I knew the radio could be monitored so I was very careful not to give away our true condition, which looked none too good."

Van Cleve called mortars to the last defensive fire position, but there was no adjusting the fire as they were as close as they could get to the hill without being on top of the company positions.

"I remember them asking me the number of the defensive fire," he noted, adding that he called in earlier with each sector having a number, written in crayon on his map. "I had no clue and certainly didn't have the map to look at. I remembered it was the last one I called

HILL 902

in so I told them that and also it was the closest sector between our hilltop and Firebase Ripcord, so I told them that. Trust me, this was difficult."

Capt. Chuck Hawkins had been with Charlie prior to taking over Alpha Company and was on Firebase O'Reilly in the early morning hours of July 2 when his radio telephone operator awakened him upon hearing the chaos coming from Hill 902.

"I listened on the command net," remembered Hawkins. "Other radios in my command post were also tuned to that frequency so others could listen.

"After a few minutes... five, 10... Van Cleve got on the radio. I recognized his voice as the Charlie Company forward observer. He began directing fire and providing succinct reports to the TOC (Tactical Operations Center). He became the de facto commander of C(harlie) Company at that point. He did an outstanding job."

Van Cleve, while attempting to communicate with the firebase, was repeatedly interrupted by Maj. Herbert Koenigsbauer, who was attempting to ascertain what had happened during the chaotic transmissions from 902.

"Maj. Koenigsbauer kept getting on the radio and asking what was going on," said Van Cleve. "I said, 'Get the fuck off the net.' I knew exactly who I was talking to. I'm just trying to live here and take control and this guy is just getting on and asking what's going on. I had antennas sticking up and I had guys zeroed in on me.

"I'm calling in flareships, I'm talking to the company on the ground and I'm talking to Capt. (Dave) Rich."

Van Cleve was discussing artillery options from Ripcord with Rich while battling the NVA soldier just meters from his position. He's working the radio, firing his M16 and considering options the entire time.

"This gook was standing literally 10 yards from me behind this big log," said Van Cleve. "I'm trying to kill the son of a bitch."

John Kuennan was with second platoon, though he had been sent down the trail and away from many of his buddies, who had dug in on top of the hill. The NVA would not attack from the trail, though.

"They had moved me down along the trail with a machine gun," remembered Kuennan. "I was pissed off because it took me away from my squad and I was in a place they should have come up."

The NVA, however, descended directly upon the command post with a barrage of RPGs and explosives.

Kuennan said he found a radio and attempted to call in support. He knew the enemy had penetrated the perimeter.

"We just got overrun, it was mass chaos. This whole thing is going on. We're sitting where we were and I'm on the radio. During the course of the night, the guy asked whether we wanted a sulphur round for illumination and I said 'yeah.' It went off and I thought, 'Jesus I did the wrong thing here because they could see us and we could see them,' but it did give you an idea of what was going on. Those are the decisions you have to make."

Manthei was blown from his guard position into the side of his bunker, which he shared with Holthausen. "My watch was 1 to 3 in the morning," said Holthausen. "I had just woken Steve up and called him back. I had just fallen asleep and Steve grabbed me and pulled me back in the foxhole. We were back to back in the foxhole. You live and fight that way. They're your brothers."

HILL 902

Manthei blew the claymores then heard the radio, which he said he immediately grabbed.

"It sounded like (Dale) Cooper," said Manthei of the radio conversation. "I told him we needed Cobras. He asked me about the CP and I said they were eliminated."

Tarbuck was awakened and grabbed his helmet, then got hit by a can of C-rations, launched by an exploding RPG sent through the company command post.

"I could see the gunner firing," remembered Tarbuck. "He got knocked out. Now I've got to cover a wider pie. I was facing south, to the west of Ripcord with the command post over my shoulder. We started firing off claymores. Fortunately where we were it was steep. You could see the heads popping up and down, they were that close. They were so close we were counting off the hand grenades. I used all my hand grenades. We fired off all my claymores."

Describing the intensity of the moment, Tarbuck said, "I could hear my heart in my ears – my blood was pumping so hard, so fast. There'd be a lot of firing, then quiet. They had already gotten into the perimeter. You could hear a lot of screaming. Guys got hit. You could hear someone screaming out orders for them. We were shooting any kind of illumination we could. When I saw them that close, that's when I thought it was over."

Cooper, who was on Ripcord with third platoon from Charlie Company, had been rotated to Ripcord in late June after spending the entire campaign to that point with first platoon. He knew the men on that hill that night.

"The guy on the radio woke me up," said Cooper. "I was in the bunker asleep and he said your company has been wiped out and they want you on the radio right now. I think probably your mind takes over, it goes into shock because those were my guys out there. I've been with these guys for almost a full year, we've all gone without food and water and we've seen our guys die and in pain, trauma, nasty things involved in war, nasty animalistic things and it comes to this - I wasn't with my guys."

It's something that weighed heavily on Cooper, and still does.

"I call and call and it goes through your mind that they've been wiped out, they're gone," he said. "It's what I was told. I don't know who I talked to, it's just hidden away."

"We were lucky," said Holthausen of his and Manthei's bunker position. "We were on the steep side of the hill. Our foxholes were right out in front where it drops really steep. There was a trail on both sides of the LZ (landing zone). They didn't come up our side, which kind of saved us in a way. Once the sappers got into the perimeter they were throwing satchel charges into everyone's hole."

Leibecke, who later labeled 902 "The Hotel" after finding abandoned foxholes, cans and other garbage, noted the North Vietnamese were smart in the attack, first hitting under the cover of darkness and second, hitting without much in the way of small arms fire, which would have given up their positions.

"There was no point shooting at them, because you couldn't see them and if you did, you'd give up your firing position," said Leibecke." We threw grenades. I didn't realize they had gotten through the line."

Manthei recounted the confusion and described the scene.

"There was so much screaming, hollering," he said. "The smell, it was unbelievable. I realized they must be inside the perimeter. I had a flare, popped it and looked southeast to the saddle and saw nothing but heads. I couldn't shoot my M-16 but I had my grenades. I lobbed them toward those heads. It was the most vicious, brutal noise. I was splattered with shrapnel. I had never been in anything like that before. It was the most intense, violent thing. I heard the guy on the chopper and answered him. I threw a trip flare as far as I could and threw the other to the southwest and told him to drop it between the two."

"You could hear the small arms fire," said Holthausen. "The sappers had already infiltrated our perimeter. Once we got hit and the enemy is in the perimeter, you're hesitant to shoot. You don't know if it's friendly or enemy. Once you have 15-20 people running inside the perimeter, you don't pull the trigger. The battle started quieting down. I was the platoon RTO (Radio Telephone Operator) and I tell Steve, 'I think we have the only radio. I haven't heard anyone else on the frequency.' It was dying down, sporadic. I said to Steve, 'I'm going to call someone on the radio. Company HQ (headquarters), Evans picked up and said 'What the heck is happening out there?' I said 'Get us some gunships out here, we have a lot of casualties.'

Two gunships approached and Holthausen turned it over to Manthei.

"We shot parachute flares over the sides. Steve guided the gunfire. Those two Cobras worked all around the LZ and made us all feel a lot safer."

As first light rose, Leibecke began to crawl up to the command post. There, the magnitude of the battle settled in.

"Hewitt was dead," said Leibecke. "I think he took an RPG. He was all blown to shit. The next morning I saw all the bodies and that's when I got an inkling they made it through the line. They got through the second platoon, they managed to decimate second platoon. There were two things I remember, a bunch of bodies around and hundreds of satchel charges, that may be an exaggeration but there were so many unexploded satchel charges just laying around. They were pretty good tossers, we had one land in our hole and went to the bottom of the hole and land at our feet. We crawled out of the hole, it was like a dream, moving in slow motion, and there were all these explosions going off and we're waiting for it to go off. It never went off and we climbed back in and threw it out. Somehow I don't remember being panicked. I remember thinking, 'It's going to be tough to come out of this alive.'"

The battle raged on for more than two hours, with sporadic contact continuing through 5:30 a.m. When the dust had settled, seven Americans were killed, six wounded and one missing. Steve Harbor was never found. Kuennan saw dozens of NVA bodies scattered about the hill.

"It was chaos, just terrible," said Kuennan. " I blew all three of our claymores. I threw everybody's grenades. We survived. There were only five of us that walked off the hill that night. There were a lot of busted eardrums from all the satchel charges. They brought in third platoon at first daylight. The shooting had stopped. By that time you have gunships around. That morning was terrible. Days like that, once you have a firefight, you walk back there and it's like you walked off the edge of the earth. Even the M-16s and M-60s had their stocks shot off. Helmets don't stop bullets. There were helmets with holes in them; C rations that are shot up, rucksacks blown up. When you get the whole array of canteens, guns, and of course the bodies, it's unbelievable. There's 37 North Vietnamese dead laying here, odd shapes, all kind of ways. There a pieces of bodies being pulled out of trees and bushes. I'm walking over to where I should have been, Lee (Lenz), who I considered my best friend, there sits half a torso from the waist down and that's all that's left. I knew it was Lee, because he wore a pair of blue jean cutoffs under his jungle fatigues. I was positive that was Lee's remains. There was no Steve Harbor. I'm rummaging around and I found a GI boot with a foot in it. I'm just out of it mentally, I'm toast. I keep saying 'Steve's not here.' In retrospect I don't know if Lee had two feet on his torso. I never told anyone about it."

HILL 902

Van Cleve had men collect the unexploded grenades and satchel charges and put them in a hole outside the perimeter. He also ordered soldiers to check for NVA bodies and blood trails. "We had choppers coming in to take out our wounded and our dead."

Cafferty tended to the wounded. He remembered searching the hill for supplies, anything he could find to patch wounds.

"I was devastated but I didn't really have time to think about it," the medic remembered. " I was trying to find supplies at the time. There was so many dead and the others, their ears were ringing from the explosions, they were hurt. It was just so confusing. You weren't real sure if they were gone. I had to keep going to patch up who I could. The IVs were all blown up."

Manthei remembers the end of the battle and the silence.

"What I realized at that time was I couldn't hear," he said. "You could see it, though. You could smell it. The first thing I saw was Hewitt. It was just his legs. There were chunks of body everywhere. Bob Radcliff was my good buddy. His face and head were gone. Harbor – I saw him take a direct hit from an RPG. I can't even explain it – human flesh and blood, smoke, stink, the sight was the most graphic you can even come by. Not being able to hear during that really spooked me, no doubt about it."

"At that point I was pretty much in shock," said Holthausen. "We had eight of our guys killed. We lost a lot of good friends"

The eight Americans killed were Lenz, Hewitt, Harbor, Richard Conrardy, Thomas Herndon, Robert Radcliff Jr., Roger Sumrall and Robert Zoller.

Kuennan remembers gathering the parts, many of which went out in ponchos.

"It was so unfortunate," he said. "You're basically deaf (from the battle) and we're looking around to make sure we got all the parts."

Manthei and another member of the company began checking the dozens of NVA bodies for anything they could use. "One of my comrades took a 100-round (M)60 and shot everything he could. The last thing we wanted was to have one of them playing dead and finish a couple more of us off. Another company came in and provided security while they got us out. Outnumbered and overrun sucks.

"I was stung and I couldn't hear but you couldn't stop me. You just go on cruise control. The thing I remember most was the sight and smell. I'd been splattered with small bits of shrapnel and my hearing was screwed up but I'm looking at my buddies with no heads, no legs, in pieces. My condition really didn't affect me. I was just stunned at what happened. You get choked up and can hardly talk."

Charlie Company troopers were numb from the pain of the battle and having lost so many of their men, however scanning the scene, and seeing the mounting numbers of NVA bodies, it was clear who won the battle.

"When the smoke cleared, we were the only ones left standing," said Manthei. "We kicked some ass there. That goes back to the type of guys we had. "When the helicopters took off there were NVA bodies scattered throughout that saddle."

Van Cleve, now experiencing the pain in his hand from the wound incurred in the initial minutes of the attack, is attempting to get everyone off the hill. "I put Hewitt on the helicopter and Leibecke helped me. I would not leave the hill until they came in with reinforcements. I took the last helicopter out. When I took the last helicopter out, they took me to Firebase Ripcord to debrief me. I got to talk to them for about five minutes and they started taking fire and they got my ass out of there. I jumped on a helicopter and we're taking 51-caliber fire all the way up."

HILL 902

Van Cleve was being ushered the hospital. He was later interviewed and later earned a Silver Star for his actions at Hill 902.

Back at Ripcord, Cooper was communicating with Capt. Charles Lieb, who was now on Hill 902 and attempting to relay the numbers of dead and wounded over the radio.

"You never wanted to reveal anyone's name over the radio, it's something the enemy could use," said Cooper. "The PAC list had been destroyed in the initial attack so he was trying to give me little hints, clues, and as I'm figuring out who it is, I'm checking them off. It's like I'm killing these guys with my pencil. It's a terrible feeling. You realize they were in so much pain, but you're so remote. You're on automatic pilot. You begin to realize what they had been through."

"I took control, deployed people to check to see what we had," remembered Lieb, a 1968 graduate of West Point. "They were pretty shell-shocked, pretty uptight. They had taken some severe hits."

Communication channels were cleaned up after the 902 attack, Lieb said.

"When that happened, it happened early in the morning and they came (to Camp Evans) mid-day," said Pete Meloro, clerk for Charlie Company at Evans. Meloro was on the helipad as the casualties and dead returned. "I was helping people off the chopper. We didn't have casualties in Charlie Company, never to that extent. A couple of us hustled down to the helipad. My memory lined up the guys who were KIAs. Hewitt was sliced in half. I thought, 'How could this man's life come to this?' There were these two Vietnamese who worked on the camp. At a distance, they walked by and I sensed they were smiling. I swear to God that if I had a rifle, I would have shot them. I was furious. I had just spent time not that long ago with these guys when they had a standdown."

REMEMBERING FIREBASE RIPCORD

Meloro is among many men who questioned the preparedness of Charlie Company that night on Hill 902.

"We were monitoring at base camp what happened," he said. "If Vazquez was there, would this have happened? I was convinced it would not and that might be unfair a little bit. The NVA would have taken that hill eventually. They didn't care how many men they lost. The frustration was, you could see we weren't going to be able to stay there or get the support we needed."

Several others defended Hewitt, acknowledging his call for his men to dig in deeper prior to the attack.

Fowler was among them. "He struck me as a pretty squared away guy," said Fowler. "I'm from Kansas, he's from Kansas. He seemed to be well-trained. It's odd he slept in a hammock. He carried a shotgun as opposed to a rifle. Other than that, I just knew he was the new captain. If I had been there, I think I would have counseled against (staying there). The word came from above. That was tough. (The NVA) knew. They took out the CP (command post) first."

Van Cleve said in retrospect he understood Koenigsbauer's desire to know what was happening during radio transmissions, but the forward observer also knew that it was not wise to be discussing the condition of the company just in case the enemy is listening.

"All hell is breaking loose and he asked me, 'How's captain?'" said Van Cleve. "I told him captain's out of commission. If the Vietnamese had any clue how weak we were, they wouldn't have cut off when they did. They would have eliminated us."

Remaining members of Charlie Company were assigned to Capt. Jeff Wilcox, who remembered meeting the men for the first time.

"When I was called up to Ripcord early on the 3rd , I think, the day after 902, I'm standing there and these choppers are fluttering in and I look at this guy, Sgt. (Paul) Burkey. He jumped off the chopper with an RPG and I just thought that's the guy who's in charge so I walked over to him and verified it. (Lt. Jim) Campbell wasn't there yet. Lt. Campbell and Staff Sgt. Burkey were the command structure and basically we were a platoon-size company. We were always understrength there, always.

"I was really nervous about taking over this outfit. They hustled us off the hill, so we marched off. They sent us some replacements that night. So we looked at each other, and they're getting us off the hill, and we're OK, old guy, new guy, old guy, new guy, so we went off the hill like that. I just was thinking, we've gotta get off the hill and we've gotta march on, drive on. I went around the familiarized myself with the guys and they all looked the same as anyone does when you're in the field, kind of a thousand-yard stare."

There were hints that the attack of Charlie Company at Hill 902 were coming. Some viewed a message that an RPG and Sapper attack was forthcoming as a possible diversion to the launch of the siege via mortar attacks. The attack, it was noted, was to be carried out between 3 and 4 a.m. July 2 against a platoon-sized element of the 101st Airborne by the NVA 29th Infantry Regiment.

Information about a potential attack was radioed to the command post at Ripcord and the information was received with a thank you and somewhat of a dismissal. That revelation prompted a visit to Ripcord by David Dike, a spec 5 working in the Operations Center. Dike allegedly awakened Lucas and provided the information in person hours before the attack on 902.

Reports indicate Lucas was continuously fed intelligence information indicating the NVA were in it to win it.

What was left of Charlie would again be tested in less than a week on Hill 1,000.

"It was extremely hard on the first platoon having gone through 902 to go to Hill 1,000," said Fowler. "I admire Jeff Wilcox to no end. I admire him. For the men, what he did at Hill 1,000 was great."

The Battle Never Went Away

Rick Thomas, a tough machine gunner, thought he was dead when he sustained wounds from shrapnel during the battle atop Hill 902.

"He said when he was wounded – because his eardrums were blown out and he was blinded temporarily – he said he thought he was dead," said Sheryl Thomas, Rick's widow. "He said he heard a distinct voice tell him, 'Get up, get up, you're not dead.' A medic grabbed him and said it was a good thing he began moving because there were so many casualties, they might have missed him. He always said God was telling him to get up."

Rick made it through the battle of Hill 902, but it never left him.

When he returned to the states, he drank. "He got a reputation for being a partier," said Sheryl. "He kind of came out of it and when we started dating he told me he was going to stop drinking. He didn't. He got rid of all the liquor in the house and kept bottles secretly. He became an alcoholic. He was at a genius level, a very smart man, but in the 25 years we were married he had about 12-13 jobs."

He and Sheryl married in 1976. They had been friends three years before exchanging vows.

The effects of war, and what Rick saw, lived with him daily. Some days were better than others, noted Sheryl, who tried to get him to seek help for years.

"Rick never talked about it," she said. "He never wanted to talk about it. Bits and pieces of it would come out now and again. I remember him saying he was down in a foxhole dug for two people and there were three people in it. He turned to the other two guys and said, in his usual sarcastic tone, 'Feel free to join the war at any time!' How could you think of something that sarcastic to say while you were firing? He was very, very affected by the guys that were killed. He talked sometimes about that."

In 1998, Rick attempted suicide. He had previously resisted counseling.

"After a while I started to realize he was struggling to get along with people and I think that was part of the PTSD (Post-Traumatic Stress Disorder). He finally got to the point where he went, because they were talking about replacing his liver. He was in the hallway crying, saying, 'I've ruined my life.' I remember him saying to me, 'You can only see so many people's heads blown off before it affects you.'"

Rick committed suicide in 2002.

"He just did not feel he could stop drinking," said Sheryl. "Alcohol is a depressant. He became very, very depressed. I didn't understand alcoholism at all. I didn't know how to deal with it. I think that his experience in Vietnam certainly began his downward spiral without either of us realizing it. He thought he was just fine.

Burl Ives, a sergeant with Charlie Company, died in 2008 after struggling with memories of Hill 902 as well, two of Ives' former company mates related. Originally from Michigan, Ives died in Texas.

10

Lightning Strikes

From left, Bob Leibecke, who was a lieutenant with Charlie Company during the assault atop Hill 902 July 2, 1970. At right, Jeff Wilcox, a West Point graduate, who was a captain with Charlie Company in July. The two are pictured at the 2014 Ripcord Association reunion in Myrtle Beach, S.C.

Bravo Company and Capt. Bill Williams were working on Hill 805 on July 3 when Capt. Jeff Wilcox and the battered remains of Charlie Company were to provide relief. As Wilcox and his men got into position, Williams directed his men to head off 805 via the southwest slope.

Frustration built as a sergeant refused to walk point, prompting a private, Robert Utecht, to volunteer for the duty. Bob Judd assumed the slack position and off Bravo One went. Utecht, reportedly still angry over the point incident, walked hurriedly and was some 50 meters ahead of Judd when Judd spotted a freshly sawed-off stump, but it was too late. Utecht was killed with a single shot.

As the rains arrived, the two companies linked. Suddenly the jungle lit up and the thought was an RPG (rocket-propelled grenade) had soared through the trees. Rains and storms could arrive and depart seemingly out of nowhere.

"They got in contact in a driving rain and a tree blew up about 20 feet above and Paul (Burkey) and I were standing next to each another," remembered Wilcox. "We thought it was an RPG, then immediately I was doubled over and Paul was sitting there with his legs spread out. It was lightning. When you get in contact, you put up your long antennas, call in artillery and that sort of thing. So the command post got stunned. We were leaving Bravo Company to handle that and they did come around and they did walk off the hill."

Williams was one of the men struck by the lightning bolt.

"We were pulling off of 805 and as we were withdrawing I was making sure everyone was coming off," said Williams. "I was at the rear. The point ran into an enemy position and was killed. Utecht, he was very popular man. He wasn't probably as alert as he should have been because there was arguing going on - not his fault. There were people that wouldn't do their job from what I understood."

Williams and (Aaron) Andrasson set up behind a tree, popped the long antennas and got on the radio. Andrasson was coordinating artillery fire while Williams was phoning superiors to assess the situation.

"It got both of us," said Williams "My radio operator said it blew me about 15 feet down the hill, and I was tied up in the cords, flinching.

Yep, it blew the hell out of the radio. I got knocked out and came to under a poncho in a driving rain. The medic picked up the corner of the poncho to check on me, then went over to take over some people that weren't doing so well. I called Wallace up, Steve Wallace, and turned the company over to him."

Four Days in a Row

Dr. Capt. James Harris graduated from medical school in 1968 and got his draft notice in 1969.

"You didn't escape your obligation," he said. "It didn't bother me that I got drafted. There were a lot of people getting hurt over there and they needed us… Some of the reaction of the medical profession was less than honorable, self-serving. I was disappointed in that. I knew when I got back I was going to have a decent life ahead of me. Some of those guys suffered a lot."

He ended up in a surgical medical hospital in Long Binh in November 1969. The Big Red One was getting pulled out and he was moved north and west of Long Binh for a while, then ended up with the 101st Airborne Division because it needed surgeons. He arrived with the 101st in May and was soon on Firebase Ripcord.

By the time July came, he noticed a shift.

"Charlie Company got hit on 902 then everything changed for us," he said. "Most of the serious casualties didn't happen on the firebase. Most of those guys are medevacked. I'd already seen a bunch of that stuff. It bothers me almost more now than it did then. We didn't have to fight that war. These guys were out there in an environment where violence and risk-taking behavior were really life-saving skills. People get hurt a lot. My job is to take care of them. If you let emotion take over, you may not do your job as well as you should."

LIGHTNING STRIKES

From July 1 through July 23 at Firebase Ripcord, four medics were killed and six others were wounded, Harris noted. "That's a 60 percent casualty rate. We had four companies riffing out in the field, four medics per company. What can you say about those guys? They will never get the credit they deserve. Those guys are getting killed out there. They were taking risks out there. We (on the firebase) weren't exposed to the same level of risk they were."

Three were wounded July 4 as Ripcord took incoming for the fourth day in a row – nine attacks consisting of 82mm and 60mm mortar rounds.

While set up in its Night Defensive Position, Charlie Company (2/501st) engaged in small arms fire with three North Vietnamese sited just west of their position southeast of Ripcord. Charlie Company thought the enemy had fled when at 12:50 a.m., an attack with satchel charges prompted small arms fire at the enemy. Three troops were wounded. No NVA were ever found.

Shortly after 6 a.m. the company was attacked again and again from the west. Eight to 10 RPG rounds and small arms fire descended upon the company. One American was killed and 14 wounded, all evacuated. A sweep of the area found five dead NVA. Five AK-47s were recovered as well as more than two dozen satchel charges as a pair of gas masks.

Near the same time, three klicks south of Ripcord, Alpha Company was engaged in a small arms fire resulting in two Americans being wounded. Artillery fire was also employed. Five NVA were reported killed.

Filling Needs

Lt. Bill Hand knew he'd end up in the military. His father spent his career in the military. Originally he thought he'd end up a Marine, but he found his way into ROTC (Registered Officers Training Corps) at the University of Houston, then to officer's basic training at Fort Benning, Ga., on to Airborne School, Ranger School and Jungle School. At age 23, he was assigned to the 101st Airborne, Camp Evans.

Things were hectic. It was just days after the massive losses at Hill 902 and Hand learned little before heading to the field.

"I knew there was some pretty bitter fighting going on at that time," he said. "Assignments came down after we finished Combat Commanders Course; they needed people there quick. Tom Rubsam filled me in on everything because he knew I'd be going to second platoon. He had been hit in the arm. I would have about 20 guys, that was my platoon. The most I ever got was 24. I didn't have a whole lot of knowledge or detail."

Only days after the lightning strike, Capt. Bill Williams was still having trouble hearing. He soon got the call to replace the S3 at Firebase Ripcord.

"I got out there on a Chinook," said Hand. "It was my first ride on a Chinook and it was treetop level. I went in and Lt. Col. Lucas was outside the TOC (Tactical Operations Center). You could tell he was worn out. He introduced himself and briefed me."

Always in the Thick of It

Alpha Company (2/506th) was attacked July 6 on all sides by an NVA (North Vietnamese Army) company, which used small arms fire and fragmentation grenades. Fifteen men were wounded.

Having served as air support for the 2nd of the 506th, Capt. Randy House saw Alpha Company's men constantly running into the enemy in the early days of July. That early contact was tough, but it was nothing compared to what would happen by the end of the month. House praised the company's leadership, which would prove invaluable later as the company would face unspeakable adversity in the jungle.

"Alpha Company, for good or for bad, that outfit was in a fight a lot in early July," he said. "Just day in and day out, keeping up with what was going on, they were always in a scrap. They were a good company, they called in their artillery well, they just did things well. They just ran into bad guys all the time."

"This is a war. This is what I hadn't seen for nine months." – Capt. Robert Anckaitis

On July 10, two more Americans were killed on the firebase, seventeen were wounded in North Vietnamese attacks consisting of 60mm, 82mm mortar fire and 75mm recoilless rifle fire.

From July 8-16, ground action around Ripcord, in the vicinity of Hills 1,000 and 805 resulted in ten Americans killed, 52 wounded and twelve NVA killed.

Robert Anckaitis was a product of ROTC at Lafayette College, Easton, Pa., a short drive northwest from Philadelphia. Having arrived in Vietnam as a lieutenant, he earned his captain's bars the first week of July on Firebase Rakkasan. By the time he arrived on Firebase Ripcord, despite having taken serious fire on Rakkasan, he knew something was different.

"I remember it was a lot different than a lot of the others I'd been on because some I'd been on, it was just us, just artillery," said Anckaitis. "Some were just a hilltop. The wire complex at Ripcord was incredible. It was just an incredible amount of fortification. Then there's the 12 guns (six 105s, six 155s), the bunkers, the stuff being built by engineers, that sort of amazed me, way out in the middle of nowhere."

Mortar rounds came in daily, at night as well.

REMEMBERING FIREBASE RIPCORD

"We'd be in the bunker where we slept and sometimes when those rounds came in we wouldn't get out," said Anckaitis. "I remember being in our hooch and hearing mortar rounds going off close, or down the hill. We'd fire hand grenades if you thought there might be gooks in the wire. A lot of those rounds that came in didn't land on top of the firebase, they landed down around the infantry bunkers, near the wire."

With 10 months in Vietnam under his belt, Anckaitis admitted he wasn't aware things could get so bad.

"To me it was a war that was eight to 10 miles away," he said. "The first 10 months I wasn't on a firebase that really came under attack. They would do their mad minutes every night in case there were sappers in the wire. I was never close to the war. I was around the weapon systems, I'd hear the rounds go off. Now, I'm at Ripcord. Man, oh man, these guys that are out there and I'm seeing what they are going through. They've got injured guys and choppers can't get to them. It was surreal. I thought, 'I'm really in Vietnam; this is a war, this is what I hadn't seen for nine months.' There's a lot of people in grave situations out here, a lot of infantry guys. I don't know how they do what they do. I had a greater appreciation of how they got around, where they were and how they got the right coordinates for fire."

Capt. Dave Rich was another hero at Firebase Ripcord. Notorious for his persistence in charting incoming rounds and returning fire, Rich was admired by all who knew him. The most decorated soldier to emerge from the Battle for Firebase Ripcord, Rich was the recipient of the Distinguished Service Cross, Silver Star, numerous Bronze Star and an incredible seven Purple Hearts.

Rich was a dedicated soldier who took pride in his craft.

"He knew artillery backward and forward," said Dr. Capt. James Harris, the surgeon on Ripcord. "The first day we started taking casualties on the hill, I saw a guy come up who had gotten hit by some fragments. We're taking care of him and here's Rich out in front of everyone saying, 'Come on people, we have work to do.' One day, we got gassed a couple times. They'd fire an 82mm mortar with some gas on it. Rich was out doing a crater analysis after some incoming. They dropped in a round right next to him. It was riot gas. He came walking into my aid station with tears coming down both cheeks. It it would have been high explosives, he would have been dead. A few days later, he got a frag somewhere in his groin and we sent him out to have someone look at it. He never really talked about that injury. When he was in Japan, set to be discharged, he had a party catered for those who were taking care of him."

Rich passed away Nov. 8, 2011, following a fall at his Maine home.

11

Lifelines

A medevac chopper lands atop the lower pad at Firebase Ripcord in July 1970. Photo provided by Chris Jensen.

Those birds, the choppers and their crews, meant many things to the men on the ground. Hearing a chopper coming meant the arrival of food, water, mail and supplies to soldiers in the field. Those who had been shot anxiously awaited the arrival of a chopper – whether it was a slick or a medevac didn't matter - in order to leave the field and receive further medical care.

The arrival of a chopper also meant your position may be compromised, however given the fact that the North Vietnamese were everywhere, that chopper's load meant more than to the men in the field than the possibility of having their positions compromised.

Flying in the Ripcord AO (area of operations) presented a unique challenge, even for the best of pilots and crews. Kenneth Mayberry was an aircraft commander with the C/158th Aviation Battalion.

"The area we were in was very mountainous," he said. "The terrain went from ocean to coastal flatlands – sand dunes, swamp, rice paddies – to rolling hills, the Annamite Range, which grew abruptly with a ridgeline running north to south as far as the eye could see. Camp Evans was adjacent to QL-1, which was the only highway in Vietnam which ran north to south along the coast. We had sand dunes and the sea on one side of us and rolling hills and mountains on the other. It was a miniature Rocky Mountain-type environment. We went from basically sea level to 2,000 to 3,000 feet in altitude. That may not seem like much to you but for helicopters it pushed them to the limit. Hovering at 2,000 feet was like 10,000-plus feet depending on the density altitude and temperature stressing our engines and rotar systems. It was not unusual to bleed RPM at those altitudes depending on how much weight we were carrying on board. Add to that the wind shear in the mountainous environment and it made for some challenging piloting."

A Chinook pilot, Dale Ireland, remembered the challenge approaching a firebase presented when winds would suddenly pick up. The massive supply choppers were critical to the establishment of firebases and in resupplying troops in the field.

"The wind really does impact how you piloted," he said. "I can remember on one of the firebases we were trying to pick a load up the wind was blowing so hard, one moment we were climbing at 400 feet a minute, then another moment we were falling at 400 feet a minute. You had to constantly work your thrust.

"We supplied ammo, water, petroleum, concertina wire, you name it we did it. When we first started with the firebase, we'd usually drop a ladder and the engineers would start cutting the jungle. Then we'd bring in a bulldozer. In the back, they'd build the bunkers. We'd take them in and drop the bunkers in the holes and they'd fill them in. Artillery pieces, sandbags - everything would be going out over several days to supply a firebase. Then it was constantly resupplying it. Every day there was a resupply. Every day there was a need for ammo."

Michael Bruce was a 21-year-old Medevac pilot while flying operations in and out of Ripcord with the 326th Medical Battalion. Medevacs carried with them four-man teams, two pilots, a crew chief and a medic. The birds were unarmed and often flew without escorts. To say that those men were gutsy, was a gross understatement.

"The medic, he did the magic," said Bruce. "We got a lot of people back that, actually to their detriment sometimes, that our medics saved them they were so badly injured. When we picked them up we'd either take them to Camp Evans, or if they were bad enough and the medic couldn't get them stabilized, we'd stop down to Charlie Medic, C Company. They had a couple doctors and other medical technicians that would work to stabilize them. We'd take them to 85th Evac Hospital, Hue, or a hospital ship, the USS Sanctuary or USS Repose."

Edward Carnes came to the 326th Medical Battalion from the Special Forces, where he received additional medical training, which made him a valuable asset to the Medevac crews.

"They loved us because our medical training was so far and above the average medic, plus I had in-country training," said Carnes. "They liked medics that had already been in the field six months and had seen it and were accustomed to the carnage you'd see on the choppers."

What Carnes was not made aware of, nor was he properly prepared for, was the sheer number of casualties he'd see flying missions in and out of the Ripcord Area of Operations. He arrived in the area in early July and boarded his first chopper en route to Ripcord on July 3.

"We were completely in the dark," he said. "When it came, we never knew what was happening at Ripcord. That first week I flew I was shot down on Ripcord. We were pulling a hot hoist and we were coming in and they opened up on us. We got it through the belly, it almost took me out and then we didn't even know we were hit when we heard the groundies say that we were on fire. I looked back and all the fuel was coming in, igniting on the exhaust. We dropped it onto Ripcord and shut it down then we got evaced out and got another chopper. We were just coming in about treetop level when they opened up on us. I told the pilot we were taking fire on the left, bank right, he blew the cable and we pulled out of there. That was my first dive."

It wouldn't be his last.

Medevacs were targets and everyone knew it. The birds had to hover, especially when dropping hoists through the jungle canopies. Carnes said the birds would take rounds through the blades, some rounds even went through the chopper. Hueys were very resilient, as were the members of the crews.

"A lot of what we did, especially in the Ripcord area, was with hoists," remembered Bruce. "We'd hover over the treetops and when we'd do that, we'd have the ground unit pop smoke for us. Sometimes you'd see two different colors of smoke, about a few hundred feet from one another. We'd call them and say, 'Hey, we see yellow smoke and green smoke,' and they'd say 'We're the yellow'. We'd go in and pull the hoist. Our crew chief and medic would be on the skids guiding us down as low as we could get at a hover. Usually we'd get within a hundred feet of the ground. We'd drop down a jungle penetrator or a stokes litter. The jungle penetrator was folded up, with three seats on it. You could get two Americans on there or three Vietnamese. If they were in pieces we'd send a stokes litter down and we could get up to two people in there, but they had to get them in right. I remember one pickup, we were on the north side of Ripcord, we were hovering down a ways when we were doing the pickup, they were shooting at us. Our medic took a shot through the pants leg, missed him. They loaded a guy backward in the stokes litter, he was almost falling out as we got him cranked up in the helicopter. We had to secure him. Once we got him in, we had to secure him. He was really bad, then we got out of there. Some of these guys, if they didn't come up in a stokes litter, they were going to leave pieces of them down there."

Dangerous situations were the norm for chopper crews. The NVA would shoot at the birds with anything they had: RPGs, 51-caliber machine guns, even their AK-47s.

Larry Kern was shot down nine times during his tour in Vietnam. His experiences in the A Shau still live with him to this day.

"On many of my first missions as a co-pilot, we were shot at and hit," said Kern, who flew with the Ghostriders of the 158th Assault Helicopter Battalion. "We were forced down a number of times, all with different aircraft commanders. This had earned me the early call sign 'Magnet Ass.' After my first few weeks, veterans of the unit thought they had jinxed me with that first name, so for my protection and their own, my call sign was changed. The old guys then renamed me 'Crash.' This name was earned from the fact that my aircraft had crashed from an engine failure caused when my instructor pilot accidentally turned off our fuel switch instead of our hydraulics switch during my first flight in country – my in-country check ride."

"Every time we'd go out there somebody would be shooting at us," remembered Bruce. "The first mission I remember going out on, we had a hoist down. I was flying right seat, I had the aircraft. When you're doing a hoist, you have to find something solid out there to hover on or the whole aircraft is going to move. If you see something solid, you're going to be able to stabilize. I'm looking out at this branch through the chin bubble, hovering on that, and you can hear everything falling apart and all kind of shooting going on. Suddenly the tree I was focused on started to disintegrate and the aircraft commander starts saying, 'Get up, get up, get up!' I thought he was talking to me, to get the aircraft up, but he was talking to the crew chief to get the guy up as fast as he could. I ended up lifting up and we had this guy hanging up on a cable. We cleared him as we finished clearing the area."

Despite the danger, the chopper crews felt an overwhelming sense of responsibility for the men on the ground and did everything they could to get to them when the call came in.

"That whole period of time it always seemed hot missions around the Ripcord area," said Bruce. "Everyone was always taking fire. We talked to each other about how fortunate we were being in aircraft and landing behind barbed wire, where these guys were always out in this stuff. We had a lot of admiration for the grunts out in it. That was the worst place to be."

"Wherever they needed us, we were there in that area," said Carnes. "We flew so much up there, there were times we never ate, we just flew and flew. You could take our flight suits off and you could stand them up in the corner they were so saturated with blood. So that's what we were up against."

"Flying was voluntary, even for pilots," remembered Kern. "You could quit if you wanted to. I was very grateful to the guys who served as crew on the aircraft. Their jobs didn't end when we touched down at the end of the day. They had numerous duties to the aircraft and often flew more than the pilots because the pilots were limited to certain numbers of hours in time periods for safety reasons, by rule. I guess we did not have good judgment or we would have said, 'Do what you want with me. I am done.' True as that was, the fact is that our pride and dedication to each other told us that was not an option. We had our job and you soon became so attached to the other young men we flew with and supported on the ground that if you quit, the guilt of leaving the others before your turn was the same as abandoning them. We had to do it. We were young and being loyal to each other was more important than being safe."

Ireland and the Chinooks flew every day. They had to, it was the Chinooks that supplied the firebases.

"We'd fly 12-14 hours a day, working three days on, one day off, mostly single-ship missions," said Ireland. "We'd get up early in the morning, grab breakfast, put our flight suits on and go to operations, where we'd be handed a clipboard with our missions for the day. It would be three or four firebases you were resupplying. We'd also recover downed aircraft. Whatever kind of heavy lift mission was needed, it would be on our clipboard. Once you are out flying your missions, you're flying back and forth, back and forth. Once you were finished, you would call in and ask if there were any add ons and you'd help your fellows out. We'd refuel hot, we'd never shut the engines down. We'd eat C rations in our seats."

Pilots and their crews knew the dangers that came with flying in the A Shau. Vietnam just years earlier became the first war in which airmobile assaults were employed. President John Kennedy ordered the test program years before Vietnam became a war for the United States. The Battle of the Ia Drang Valley proved to be the first troop on troop battle of the war, as well as the launching point for America's newest battlefield strategy – airmobile assault.

UH-1s or Hueys were the birds transporting troops, supplies and serving as medevacs. Both medevacs and slicks flew with four-man crews. Each had a pilot and co-pilot. Medevacs were unarmed and staffed in the rear with a medic and a crew chief, who typically manned the hoist. Slicks had two door gunners in the right and left rear cabin.

"There's an inherent danger when you're sitting there hovering," said Carnes. "We weren't armed. We had personal arms, but no M-60s. When they'd call an urgent, we'd do everything we could to get in there. We made one pick up where we picked a guy up and they kept saying he was bad, bad, bad. We picked him up and the whole front of his head was blown off. He had taken an RPG to the face. Obviously he wasn't alive when we got him. I think they just wanted to hurry up and get him out of there. It was a morale problem (in the field) when that happened.

Life on the Medevacs was chaotic at times, frightening and often simply heart-wrenching. Crew members saw the effects of war firsthand. Each dealt with what they saw in different ways.

"When we got him up, we had a medic that had just gotten into the unit," remembered Bruce. "Normally you look and you acknowledge what you see and you get back to doing, what you're supposed to do on the aircraft. This poor guy, he looked and psychologically he fell into the wound I guess. He ended up having to leave the unit. Some people just couldn't take it. The thing was we'd get back and the medic would clean up the aircraft and we'd go into our hooch, break out some C rations and play hearts and wait for the next call. We were back safe and we got a break from what those guys couldn't get a break from."

"There's a place in your mind you had to go, thinking that you're doing more good than harm," said Bruce. "You're trying to make a bad situation better and by keeping that in mind it helped immensely."

For Carnes, the toll of the missions weighed on him, the effects of seeing soldiers ripped to shreds was something he couldn't just put away each and every night back in his hooch.

"I had a scrapbook I was keeping, writing down names of dead and that died, kind of what was going on," he remembered. "I stopped it mid-month, I think I got burned out thinking that none of us were going to make it. There was one thing that I tried to do one time, the first day I was flying I picked up a guy, we flew a hot hoist and we picked up one soldier, he had been hit by a booby trap, it mangled both his legs, and one arm was gone. I got him in the chopper and kept him alive. We took him out to the hospital ship and dropped him off. When we got back, the chopper was just pools of blood, just floating. We washed the chopper out and found this cross that he had on his neck. So I kept that thinking that I knew we'd go back to the hospital ship. I went back, it was that week, and asked what had happened to the guy. They said they had amputated both legs and an arm and sent him to Osaka, Japan. I said see that he gets this. Whether he did or not I don't know."

Having come from Special Forces, Carnes had taken part in clandestine missions in and out of Cambodia and Laos. He was privy to information few others knew. His time at Ripcord, though, weighs heavily on him to this day as he recounts the horrors he saw in the field.

"When I went to dustoff, the thing of it was it was so much it was like a daily barrage, it's all we dealt with," said Carnes. "I had everything from massive amputations to I had one guy, it was a night flight, they had set up their night camp and somehow somebody triggered a booby trap. It killed a couple of them. One guy was busted up, his mouth from his nose down was just gone. His face was just awful. They threw him on the chopper and I could see him gurgling. I told my crew chief you gotta help me and I told the pilot put the pedal to the metal, we gotta get this guy in fast. I gave him a tracheotomy in the chopper at night, put a tube in him, gave him mouth to mouth until we got him to the Charlie. I told my crew chief to grab a rag and stuff it in his face, the air was coming back out through what was left of his face. He didn't make it. So that's what we dealt with. I think most of the guys felt like we were making a difference, we were doing something worthwhile."

Carnes lost 13 crew members during his time in Vietnam. From day one in the Ripcord Area of Operations, he admitted he did not think he'd make it home alive.

"One night it was raining, cold," remembered Carnes. "I woke up in the middle of the night and sat up in my bunk and there was the grim reaper looking right at me. Never said anything, never moved. I knew right then and there I wasn't coming home. I wasn't drunk, I wasn't stoned, I was as lucid as can be."

These men came from all walks of life. Kern was an art major and war in the jungle was the last thing he thought he'd be mired in as a 22-year-old in 1970.

"I wasn't your average airborne kind of guy. I wanted to make paintings and chase girls," he admitted. "I had often wished that there was a college major named 'Painting Girls 101.' I never wanted to go to war. I blew my college deferment by dropping a class one semester because I could not get to my job in time. I thought that I could make it to the next semester, register for a full load (12 units) again and then it would be 'Joe College' again and no worries. It didn't work that way. I received my draft notice.

"After receiving my draft notice I volunteered to go to flight school because I knew the training took a year and the war might be over. I also thought that being a pilot would allow me to live like those guys in the movies. You know what I mean – nice living quarters, wild women and a wild life in the rear. Boy was I wrong. Camp Evans was better than being in the field but the conditions were much like the movie 'Mash', very Spartan and often under attack."

Kern would become a big part of the battle, and the battle would forever become part of Kern's life, something that lives with him every day.

Four-Legged Screaming Eagles

Early the morning of July 6, Bruce Bond was alerted by Jim Dandy, his German shepherd Scout Dog, that there was danger in the area.

"We were in a night defensive position and we were getting ready to saddle up," said Bond. "Jim alerted to my left and when I saw him alert, I picked up my CAR-15 and was getting ready to alert the CO (commanding officer) when a satchel charge came in. There were 18 of us wounded. When the first satchel charged went off the lieutenant saw several of the VC and everyone started shooting at that time."

It was around 6:30 in the morning. Bond was hit in the left foot, right leg, right arm, back lung and heart.

"Jim wouldn't let me be hurt," said Bond. "Angry was not the word for his reaction. During contact he got really aggressive toward everyone. I had to wrap his leash around his nose so the medic could work on me."

Bond and Jim Dandy were working with Bravo Company, 1/506th, southwest of Ripcord.

The 58th Infantry Scout Dog Platoon was part of the 101st Airborne Division stationed at Camp Evans. The platoon had its own area at Camp Evans, its own hooches, its own training area. Scout Dogs were trained to find spider holes, snipers, bunkers, booby traps, trip wires, basically anything that would cause their handlers, or other troops, harm.

Bond arrived in Vietnam in September 1969 and was assigned to the

LIFELINES

101st Airborne, ultimately with the 58th. Training consisted of 12 to 14 weeks stateside, at Fort Benning, Ga. Bond had but three weeks with Jim Dandy.

"When I got there, they were short," he said. "They only had 20 dogs at Camp Evans They were all shepherds, or shepherd mixes. Later in the year we received a mine dog, a narcotics dog named Marc the Narc. They were Labradors."

Jim Dandy had been with other handlers and was known as an aggressive dog. He had attacked his handlers previous to Bond.

"He did not like other people," said Bond. "When I got there, I just liked him. I asked the lieutenant if I could have him. I liked the way he looked. It took me about two hours to get to know him. I did two weeks of training with the handlers to know how to read him. I'm the only handler he did not bite. He was with me 24-7. The only time he was not with me was in the mess hall, then he stayed in my room. He was an equal opportunity biter, so I had to keep a sign on the door. I had to keep a tight rein on him. He bit his last handler pretty bad. No one knows why, he just liked me for whatever reason."

Training included taking the dogs through obstacle courses and night perimeter duty at Evans. Training also included local village children, who were hidden for the dogs to sniff out and locate. The children were put in holes and stationed in trees.

"I would have someone put out a trip wire and Jim always found it," said Bond. "He was the man."

A Scout Dog and his handler were guaranteed to walk point, an extremely dangerous job in the A Shau. Despite having a job that carried with it a life expectancy of just minutes, Bond remembers feeling invincible around Jim Dandy.

"At my age, I was very naïve," he said. "I couldn't be hurt. Jim knew his job. He kept a bunch of us safe and he never let me down."

That included the day he was hit. Scout Dogs and their handlers were never separated. That included any insertion or extraction. The handlers were outfitted with D-rings used to strap the dogs to their handlers in the event of an extraction. A jungle penetrator could be lowered to collect the handler and the dog would ride up clamped safely to his handler. That morning, July 6, Bond was severely wounded and was one of the first to get out on a medevac; Jim went with him. There were 18 wounded in the attack.

"Jim hooked to my gear," remembered Bond. "They sent me to the aid station at Evans. My lieutenant and sergeant were there. My first thought was to take care of Jim. I was not going to leave him. The doctors and nurses wanted to take me in. I took him to his hooch and fed him, gave him water, then they took me."

The bond the two shared was deep. Bond didn't want to leave Jim, knowing he wouldn't react well to others. It was more than that, though. He still tears up to this day remembering those final moments before being airlifted for medical attention. He didn't want to leave Jim, but he had to. His foot was shattered and he was in danger of losing it, if not worse.

"They wanted to send me to the 95th Evac," remembered Bond. "They gave me a shot (to sedate him) and I woke up on a C-130 going to Japan. I never saw Jim again. I spent two months in Japan and went to Walter Reed (Medical Center) from there. My left foot was shattered.

"To say I was upset is an understatement. They tried to get him to go with another handler. Jim basically ate him up. He got so mean and nasty, then somehow he broke loose. I've been told he went back up to the aid station. He was so aggressive that they had to use catchpoles to catch him."

LIFELINES

Jim was put down. He was buried at Camp Evans in the Scout Dog Cemetery.

"I can't imagine what he was thinking. He was suffering from PTSD (post-traumatic stress disorder)," Bond said of Jim. "His whole world ended on July 6. One minute I'm there, the next minute I'm not."

While in the field, handlers carried supplies for themselves as well as their dogs. At night, the two would sleep together.

"We'd sleep curled up together," Bond said. "He'd lay his head on my chest."

The work of the Scout Dogs was invaluable to soldiers in Vietnam. Dogs, with their handlers, sniffed out danger in its many forms. In the A Shau, dogs with the 58 Infantry Platoon stayed busy, answering the call wherever and whenever they were needed.

The history of the 58th is rich and dates back to 1951. It was first deployed to Vietnam Feb. 16, 1968, where it was assigned to the 3rd Brigade, 101st Airborne Division at Phuoc Vinh in III Corps, just northeast of Saigon. Training was following by operations in support of the 1/506th, 2/506th and 3/187th around Phuoc Vinh. Soon operations expanded to the Cu Chi area.

By September 1968, 1st and 2nd brigades of the 101st were in I Corps while 3rd Brigade remained in III Corps. When the division combined, the 58th moved north as well, loading onto C-130s for the flight to Phu Bai. The platoon set up shop at Camp Rodrigez at Camp Eagle, where sister unit, the 42nd Infantry Platoon Scout Dogs were nearby in support of 1st Brigade. The 47th Infantry Platoon Scout Dogs operated in support of 2nd Brigade north at Landing Zone Sally.

The 58th relocated to Camp Evans on Nov. 1, 1968. Handler Oscar McGhan was wounded Nov. 11, becoming the first 58th casualty in I

Corps. His dog, Bo Bear, was killed and buried in the unit cemetery at Camp Evans. By April 1969, the 58th was sending teams into the A Shau Valley and was working in support of two brigades. On July 19, 1969, Raymon Draper Hales and his dog, Rebel, were killed in action. A second handler, William Clayton Ray was killed just two days prior to Bond getting wounded, on July 4. Ray's dog, Fritz, was wounded.

"The week I was wounded we found three or four spider holes, some bunkers," said Bond. "During our rotation, our standdown was supposed to be five days but there was such a demand, we were going out every five days. On several trips we found trip wires. The 58th Scout Dog Platoon, the guys were just phenomenal. The dogs were their best friends. The companies were glad to see us when we went out because they knew the capabilities of the dogs."

Others knew the capabilities of the dogs as well. The North Vietnamese had bounties on all the dogs and their handlers, noted Bond.

Demand for the dogs was so high by August 1970, it was difficult to keep up with requests. By that time, the 58th was supporting five battalions. On July 21, 1971, the 58th was inactivated, having served in 10 campaigns during the Vietnam War.

Once Bond ended up at Walter Reed, he had to learn to walk all over again. It was a 12- to 14-month process, during which one of the surgeons felt he may lose his foot. When he finally left the hospital, Bond wound up at Fort Gordon working with MPs and their dogs. After that, he went to the police academy and worked at the Florence Police Department in South Carolina.

Today, Bond is dealing with the effects of agent orange. He remembers walking through the jungle with the choppers floating by and spraying chemicals, standing there with Jim Dandy as leaves fell to the ground almost instantaneously. In addition to the effects of agent orange, Bond suffers from PTSD. He still tears up talking about Jim. To this day, Jim Dandy's dogtags dangle alongside his own.

"I miss him," said Bond. "I never got to say good-bye."

Nearly 300 dog handlers were killed in Vietnam. Nearly 290 Scout Dogs were killed.

Bond said the lessons he learned in the 58th, from both the dogs and their handlers, live with him to this day. Their courage continues to inspire him.

Direct Hit

Atop Firebase Ripcord, Clem Neiderer was part of Headquarters Company, 2/501, stationed in Phu Bai, futher south. He and several others were sent to Ripcord to supply radios to the Tactical Operations Center.

"I was in the communications section. We did a lot of work with field wire and radios. We used to repair radios," he said. "I worked as field wireman, and usually worked with the generator mechanic. I ran wire line from the TOC to the generators. We stayed on the firebase about 14 days."

Neiderer routinely hopped from firebase to firebase and remembered stops at Brick and Bastogne. Ripcord was much larger than other firebases and he noted its elevation, as it stood much higher along the western edge of the A Shau than other firebases located at lower elevations.

He and his platoon sergeant were among those flown from Phu Bai north to Camp Evans. There he noted the fury of chopper activity bringing troops in and troops going out.

"They were coming in one after another," he said. "We finally got a ride out to Ripcord. "On the way in I remember the copilot told me they weren't going to go all the way in, they were going to hover on one side of the hill. We had to kind of hump up the hill of the firebase. There was a helicopter shot down sitting down on the pad up top."

It was July and the firebase was routinely taking incoming rounds. July 10 stood out for Neiderer as he was working with men around the mess hall, chatting and drinking coffee.

"That morning I was there, I was supposed to lay wire for the generator mechanic," he said. "I was talking to those guys and the mechanic, we were shooting the breeze, talking about what we were going to do back home. The generator mechanic came to get me, I was drinking coffee, we left and no sooner I left it hit the mess hall."

Anthony Critchlow had been a cook atop Ripcord since April, in the days after the firebase was established. He recalled the blast.

"I was on the pad waiting for the first bird to leave," said Critchlow. "Someone came up to me and said there was no need for me to go, that the mess hall had been hit and there were dead there."

He quickly moved to the site of the blast.

"There was no mess hall anymore," he remembered. "So I went back to the orderly room to see what was up. (Victor) De Foor was getting two cups of coffee in the bunker. As he walked out the front door to the bunker he was hit in the chest or head with a recoilless rifle round. There were two cooks and three other soldiers getting coffee. What was left of De Foor was blown back into the bunker. The three guys in front of the serving line were blown out the back, along with a full pot of hot coffee. The cooks helped the three soldiers to the aid station. Everyone was hit with body parts and shrapnel. "

The hit was a 75mm recoilless rifle round that slammed through the door of the mess hall, killing Victor De Foor immediately. His lifeless, burned body was thrown back into the bunker, where several others were wounded.

"I wouldn't be here today if it weren't for the generator mechanic," said Neiderer.

Three others were killed July 10, including Patrick Bohan, Frederick Raymond Jr. and Daniel Hively.

Critchlow served soldiers on Ripcord near the entire time the firebase was open. He said moral remained rather high, even in July when incoming mortar rounds increased on the firebase.

"When the companies in the mountains around us were getting hit and overrun, things were not so good," he said. "The guys were mad we were sending people out to die for no good reason. It was stupid. Everyone thought we should leave Ripcord before we were overrun. We expected that to happen any day. All of the books say we started to get mortared on 1 July, but I remember it started the last week or two weeks in June. It started with one round in the morning, always about the same time. Then it was two in the morning and two in the afternoon. Then, by July, it could be any time of the day. In July they started shooting at us with the recoilless rifle. On 4 July I was standing outside the bunker cooking steaks. We could hear the rounds flying over our heads.

12

The Delta Raiders

On July 11, the 2nd of the 501st was sent to Camp Evans before returning July 12 for assaults south and east of Ripcord, in an area that proved problematic throughout July – Hill 1,000.

The Delta Raiders have a unique history within the 101st Airborne Division. Capt. Charles McMenamy was a Green Beret in the Army and was nearly killed leading a group of Rhade Montagnards in 1967 near the tri-border of Vietnam, Laos and Cambodia during an intelligence gathering mission (Project Omega). He was dropped into the jungle with a Montagnard bodyguard during an aborted insertion and survived ambush and five days before being discovered and flown to safety.

Back in the states, McMenamy was offered a rifle company that he would form from scratch at Fort Campbell, Kentucky, home to the 101st. There he commanded Delta Company, 2nd Battalion, 501st Regiment.

Delta was the fourth rifle company added by the Pentagon in late 1967, a need that arose due to an escalating war and mounting casualties. A fourth company was needed, especially in the areas where firebases

THE DELTA RAIDERS

required an entire company to secure the perimeter, leaving just two to patrol. With that, approval was granted for the fourth company and so the Raiders were born.

Small numbers of men from Alpha, Bravo and Charlie were incorporated, but the remainder of the Raiders were pulled from wherever the Army could get them, including the stockade.

Under McMenamy's leadership, the company thrived. The Raider name came from battalion Commander Lt. Col. Richard Tallman, and McMenamy used the moniker often to instill a sense of pride and determination in the men. They saluted and acknowledged each other with "Raider, sir!" as Peter Maslowski and Don Winslow so thoroughly pointed out in their book, "Looking for a Hero: Staff Sergeant Joe Hooper and the Vietnam War."

Raiders were different, and they operated differently than a typical rifle company in the field.

With Ripcord under near constant attack, July 12 marked a period of several consecutive days of heavy action around Hill 805 as Hawkins' Alpha Company, and Delta Company (2nd/501st), the Raiders, under Capt. Chris Straub began working in the area.

"I flew to Ripcord, it was my first time on that firebase and met my new commander, Andre Lucas (July 11) and his S3, Herb Koenigsbauer, and they gave me a briefing," remembered Straub. "They told me to take my company and land at the base of 805 and go up, fortify the top and dig in the best I could because it was a high likelihood we would be attacked up there. They explained it to me and it was obvious to me that having a strong point on 805 was important to keeping the enemy away from Ripcord."

Delta Company combat assaulted into the area via a small landing zone.

REMEMBERING FIREBASE RIPCORD

"It was quiet, too damn quiet!" wrote Sgt. Ray "Blackie" Blackman. "You could feel the gooks. I walked rear security for the company and never felt so alone in my life. We could hear them prepping 805 in the distance and the explosions were getting louder as we got closer.

"After reaching the base of 805 we were told to form a line and move up. Just like in the movies, we assaulted the hill in waves. Thank God for the heavy prep. We got to the top without contact and started checking things out. There were a few blown up bunkers and a couple NVA (North Vietnamese Army) bodies. In a way there seemed to be a feeling of relief. We had CA'd (combat assaulted) into this bad fucking AO (area of operation) and John Wayned it up one nasty hill without contact. All right, there's nothing here, let's go back to the bush.

"That, however, wasn't' our mission. We started digging in."

Lt. James Noll, Alpha Three, knew 805 well.

"I don't know how many times I was up there," Noll said. "On one of the operations we had earlier on 805, we had some North Vietnamese come around patrolling and they got shot up. We kept finding bunkers and foxholes all over the place, but were they all made by the North Vietnamese? I don't know. Other American troops had been there too. The South Vietnamese had been there. Some of these things were even years old. There had been fighting in that area years before. We found a tree with the 1st Cavalry patch carved on it. They had operated there."

Alpha Company had been moved in June to Firebase O'Reilly in order to build up company strength. When Charlie was depleted at Hill 902, the decision was made to move Alpha Company back into the area of 805, which was just north and east of 902.

"We were CA'd out of O'Reilly to that special ridgeline again," said Noll. "Charlie Company was there. I talked to (Capt. Jeff) Wilcox and (Lt. James) Campbell for a few seconds on the landing zone when I flew in. They hopped on the chopper I came in on. They were the last out from Charlie.

"I immediately took patrol while the rest of the unit was coming in. We went down this ridgeline and were heading toward a spot where we had set up before. At this time, a CH-47 was coming into Ripcord. The North Vietnamese opened up with a couple of what we call 51 calibers. As we're patrolling down this ridgeline, a finger tangent broke off and went down further. I could hear the machine guns going off every time a helicopter would come around. I started taking my little patrol down that way and there was an NDP (night defensive position) site. I got several guys to my right and several to my left. We were snooping and pooping. I hear this clink, clink, clink noise and I'm wondering what the hell it is. I signal to my guys left and right to circle around this NDP and cover me because I'm walking into this clearing. I have my M-16 on full auto and I'm about to crap my pants. I creep up and hear this sound deep in a foxhole. I just start to put the barrel up to the hole and out of the hole jumps a squirrel. It was at some ration cans that had been left. That broke the tension."

Noll remembers cutting several landing zones in the area of Hill 805 and it wasn't unusual to find a freshly cut LZ had been booby trapped by the North Vietnamese.

"We found a landing zone that we hadn't cut," he remembered. "It was very fresh, within a week or so, and it had been booby trapped. They had taken 60mm mortar rounds, buried them halfway into the ground, and daisy-chained them. There were tripwires. Their idea was to have a helicopter come in and set off these booby traps. The cords they used were red and stuck out like a sore thumb. I went very carefully, dug up the mortar rounds and disarmed them. We didn't want to set them off, because it would let them know we were there."

Noll was nearing that site when he heard the 50 calibers again. He pondered taking his patrol toward the shooting, then though with two heavy machine guns, how many NVA could possibly be there.

"Probably more than I had," he said. "I opted for caution and went back up to the rest of the company. I called in artillery. They stopped firing and they never fired again. I assumed we knocked out those machine guns. I could hear North Vietnamese speaking, yelling at each other."

A veteran platoon leader, Noll and Alpha three typically worked alone, away from the company. This week, Noll's platoon had teamed up with Capt. Chuck Hawkins and the rest of Alpha Company for the mission at 805.

Noll, given past history and the knowledge of the machine gun position nearby, knew something wasn't quite right.

"We killed some North Vietnamese that were coming around the 805 complex, but I was so dog-gone certain we were going to get hit the next day that I had it set up for another platoon to have a machine gun set up. I had all my guys ready, alert. I knew we were going to get hit. By golly, about half my platoon was outside the perimeter and we got hit. I went charging up the hill, Bruce (Brady, Noll's radio telephone operator) comes with me, and my guys were all supposed to follow. That's how it was briefed earlier. 'When we get hit, you're going to charge forward, we can't stay in this one position. You understand, you have to rush into the enemy if we're hit,' they were told. None of them did. I had a brand-new platoon sergeant. He had never been in combat. We had so many replacements that had never been in combat. I went up and found the point man and asked what they hell happened. He said a North Vietnamese jumped out and shot at him. I said, 'Well, did you shoot him?' 'No,' he said. 'I ducked down behind a log.' I asked why he didn't shoot him and he said he was too scared.

"I realized that Bruce and I are up there by ourselves. I go back down the hill and start grabbing kids and going back up the hill, kicking them in their butts. We start charging up the hill. I'm shooting and a little North Vietnamese pops up and I try to shoot him. My gun is empty. He ducks and goes under cover. I turn around and start hollering, 'Get your butts up here,' and boom! I get hit."

Alpha Three walked into an ambush in a saddle heading up to 805 and both Noll and his radio man, Brady, were hit. Small arms fire and RPGs rang through the bush as several NVA were spotted.

"We were going a little bit of an incline and hit a clearing," remembered Brady. "That's when we got hit. The point man opened up. Noll took off to my right. I hit the dirt, I had to get the radio off my rucksack. I low-crawled over to Noll. We had been in that area before. He was in a little foxhole and had his leg out. I came in on his left side. I called in to the rear and said we were in contact. He pointed off to my left. I started firing off to the left and it wasn't too long after that there was an explosion. I got hit and he got hit. We think it was a grenade.

"It just picked me up and threw me," said Noll. "I landed so my left leg from my knee down was under my butt. It hurt so bad and to me it was like the jolly green giant took a red hot poker and slammed into the back of my leg. It burned. I'm trying to find my left leg and I start to feel behind my left kneecap and of course my middle finger goes right into the bullet hole and I pull my own meat out. I got scared. I hollered, 'Medic!' Mark Draper hollered, 'Lieutenant, I'm not coming out into the open. You're not hurt that bad, crawl back here.' At that point, Baldwin hollers, 'If you die can I have your K-Bar knife?'

"I crawled into a foxhole with Bruce. I realized I had my leg but I couldn't bend it. I had to keep part of my left leg out of the foxhole. There, I started calling in Cobra helicopters. Of course the machine gun from the other platoon I set up did a good job of covering fire, discouraging the North Vietnamese from charging up the other side of that hill. We're throwing a few hand grenades down and shooting. I've got the mic to speak on the radio and finally the rest of the platoon got up there and I called the gunships off."

Noll's platoon secured the top of the noll en route to 805. Hawkins and the rest of Alpha arrived about that time. Draper began working on Noll and Brady.

"Bruce and I went to the landing zone with security, the landing zone I had taken the booby traps off of," said Noll. "We went back to Camp Evans. Bruce got hit in his hand and had metal stuck in the bones. It needed pretty serious surgery."

"It was like a hammer hitting my hand. There wasn't any pain. I knew I was hit though. Noll was yelling for a medic. Everyone behind us hunkered down. He was yelling for Doc (Mark) Draper to come forward. Draper told me the firing had slowed down. There were only a few rounds coming from up front. He'd dropped his rucksack and told me to get out of the foxhole, because the lieutenant comes first. I crawled to what I thought was a secure spot. Doc came over and bandaged me up. He said, and I'll never forget this, 'Brady this is your ticket out of here.'"

Once Noll's wounds were dressed, he arrived back at the company area of Camp Evans. That's when he learned his radio man was en route to Japan for surgery. Noll could walk, but needed the help of a cane. He was out of commission for several days then arrived back at the chopper pad, where he waited for next ride to Ripcord. There, a couple of lieutenants arrived and pulled him into a jeep. His second Purple Heart was enough. He was now going to work for brigade as a night duty officer in the underground bunker.

His experience and leadership in the field would be impossible to replace.

"Simply outstanding as a leader of men," said Capt. Chuck Hawkins,

Alpha Company commander. "He was savvy, he knew things the average guy never learned – marks on enemy small arms shell casing would indicate whether they had been fired from a RPD machine gun or AK assault rifle. Noll led from the front and by example. He was not shy about sticking his nose in a firefight and knew how to go about it – fix the enemy to the front, flank them to one side, destroy them."

The heat at 805 would only intensify in the coming days.

Capt. Straub's Delta Raiders saw no direct contact, though there was a sense they were being watched. Tired from humping throughout the heat of the day, Delta set up a Night Defensive Position and settled in that evening.

"While we humped up the hill, we were anticipating something," said David Mitchell, Delta Company. "The powers that be anticipated relatively severe resistance and we walked up, and nothing. We did not hit any contact."

"We were always running into contact in the Ripcord area on previous trips there," said Blackman, of Delta Three. "We'd heard rumors about heavy contact and Ripcord being constantly shelled just prior to us going to Hill 805. And, we got a few packages from home during the previous days log along with a lot of extra ammo, frags, etc. Basically we were told it was not going to be good and to be ready."

Delta Raiders were known for their ability to work in and out of areas, finding the enemy and getting out. The company was good at it, too.

"Our company prided itself on surprising the enemy and being where it didn't think U.S. forces were supposed to be," said Straub. I didn't like being up there where the entire world could see us. Offense is the way to go. Defense is not the way to go. You don't score many victories on defense."

"We didn't like it on LZs during log days or pulling security on firebases," added Blackman. But we especially didn't like that hill. We'd always run into contact in the Ripcord AO (area of operations) but never stayed on bald hills. We were good at moving into an NDP late and quiet. They never knew exactly where we were at night, but they knew we were on that hill."

The Raiders, tired from a daylong hike, settled in atop the hill, assuming some positions the NVA had manned while assaulting Ripcord.

"Hill 805 had been blown all to hell," remembered Blackman. "There were a few large boulders at the very top and ragged tree stumps everywhere. Blown up trees and branches covered the sides of the hill providing a million places for the gooks to hide. At the bottom of the hill there was a wall of green jungle. We were, to say the least, extremely vulnerable."

The first attack came around that night from an enemy force northwest of the hill, according to Blackman.

"As far as I remember everyone was still awake," wrote Blackman. "We were on a self-imposed full alert. Another man and myself were sitting near the top of the hill just below one of the big rocks. After such a long day and not much sleep the night before it was nice to kick back a little. It was real quiet and peaceful."

"We always had small-arms fire," said Mitchell. "It ended with us repelling whatever the force was."

Shortly before 9:30 p.m. the jungle erupted as Delta sat atop the hill. RPGs did immediate damage and small arms fire continued for another hour northeast of the company's position.

With RPGs (rocket propelled grenades) slamming into the hill by the dozens, the Raiders took cover.

THE DELTA RAIDERS

"As we ran toward the foxhole below an RPG went off behind us and the guy with me got some shrapnel in his back," Blackman wrote. "The battle was in full force before we ever reached our position with loud explosions and small arms fire hitting all over the hill. Delta Company opened up with everything we had. It was in impressive display of firepower that a line company with full supporting fire is capable of producing. I guess the thing that struck me the most was how damn loud it all was.

"Mortars from Ripcord, Cobras, air strikes and a flareship were called in. Capt. Straub was doing his job well. The belching sound and steady stream of melting tracers from the mini-guns that ripped into the jungle wall below almost made us cheer. The flares had made the trees and stubble below do a shadowy death dance that I'll never forget. I have no idea how long the firefight lasted, but it seemed like hours."

Delta fought off the attack and aerial rocket artillery, air strikes and a flareship was employed. Three Delta Raiders were medevacked that night and 10 more the next morning, among them, Barry Barnes, Jackie Brumbelow, Keith Cluff, Larry Ertel, Willie Lewis, James Poulard and Carl Robinson.

There was a sense of shock amongst the Raiders after the intensity of the attack.

"We had small-arms fire, rockets, mortars. We got it," said Mitchell. "It ended with us repelling whatever the force was."

"We had expected contact at the LZ during the CA (combat assault), along the way to Hill 805 and when we assaulted the hill," said Blackman. "We were relieved that we hadn't run into contact and let our guard down a little while digging in. I guess we thought we'd spend a quiet night there and then leave."

Blackman recalled that the eery quiet after the battle was such that it made his ears swell until he thought they may burst.

REMEMBERING FIREBASE RIPCORD

The next morning, the Raiders found evidence of enemy activity in the area, namely RPGs, all of which were destroyed. Evacuation of the remaining wounded also commenced at first daylight. Morning also brought new supplies and knowledge that the company would be staying on the hill.

"The company was shifted slightly around the hill and we began building our bunkers," remembered Blackman. "Busted up tree branches were placed in front and on top of our new position. Wire was strung and claymores put out. The rucks of the wounded were stripped of ammo, food and water. Everyone worked on their fighting positions with silent determination. Then we waited."

Little did they know what the succession of nights atop that hill would bring. The Raiders would be hit every night they were set up on Hill 805, through July 18, when they were choppered out.

"Everything we got hit with was after midnight," said Mitchell, "throughout the whole time we were at 805."

As night fell, the men settled in.

"The first platoon sector faced a saddle leading to a small LZ with Ripcord beyond," wrote Blackman. "Second platoon faced the ridgeline leading up to Hill 805 and third platoon completed the perimeter along a steep dropoff. It was just about dark when we got the word to keep our heads down. Straub was walking our DTs in as close as possible. He was to show the NVA that we were ready and to show us that we weren't alone. Shrapnel from the friendly fire whistled over our heads. It made me feel better."

Just after 1 a.m. on July 14, Delta again set up in Night Defensive Position when it began to take rocket-propelled grenades, satchel charges and small arms fire. The attack came from the northwest, which faced a saddle beyond the crown of the hill and a landing zone

THE DELTA RAIDERS

in the distance. Delta returned fire and received artillery support from Ripcord.

"The hill exploded," said Blackman. "This time, they were close... very close. I started rolling grenades down the hill and filling magazines for the other guys in our bunker because my fucking gun had jammed. I was pissed! The M-60 to our left was sending a steady stream of tracers down the hill. It's barrel was bright red and I could see the piston pumping. Airstrikes, flareship, ARA (aerial rocket artillery), quad 50s, artillery and mortars from Ripcord and another firebase pounded in around us. Cobras were circling us like vultures. Such firepower, yet they kept coming."

Blackman wondered what it was that drove the enemy. Then there was silence. First platoon had been hit hard and there was a need to reinforce the side of the hill.

"We went up the hill and around the big rock at the top," wrote Blackman. "As we started down into the first platoon area I stumbled, stopped, then looked down. There were three men lying in a row. I thought they were asleep. After looking at them for a couple seconds I realized that they were dead. Then I turned and followed my platoon sergeant to an empty foxhole."

Medic Paul "Rat" Guimond had been wounded, but was reportedly still alive. Blackman and another soldier went to retrieve Guimond and pulled him up the hill.

"He had been shot in the head but was still alive," remembered Blackman. "Doc came and put a field dressing on his right temple. I held the bandage until the medevac came."

The battle had ended after a little more than an hour. It was nearly 4 a.m. when a medevac arrived overhead. The litter came down and Guimond and another were placed on it and hoisted from the jungle floor.

Guimond didn't make it. As the sun rose, five NVA were found dead while Delta suffered six killed and nine wounded. In addition to Guimond, William Jones, John "Red" Keister, James Hembree, Lt. Terry Palm and Keith Utter were killed.

Palm, who spent the night running from position to position checking on his men, was shot and killed and later posthumously presented the Silver Star.

"At first light I started the long walk back to my platoon," wrote Blackman. "There were guys moving around but nobody talked. I tried to rub the blood off my shirt. Fuck! There had been nine men wounded and six killed. I wanted to sit down and cry when I reached my squad but couldn't.

By this point, Delta was down 29 men. Lt. Ralph Selvaggi choppered in with 12 additional troops, seven of them being new to the field, to reinforce Delta. Selvaggi succeeded Palm.

Delta knew they were surrounded. "Under us and all around us," is how Blackman explained the enemy position. "There were a few bunkers just below the second platoon sector in a draw and we thought there were tunnels but didn't find any. There was certainly a lot of activity in the area. We put a lot of MAs (mechanical ambushes), trip flares and claymores around those bunkers and all around the hill."

Patrols were sent out to repair the wire. Troops found RPGs, an RPG launcher, an AK-47, a bag containing 10 ½-pound satchel charges and five NVA bodies. Two airstrikes were called in on suspected NVA positions around the hill. Ammunition, additional wire, food and water was flown in to the battered Raiders. The men were working on no sleep.

North Vietnamese attacks would resume just before 11 p.m. July 14 and continue into the morning hours of July 15 as Delta took mortar rounds yet again. Artillery was called in to the west.

THE DELTA RAIDERS

The attack came from the south and southeast this time.

"I started rolling grenades again," wrote Blackman. "Mortars, artillery and the quad 50s on Ripcord created a wall of protection for us until the ARA and flareships were on station to help. The support we got was fast and fantastic. The NVA withdrew in an unknown direction."

Three trip flares went off shortly before 4 a.m. 15 meters to the west of 805 and the Raiders opened up with small arms fire.

Six were dead and eight more medevacked out following the fighting on the 14th. Just before 5 a.m., Jack Godwin was flown out after having his foot blown off by a satchel charge. Rodney "Nose" Collins was medevacked out just before 8 a.m. An additional six – Joseph Adams, Bruce "Tony" Chandler, Terry Cooper, Warren Hanrahan, David Weaver and Bobby Hill were choppered out before 10 a.m.

"I had never taken those kind of casualties, period," said Straub, who had not lost a man prior to the insertion at 805. "We always surprised the enemy. Certainly I was disturbed and still am to have Americans killed under my command."

At daylight, the Raiders discovered a number of enemy bodies had been dragged through the area. Additionally, clothing and a wallet with documents and photos was recovered. Blood trails lead southwest before ending. Gary Lee Schneider was killed that night and James Plenderleith wounded.

"By now I had become numb with fatigue and time had lost all meaning," remembered Blackman. "Fear and hatred had come and gone. All I wanted to do was leave this hill with no more pain to my family – my Delta family!"

That afternoon, around 3:30 p.m. a logbird sent to resupply Delta crashed and the pilots evacuated via Chinook soon thereafter. The door gunners ended up spending the night on 805 with members of Delta Company. Mortar rounds began arriving just before 7 p.m.

Lucas landed with supplies and visited with Straub, then the rest of the troops.

"He certainly did what a good commander would do," said Straub. "He correctly divined that we were shocked by the events of the night before and our morale was a little low. He came around and talked to me and went around to every fighting position and talked to every soldier, just brief bucking up, which was a very fine thing for him to do. It's exactly what I needed at the time. I started to buck myself up and I think everyone else did too."

Still, questions persisted and morale was low. The Raiders knew setting up on a hilltop was not what they were built to do.

"Of course we were questioning (policy)," said Blackman. "It just wasn't our style. We knew it wasn't Straub's idea though. We just didn't understand the reasoning behind it. We could have NDPd (night defensive positioned) in the jungle nearby and taken the hill each morning to keep them off, or airstrikes could have kept them off. I mean, we knew the NVA were using the hill to shoot at helicopters, but I think there could have been other ways to prevent it than wasting a company."

In the early morning hours of July 16, a mechanical ambush Delta had set west of its night position went off on Hill 805. Raiders fired and then took 30 RPGs, small arms fire and several satchel charges from enemy located west, south, southeast and southwest of its position. The 15-minute barrage ended with no American casualties.

It wasn't over, though. Enemy was again spotted north, but did not return fire. By shortly after 4 a.m., another mechanical ambush erupted, this time to the north. Again, no return fire from the NVA. A search produced two dead NVA, a couple of AKs and five full magazines, two

THE DELTA RAIDERS

5.5-pound satchel charges, 50 AK rounds in a leather pouch, a knife, several Chicom grenades and several bottles of some sort of liquid.

Later that night, Col. Lucas reported that intercepted NVA radio communication indicated the enemy was prepping for an attack of the hill. Three hours later, another mechanical ambush went off to the west. Nothing was found.

Later that morning, first platoon secured the logbird and reported it appeared to have been tampered with.

By 9 that night, Lucas reported that intercepted radio transmissions from the NVA indicated a planned attack on Hill 805 was imminent. Just before midnight, another mechanical ambush was detonated 150 meters to the west off Hill 805. Artillery and mortars responded. Another mechanical ambush detonated at 2:30 a.m. in the same area and aerial rocket artillery joined in the fray with artillery and mortars. Delta took a round of CS gas shortly thereafter.

At first light, a check of the area resulted in nothing found.

Still Waiting

High winds forced the postponement of the planned extraction of Delta at Hill 805.

At 2:30 a.m., enemy movement was spotted to the north and west and a mechanical ambush went off to the west. The enemy returned small arms fire and threw satchel charges before withdrawing.

It was 4:30 that afternoon when Delta began moving off. Second platoon stayed behind to destroy the remainder of the confiscated gear. Relief settled among the battle-weary men of Delta.

"I remember walking through the first platoon sector where we had been hit so hard on the second night," wrote Blackman. "I thought about Rat but still couldn't cry. We moved down the hill past a couple NVA bodies that had been blown to shit. We would stop on the other side of the LZ and wait for second platoon to re-join us. We were off the hill, but not out of the woods yet."

It was around this time that a Kit Carson scout attached to third platoon pulled a pin on a hand grenade, killing himself with troops all around. Amidst the confusion, the company engaged the perimeter, thinking it had fallen under mortar attack.

Raiders David Beyl and Wilfred Warner were medevacked out, however both later died from wounds taken in the grenade attack. Three others, Sgt. Mike Cooksley, Drew Gaster and Ron Grubidt, were flown out on a loach. Straub was also injured in the incident.

Of the scout's suicide, Blackman said, "I think he was so afraid that we'd be overrun when we left the hill that he killed himself as we were moving through the CP (command post) to take point or he thought we might leave him behind and he was afraid that he'd be captured as a traitor so he decided to end it all. Who knows for sure?"

Blackie's third platoon set up a small NDP. They would be flown out at first light.

"I'm not sure if the NVA didn't know where we were or just decided to leave us alone, but we weren't attacked that night."

Those days on 805 left their mark on the men. They share an incredible bond.

"They were really fierce," Straub said of his troopers. "They would absolutely not give ground. When we did have a situation in the first platoon area where we lost ground, the second platoon sergeant immediately rallied to them. They were incredibly alert and incredibly prepared. They really rallied to that. I can't say a negative thing about anyone in the whole company as far as their attitude. They were so determined. They were fantastic. Everyone recognized they were in an unusual, for them, survival situation because we always ambushed successfully, we didn't get ourselves ambushed and we didn't' get ourselves in situations where the enemy knew where we were until we were ready to reveal that. That was their custom. There they were suddenly in this completely different situation, but they really grew, they really rallied to it because they were determined to win up there. At one point, I could not reduce the number of people I had pulling triggers and throwing hand grenades anymore because we'd evacuated so many people and at that point had six people killed. So I just decided no one is getting medevacked out of here unless they are in danger of losing an eye, or a limb, or a life, one or more of those three. The troops, no one said 'boo' about that because they understood without even having to be told. If you have some shrapnel but you're a machine gunner and you can still operate your machine gun effectively, we need you. That's what they did. They were brave."

Those days at Hill 805 were brutal for Delta and the reasoning behind placing the Raiders on the hill in a defensive position raised many questions. By the time it came for Delta to leave 805, the feeling amongst the Raiders was bittersweet as they had fought so hard for the ground they held and now they were leaving, after so many had bled and died.

"We had to go," remembered Straub, "but we didn't want to leave land we bled over and died over. That was tough to leave a piece of land we had done all that over, especially when nobody was going to take it over again. That was hard to understand, for a lot of us to understand, for me to understand. If we had protected the firebase from Hill 805 on the 13th of July, then why on the 18th, 19th and 20th of July was that protection not needed?"

Straub wasn't the only one angry at the time.

"That was kind of a bittersweet moment for all of us, but that's the way it was," said Mitchell. "We had 13 killed. I will tell you everybody that was up there was probably wounded."

"It was very tough taking casualties," said Blackman. "We'd been so good at only having a guy or two wounded now and then it was shocking when we lost so many at once and then had more picked off every night. Our morale was low, but we were determined to make it. It was especially low after the scout did what he did."

Straub clearly felt his troops should have been refreshed by a new company to hold the high ground the Raiders had secured.

Once the Raiders were choppered back to Camp Evans, Gen. Berry arrived at the 85th Evac Hospital to present Purple Hearts and got the brunt of Straub's frustrations over the mission, and the loss of men. Straub admitted his frustrations were better aimed at Gen. John Hennessey, who had left Vietnam July 15 for R&R that had been planned long before the Ripcord mission and included the marriages of his two oldest children, his son and daughter.

"I was really sorry about that," said Straub of his word with Berry. "I was a jerk. He was a truly great guy. He came in there, got off a plane and was handed this problem because the division commander (Hennessey), as I recall, was out of the theater, which was an odd place to be when there's a war on and you're the commander of an army division of combat and it's the biggest battle of your service. Out of the theater is probably not the place you want to be but the army of the day permitted that. Here Sid Berry gets this mess and he did everything he could do. And he was very kind to listen to all my bitching. He knew it was a captain letting off steam and he permitted me to do so. We had dinner years later in Washington and I apologized."

13

Hill 1,000

Hill 1,000, despite its close proximity to Ripcord – considering the North Vietnamese point of view, entirely because of its proximity – was never controlled by American troops during the Ripcord campaign.

How close was it to Ripcord?

"Hill 1,000? I could hit it with a golf ball from Ripcord," said Rex Flansburg, Delta Company.

Brigade, and the soldiers that had humped through the area and worked at Firebase Ripcord, knew there were North Vietnamese troops entrenched on Hill 1,000, especially atop the hill that held a strategic view over Ripcord, and to its east side, away from binocular sight. During the first week of July, an attempt to secure the hill was made by recon troops from Echo Company as well as a dual-pronged assault by Delta and Charlie companies.

"We walked off Ripcord (after pulling security for most of June) on the sixth of July," said Lt. Jim McCall, Delta Company. "As we were walking off Ripcord, the recon team got hit. Our first mission was to rescue the recon team and we did that."

Recon (Echo Company) had been inserted on Hill 1,000 on July 5. Members of the team spent a silent night listening to the North Vietnamese firing mortars, preparing for an assault of the hill, ordered by Lt. Col. Andre Lucas.

"Black Spade (Lucas) wanted us closer," remembered John Schnarr, a member of the recon team." We told him every time the rounds were coming they were above us. He wanted us to secure the hill. To begin that day he wanted us to go up top and we protested pretty hard. We moved as close as we dared, to where the vegetation stopped. The hill was pretty shot up. We settled in a pretty big bomb crater. The hilltop was maybe 75 yards above us."

From there, Lucas continued to press the team to push toward the top, to which the team protested repeatedly, noting there was no need to sacrifice the entire team, especially given the fact no one knew exactly what was on top of the hill or how many North Vietnamese were waiting.

"I said I'd take one person with me and the rest could stay in the (crater)," said Schnarr. "Myself and a guy named Dixie Gaskin, a good guy, a kid from the Carolinas, we decided that it wasn't worth risking the whole team. The two of us snaked our way up. It was pretty well just bare ground above us and I found little ravines and pockets of brush by skirting around to the north side a little more. We found no real cover, but we found areas that weren't bare ground. Dixie was behind me. We were low crawling up and got pretty close to the top, going real slow and just kind of looking and listening."

Schnarr knew he was close to the top when he heard a North Vietnamese soldier. He glanced to see a head, instantly recognizing one of the pith helmets the NVA regulars wore. He began to ponder his options.

"He was about 20-30 feet ahead of me," said Schnarr. "You get mixed reactions. He was in profile and I thought, 'I think I can take him.'

Then I realized he was talking to a couple more nearby, then I heard a couple more and then I realized I didn't have the numbers. So I motion to Dixie to back crawl. I said, 'They are right there, right on top.' We started to scoot down."

Perhaps anxious from the encounter, Schnarr recommended the two avoid the deliberate path they took up the hill, opting instead for a shorter, more direct route back to the crater, where they could inform the rest of the team what they had discovered.

"Just as we got to the crater where the other guys were, they hit us with RPGs (rocket-propelled grenades), three of them, just boom, boom, boom, all at once," said Schnarr. "It sent us all flying. Everyone was hit. Dixie got the worst of it, tore him up pretty bad. We kind of came to our senses, if you will."

As it turned out, the warnings to Lucas ahead of the advance proved enough that the lieutenant colonel sent Delta Company in to rescue the team.

"Everybody was hurt," said Schnarr. "We had a medic with us and a piece of shrapnel had nicked his jugular; he was spurting blood. Granberry was team leader, I was assistant team leader. (Granberry) said he was going for help. I said he needed to stay, that they'd come to us. He went trekking back and the rest of us were there and trying to get things together. Dixie had a lot of holes in him, bleeding pretty bad. We had no communication. We decided the best course of action, we still had a grenade launcher, was to put some rounds up there. I was concerned they would come down after us. I was strong enough then that I just put the medic on my shoulder and headed down the hill toward Delta Company."

Sgt. Gary Radford, nearing the end of his tour, led a Delta Company team up the hill to link up with the battered, bloodied recon team.

"I explained to Gary what was going on," said Schnarr. "We left our rucksacks and everything up there. We had a starlight scope in one of the rucks. Gary said he'd take his squad, maybe 10 to 15 of them, and we said we'd show them where it was. We started our way back up and (the NVA) had come down. We started to take fire and backed off, thought it wasn't worth it."

"Lewis (Howard Jr.), myself and five other men went to assist the recon team," Radford wrote. "Recon was able to break contact and pull back leaving equipment behind. Half our squad helped recon back to our company position to be medevacked.

"Lewis, myself and the rest of the squad went to try and retrieve the equipment left behind. As soon as we were at the area, we were hit with RPG and small arms fire, AK-47s. We took no casualties. We pulled back immediately to the next hilltop, where our company had set up an NDP (night defensive position)."

Meanwhile, the medevacs had made their way to a safe landing zone and had successfully extricated the wounded. Schnarr went back to the night defensive position set up by Delta Company and spent the night before being flown out the next day.

"We had guys scattered all up and down that hill," said Flansburg, who had been given a radio that morning. "We weren't sure where we all were. We had two white phosphorous rounds come in on us, feet from us. I sort of snapped at him (Lt. Col. Lucas), I really snapped. I called him names. He wanted to know who was on the phone. We just about had everyone off the hill. I told him we had everything under control. We saw 50 calibers going over our head. My thought was, 'Stop shooting at us or we start shooting back.' I got back to Rollison and had to give the radio back. I did what I did to keep him from killing us. Rollison told me to go back to my position. He was a good guy. I think he understood."

Radford talked with his men that night, knowing they would have to make a second attempt the next day.

"I remember talking to Lewis and the other men (saying) we would have to take the hill the next day," Radford wrote. "I don't think any of us got much sleep that night. The next morning we moved out in company force, about 60 men. Our platoon was on point (lead element) with Lewis in the lead."

"Why him and not me?" – Dennis Stortz, Delta Company

As hammered as the hill had become, artillery barrages continued ahead of another assault July 7. Conditions were tough.

Dennis Stortz, a draftee from Emmaus, Pa., was like many pulled into service at that time in that he never saw action outside the triple-canopy jungles surrounding Ripcord.

"I put 12 months in Vietnam," said Stortz. "I never saw a rice paddy or a village. We were up in the mountains, in the jungle the whole time."

And he, like most, saw plenty. Stortz, assigned to Delta Company, third platoon, headed for the NVA-occupied Hill 1,000 July 7 and 8.

"We left the firebase to assault 1,000," remembered Stortz. "Lt. (Jack) Flaherty was hit. That was the first day in Vietnam I didn't have a radio on my back. The guy that was carrying my radio was shot and killed."

Michael Grimm was shot through the heart just before 10 a.m. He was killed instantly.

"He was right next to me," said Stortz of Grimm." The question I ask is, 'Why him and not me?' Was it because he had the radio? It was a hard day. "

"The first man we lost was the radio operator on the point," said McCall. "We were operating with less than company strength, about 80 percent. We got up close to the top of the hill on that push. It seemed like every time we'd eliminate a fighting position, it would revive somehow or start firing at us again. That happened a number of times and we'd have to go back and eliminate it again."

"That was Grimm's first day carrying a radio," said Flansburg. "We got to know that area pretty well. (The hill) went up so far then it made a break to the left. I remember Grimm was in front of me. There was fire to the left, fire to the right. I took fire where (Tom) Gaut and Flaherty were. I heard, 'Medic!' I had my head down. I crawled up and asked George Strasburg about it. It was Grimm and they said he was dead. He was sitting up against a tree, no blood anywhere."

Skinner, who had left Delta as June closed with the company pulling security on Ripcord, never got to say goodbye to Grimm.

"Sgt. Jerry Pounds came to visit me and told me Mike Grimm had been killed going up that hill," said Skinner.

As Flaherty's and McCall's men came under fire, Delta Two, under Sgt. Radford, pushed forward. Lewis Howard Jr., drew short straw that morning and quietly assumed point. Several men protested the process, throwing their straws to the ground. Howard had been Radford's radio man. Howard led Delta Two to a rocky formation and awaited word from McCall, just ahead.

Rocket-propelled grenades soared through the group. Howard took the brunt and went silent. Radford, who had been near the rear of the group, grabbed a squad and surged forward in an attempt to rescue Howard. RPGs continued to soar above their heads and satchel charges were being lobbed in front of them.

"When we were getting close to the top of the hill the North Vietnamese hit us with RPGs and AK-47s," Radford remembered. "The lead element of our platoon, the four men, was hit on the initial contact. The second, third and fourth men were seriously wounded but were able to crawl back."

The squad withdrew, and soon learned that Charles Beals, the assistant machine gunner, was missing. Radford was determined to retrieve Howard and Beals. He headed back toward the boulder from the cover of the trees. Beals was face down, having been shot. Radford grabbed him, then went unconscious after having a satchel charge explode near him. Eardrums busted, Radford came to as his radioman, Joseph Gibson, began dragging him to safety.

"We took heavy casualties trying to get Lewis," Radford wrote. "In the meantime the first and third platoons were trying to sweep up the hill from the back side. They were also under heavy fire, taking many casualties. By late afternoon we were not able to get very far. I took the rest of the platoon to the left of the initial contact, however I was not able to advance any further.

"Orders came for the whole company to retreat. As our platoon regrouped, Charles Beals was missing. I crawled to Charles' last position to try to find him. I saw him lying face down. As I tried to reach him, I was hit by a satchel charge. I was knocked unconscious."

Lead Flying

Delta, scattered across Hill 1,000, knew a tough day was ahead. It was July 8, hot as hell and the men were still reeling from fierce combat the day before.

Combat in Vietnam was escalated for the average infantryman due to the mobility provided by the helicopter. It's something few have considered when comparing the action saw by men in Vietnam compared to other conflicts throughout America's history.

According to the Department of Defense, the average combat soldier in Vietnam saw 240 days of action in his year of service. Compare that with the average infantryman that served in the South Pacific during World War II, who saw an average of 40 days of combat over four years.

Tom Gaut, a draftee from Oklahoma City, was tall and lean. His platoon mates remembered he was scared of nothing, an easy-going guy that had a good sense of humor. The day before was his first as Flaherty's radio operator. The night before they had dug in at the edge of the hill.

"That's when the recon platoon had its first contact on Hill 1,000," said Flaherty. "Of course, the next day, we assaulted Hill 1,000. Talk about going from the frying pan into the fire, we did."

"I had no idea we were going up there," remembered Gaut. "I was thinking we had walked right through there before. We saw a sniper team come through, right down the trail. It wasn't long after that we heard the gunfight. They dropped their rucksacks when it hit. They got pinned down so we sent a squad there to help cover them that evening. They pulled back. It was dark and there was not more action that night. We knew we had to go get them the next day."

Once the recon platoon found the enemy, artillery was called in and Hill 1,000 was blasted throughout the night. The next morning came and brought with it hot temperatures as the men of Delta Company prepped for an assault.

Flaherty, who had volunteered for the draft, led Delta Three up the right while Delta Two and McCall advanced up the left side.

"There was all kinds of deadfall, trees being blown down, so it was extremely difficult to see the enemy firing positions," said Flaherty. "I don't think I ever saw an enemy soldier when I was on Hill 1,000. I never could see them. I knew where the fire was coming from, I knew where the grenades were coming from but I never did see them. To try to assault that hill, we were climbing over deadfall and trees. It made it very difficult to one, move; and two, to see. It was almost like you were doing it by braille."

"We start walking up the hill and I remember walking past a rucksack and I had a funny feeling I was being watched," said Gaut. "We went up and all hell broke loose. I got down and I got a call; the captain (Rollison) and his radio man were pinned down."

Flaherty and Gaut were behind Flansburg as they made their way up.

"They blew the top of the mountain off," said Flansburg of the preparatory fire. "We're going up and jets were flying overhead, dropping bombs. The trees are flying back."

Bomb drops were made hundreds of feet from where soldiers were suspected of being so as to reduce the likelihood of friendly fire, though friendly fire was not uncommon. It was more prevalent with the Cobras, than with the fast-moving fixed-wing aircraft that delivered the 250- and 500-pound bombs.

Gaut and Flaherty made their way toward Rollison when they came under heavy fire.

"Lieutenant and I come along and there was a great, big log," said Gaut. "I got over top of the log, a little too much. I felt (a shot) go through the palm of my hand, through my (belt) buckle. I'm hit and thought, 'Oh shit, don't go down with a full magazine, so I open up. So now I'm supposed to fall down, but I remember it's not a good place with all the stumps sticking up. I went 15 feet back and was ready to fall when I found this little crater. I fell in the crater. Then Flaherty is falling on me. He landed on my rifle and I said, 'Get off me, you're on my goddamn rifle. He raised up a little bit and I said, 'Thanks, get a medic.'"

The medic came and Flaherty moved over a bit, continuing the assault, continuing to take fire.

"I gotta give him credit," said Gaut. "He was firing that shotgun, and reloading."

The medic was scared, his teeth chattering, remembered Gaut. Between the two of them they managed to patch the wounds amidst Gaut's periodic bursts of fire aimed toward the enemy.

"He's picking shrapnel out of my gut and lead is still flying," said Gaut. "I'm shooting over the log, must have went through two or three magazines while the medic was picking shrapnel out of me. I had a pile of six or seven frags. I threw some to Flaherty."

The medic was Puerto Rican, remembered Gaut. There were racial tensions at the time and Gaut said he used it to his advantage with the medic, who was doing his damnedest to help.

"I picked up a frag and the medic is sitting there," he said. "I can't use my finger, so I ask him to pull the pin. I pulled and his hand came with me. I thought what is going to convince him to pull the pin? I said, 'Pull the pin nigger! He tensed up and it came out and I threw the frag. There were tensions. I used them in battle. The medic did a pretty damn good job."

Flaherty continued firing until he was out of ammunition. He motioned over to Gaut for his M-16.

"I mouthed the words, 'Fuck you. We're in a battle,'" said Gaut, recalling the story with a grin on his face. "He said, 'I can use it better than you.' I thought, 'He's right.' I said, 'Give me your .45' and we traded out with the medic's help. He said, 'Give it back to me at the end of this, It's checked out in my name.'"

"We got pretty close to where Tom had gotten hit," said Flansburg. "We had three squads, Flaherty sent one squad to the left, one to the right and one into the bombed out zone.

When Gaut was hit, his radio was destroyed. It may have even helped save him from additional injury. That left Flaherty with no radio, though.

"George said Gaut's been hit and lieutenant needs a radio and hand grenades," remembered Flansburg. He was going to have to get the radio off Grimm's back.

"I went over," he said. "Grimm's a little taller than I was. I was trying to get the band off and I couldn't get it off. When I stood up, three shots fired off and those shots were meant for me. George asked if I had been hit. I remember saying, 'Jesus Christ, that was close!' About that time I looked at Grimm. I couldn't look at his eyes, so I shut his eyes. I pulled him to the side and pulled the radio off him."

Flaherty was still battling the sniper who shot Gaut. Out of grenades, Rollison crawled over to within 10 or so feet from Flaherty. Lucas, floating above in a Loach, began aiding Rollison in the tossing of grenades. Rollison tossed while Lucas coached his direction, right or left. One landed too close to Flaherty, who took shrapnel in his back. Rollison soon hit the intended mark and Flaherty emerged, shotgun blazing.

Amid the confusion, Flaherty grabbed Gaut and retreated where Flansburg was able to pull him further back. Flansburg pulled Gaut out and Flaherty was provided with the radio and four extra grenades, thanks to Flansburg's efforts.

Flaherty again linked up with Rollison as the two attempted to take out the enemy position. Rollison fired LAWs (light anti-tank weapons), apparently taking out the position, only to have it reinforced through

REMEMBERING FIREBASE RIPCORD

the maze of tunnels that ran through Hill 1,000 and across its backside, in relation to Ripcord. It was nearly noon and Lucas continued to hover, providing instruction and direction to the men below.

McCall and Delta Two inched their way up.

"I realized the fighting positions had to be connected," said McCall. "We got up there, close to the top and realized we were outnumbered and outgunned. I carried as many hand grenades as I could on that first trip and ran out. A helicopter, I think Col. Lucas was on board and Fred Spaulding, they got in touch with me. I was pinned down with a machine gun firing from a bunker. I was throwing grenades at them and they were throwing grenades at me. They said, 'We'll hover over the bunker and get the guy to stand up and fire at us. You think you can take him out if we do that?' I said, 'Yes.' I took him out."

It's all McCall would need to quell the threat. It wasn't the end of his problems, though.

"The helicopter got hit it got so close," he said. "They came back and dropped a gas mask full of grenades for me. My machine gunner had been hit and my assistant machine gunner was killed. The most powerful weapon I had was the push-to-talk button. I could say 'Help' and you would get help from somewhere. I got pinned down again and called for the gunships. A Cobra gunship came on station and asked if I could mark the target. I threw a smoke grenade and he said I was too close. 'If you're that close, I can't make a run.' He rolled in and about the time he started firing I took off running. I ended up taking shrapnel in my elbows."

Flansburg and Dennis Stortz were caught out in the open and began taking fire.

"We were lucky," Flansburg said sarcastically. "We get to go into the bombed out zone. I'm thinking, 'What are we doing out here?' There's four or five of us in the open, four or five pulled back. Spade was flying over. I was out in the open and three others are down a bit from me, a little more protected. The door gunner (in a chopper) threw out a smoke canister; it hits six feet in front of me, rolled down and hit me in the foot. They marked us as the enemy, red smoke. I think to myself, 'If they start shooting, I'm going to take the helicopter out.' We get to the edge of the ridge and we hear small arms fire. The helicopter twitched as it took small arms fire. That NVA soldier (that fired on the chopper) saved all our lives."

Delta retreated and the wounded were taken care of. Lucas got on the horn with Rollison and planned a two-pronged attack of Hill 1,000 with men from Charlie and Delta companies.

"If you're going to attack a defensive position, you need a three-to-one ratio," said McCall. "We had less than a one-to-one ratio."

"We went back down, the next day we went back up and did a repeat," said Flaherty, "the same thing all over again. Day one the top was lush jungle. Day two it was bare dirt. They pounded that hard all night and they were still there (the next day). They would shoot down on Ripcord from there. They'd shoot and you never knew where they were coming from. You never saw anyone but you heard them shooting at us."

Meanwhile, Gaut was on his way home.

"He pulled me off the hill," said Gaut, recounting his trip down the hill with Flaherty. "He looked at me and said, 'How are you doing son?' I said, 'Fine sir, I'm going home.' About that time a sniper opened up. I left that hill with a compress, a steel pot and a .45."

Yes, it was his lieutenant's 45.

Settling in for a Fight

Ripcord veterans, front from left, Fred Gilbert (Delta Company) and David Corradetti (Charlie Company). Middle: Frank Marshall (Alpha Company) and Pete Meloro (Charlie Company). Back, Lee Widjeskog (Alpha Company), James "Tiny" Aanonsen (Alpha Company), Dennis Stortz (Delta Company) and Dennis Bloomingdale (Bravo Company). Photo provided by Chris Brady.

Dennis Bloomingdale, of Philadelphia, was drafted in April 1969 and he knew he'd at some point end up in Vietnam. He wanted a say in the matter, though.

To do that, Bloomingdale, and many others, attended Non-Commissioned Officers Candidates School, where the Army prepped bright young men quickly to meet the growing demand for NCOs in the field. It was that, or continually bring back senior officers.

"In a year's time I went from a civilian to an E-5 sergeant," said Bloomingdale." They called us shake and bakes. It was a pretty good program for those of us that went through it. I figured if I'm going to Vietnam, which everyone was at the time, I wanted to have a little something to say about what was going on and I wanted to make sure I was as well-trained as possible."

A year after being drafted, he touched down in Vietnam and was assigned to the 101st Airborne. He was on his way to Firebase Ripcord. His first taste of the Ripcord Area of Operations came when his chopper landed on the firebase nearly midway through April. From there, he humped out to meet his new company commander, Capt. Bill Williams.

"We got up on Ripcord late in the afternoon," he remembered. "Company B was already out there in the field, but they weren't far away, so we humped out to where they were. We get out there and it's just about dark and I meet Capt. Williams and he introduces the sergeant. They stuck me in a squad with five kids that didn't have a platoon leader, didn't have a sergeant. That squad was in the middle of digging up an old grave, so that was my welcome to Vietnam, the smell of dead bodies. You never forget that. They just dig them up and find what information they can. I was the cherry sergeant and they had already started digging it up so it was 'Go over there and supervise it.' It was pretty disgusting."

It was early July when Bloomingdale got a call from the TOC (Tactical Operations Center) notifying him that Charlie Company would be moving into the area Bravo had manned recently. Bloomingdale had set mechanical ambushes in the area and would be needed to dismantle them.

"Since I was the one that set it up and knew where the batteries were, it was logical, so I said 'Sure,'" Bloomingdale recalled. "They told me to take two guys. I took my machine gunner, who volunteered. I asked for volunteers, and Bob Judd volunteered, so there were three of us. We flew out to the LZ (landing zone) where Company C had come in. I got out there and we were on an LZ but we were about two klicks from where we needed to be to disarm this thing."

It was early in the morning, July 7.

Bloomingdale knew there was plenty of activity in the area and he was concerned with the small number of men he had with him. By the time the group had reached the bottom of a ravine, they had run into a patrol and opened fire on the enemy. After firing, the squad-sized element backed up a bit.

"I called (Charlie Company Captain Jeff) Wilcox and said we ran into a patrol," said Bloomingdale. "I said, 'What do you want me to do?' and he said 'You need to go up there and disarm it.' I said, 'There's gooks up there.' Wilcox said he'd send more men and I'm thinking, 'I don't think that's going to help.' The complex we had been going through was huge. They had stored rice and ammunition and all kinds of stuff, probably stockpiled stuff that they were storing for the assault on Ripcord. We had gone through it and ruined it. It was huge. It took us a couple days to go through the whole thing. The idea of going back up there with six or seven guys wasn't a good idea, but he thought it was necessary, so I said to send out some more guys. We knew we were walking into some shit, we just didn't know how much. Generally what happens is you make contact and they disappear, unless they are ready for contact and they do that on their own terms. So I was kind of hoping that was the case, that it was a small patrol. We shot them up pretty bad and off they ran, so he sent out a few more guys. Now we're probably 13-14 guys, we're back up the ridgeline. So at that point, I had decided I would walk point because I knew where the tripwires were. I got about halfway up and I saw a gook stick his head out of a hole. I saw him and he saw me and I switched to rock and roll and he dropped back down in a hole and I dropped behind a tree. He was in a hole, it was a bunker, an underground bunker. So I'm deciding what I'm

HILL 1,000

going to do because it was an open area. I think they were using it for a mortar position or something. I'm tucked behind this huge tree, roots are beside me and I'm pretty secure here. I open up on him and I know I hit the gun, I don't know if I hit him, but it was enough to grab the attention of whoever was on the hill. Since we started firing on them, the whole ridgeline opened up. They had us on our flank. They had all kinds of shit. They were firing through the trees, firing RPGs (rocket propelled grenades) into the trees, they would explode, send shrapnel everywhere. An RPG came down and hit the open ground probably 10 feet from where I was and it just picked me up and threw me."

Bloomingdale was knocked out and seriously injured. The rest of the group had retreated, moved off the hill. When he came to, Bloomingdale found himself out in the open and quickly decided to seek cover at the tree from which he was blown.

"I kind of crawled back into the tree and at that point I started taking stock and I realized I had been hit," he said. "I'm looking and I'm bleeding everywhere, just not a good thing. All across my left side, all across my chest, I just got ripped up, both my arms, my left lung was punctured. The worst part was my left leg, a big piece of shrapnel had gone through the tibia, shattered the tibia, and came out the other side. So when I looked down I could see meat and shattered bone. The knee, the ankle was hit, so I knew I wasn't walking out of there. And I knew I was in pretty bad shape and there I was. At that point, I pretty much decided where I was where I was going to die because there was no way I was going to get off that hill by myself. I was too beat up, too chewed up. I don't know what shock is and I don't know if I went into shock. It was just perfectly clear to me. I was actually OK with it. The only thing I told myself over there was I was not going to let them take me prisoner."

Entrenched behind the tree and surrounded by its root structure, Bloomingdale settled in for a fight. Resigned to die on the floor of the jungle, Bloomingdale was unaware a soldier from Charlie Company, one of rather uncommon valor, was on his way.

"I don't know how long it had been," said Bloomingdale. "There was still firing and every once in a while I'd clip off a couple rounds to let them know I was ready to fight. All of a sudden I hear this crunching through the jungle and I look up and see this sergeant who said, 'I'm going to get you out of here.'

It was Sgt. Paul Burkey, from Charlie Company, another shake and bake. Burkey left Vietnam with immense respect from those he served with as well as four Bronze Stars.

"He was smaller than I was and he tucked himself under my right side, which in hindsight was the wrong side because it was the left leg that was shattered," said Bloomingdale. "He started to drag me down, through the jungle where he had come up. He couldn't carry me. Every time I tried to put weight on the (leg) I'd shout out and every time I'd do that, we'd draw fire. I do remember him saying, 'Shut the fuck up or you're going to get us both killed.' He finally got me off the hill. They shot me full of morphine, put me on a stretcher they put together. I remember laying on the LZ. There were a couple guys that had been hit, one guy was killed. I remember them bringing him back up in pieces. He took a direct hit from an RPG or something, it was really bad. I could hear the medevacs coming and I'm thinking I may make it. Someone said 'Put the worst ones on first' and with that they grabbed me and I'm going 'Oh fuck.' I'm thinking 'Maybe I'm not going to make it.' The medevac took off and it was such a relief."

As the morphine kicked in, Bloomingdale began to fade. He remembered crews cutting his pants and boots from his injured leg then 11 days later he awoke in a hospital bed.

For decades Bloomingdale never knew who the man was who risked his life to drag him out of the jungle and to safety. It wasn't until 2001 that he learned it was Burkey that risked his life to save him from certain death on the floor of the jungle west of Ripcord. The two had a phone conversation and later met to share their stories in private. After the initial meeting, the two were part of a feature on Fox News recounting the heroism of both in Vietnam more than 30 years prior.

"If he hadn't come up there, there wasn't anyone tripping over themselves to come up there," said Bloomingdale. "I would have liked to think I would have had the balls to do it, but I'm not sure I would have either, especially for someone I didn't know. You have to give the man a lot of credit for that, but apparently that was his character; hearing some of the stories, it didn't surprise anyone."

Later on July 7, Lt. Jim Campbell gathered a group of men to provide assistance to Burkey and his men. The first volunteer was Gerald Risinger, a 10-month jungle veteran about to go home. No one realized his tour was so close to winding down or he likely never would have made the trip to reach Burkey and his men.

"Campbell is asking for volunteers and racing down the trail, this guy, Risinger, was supposed to have been taken out of the field by then," remembered Wilcox. "He said, 'Fuck it, don't mean nothing,' and he got killed. Also Bob Judd was there. I remember bringing in the medevacs and putting both those guys on there."

As the team reached Burkey's position, Risinger got down about 10 feet away when an RPG (rocket propelled grenade) ripped through the area.

Judd had been peppered with shrapnel. Risinger was ripped apart in the attack. Campbell and Burkey called in a medevac as the enemy fire ceased. The chopper lowered a litter basket as the two badly wounded troopers were in no shape to hang on to a jungle penetrator. Burkey kept the mortar rounds coming and a pair of gunships hovered to protect the medevac.

Campbell had been unaware of Risinger's fate. When he found the young man from Kentucky, he had several men ensure his body was collected, some of it wrapped in men's shirts. The battered company continued to make its way to a landing zone. One was dead and there were 15 wounded.

"They looked like ants coming up the back side." – Fred Spaulding of the North Vietnamese at Hill 1,000

An assault on Hill 1,000 was planned for early the morning of July 8 with Capt. Jeff Wilcox and Lt. James Campbell leading the way for Charlie Company. Preparatory fire began early.

The days leading up to the assault of Hill 1,000 were a whirlwind for Campbell.

A Louisiana State University grad fresh out of Officer Candidate School at the age of 22, had arrived back from rest and recuperation (R&R) in the A Shau expecting a job in the rear. When he landed at Camp Evans, he discovered his rucksack packed and ready to go. Within 10 minutes of touchdown, his head was swimming as he was headed back into the field, and back into battle. As if that wasn't enough, he'd just learned his company had nearly been wiped out just days earlier on Hill 902.

"I was supposed to go to the rear," Campbell remembered. "Col. Lucas told me he wanted me to go out and break in a new captain for 10 days and I did. I was on R and R when 902 happened. .. I wasn't led to believe, they told me (I was going to the rear). Shit happens. I thought I was going to have a job in the rear, that's what they told me. I left thinking I was never coming back. When I came through the front gate, they had MPs waiting for me. They had my rucksack ready for me. I wasn't there 10 minutes and I was headed back into the field. I found out later what happened (on Hill 902) and of course I was shocked by it - couldn't believe it. (You) Gotta do it, it's part of being a soldier. In war, things happen and they're uncontrollable, events change, people get killed and people get wounded. I thought I was out of the field. I thought 'Goddamnit how did this happen?' I thought I was out of the field. (At that point it becomes,) Move on, you're back in the field."

Charlie Company flew in early and began the trek up Hill 1,000 before 7 a.m. The hill had undergone tremendous artillery prep, making the ascent tough as sand shifted under the men's feet.

"The fire that was put on Hill 1,000, they probably put as many rounds on Hill 1,000 as they did on Iwo Jima," said Campbell." They prepped that hill forever with everything the Army had in the arsenal. Bombs, air strikes, napalm, 175s, 105s, 155s, all this artillery, air strikes, When you made the assault, the hill was pulverized. The top was decimated. It's like a beach. It's sand. You slide back down with your feet."

The men had but one canteen of water and the temperatures that day soared to 105 to 110 degrees with sweltering humidity, Campbell noted. Still, the soldiers carried out the mission. It was what they were ordered to do.

"That was a brutal fight, the assault of Hill 1,000," said Campbell. "When you look at a map of Hill 1,000 you'll see that it's two knolls with a saddle between. Charlie Company had about 30 men that day because we lost a bunch of men that day before. Delta Company had about 70. We were given the far knoll, the western knoll to attack. We attacked and made it up to the top. Delta Company didn't attack the hill and that's what caused all the problems. Then we were given an order by Col. Lucas to attack the eastern knoll across the saddle, which was insane. It was a direct order that was given, Jeff was the company commander, he tried to carry it out and it was futile. Then we were told ultimately to get off the hill and go back to the original LZ which lay between Hill 1,000 and Ripcord."

It was just after 10:30 in the morning as the confusion set in.

Wilcox questioned the order from Lucas, who was flying above the action and sending orders down to the men in the heat of battle. When told of Lucas' orders, Campbell agreed with Wilcox, but it made no difference, Lucas wanted the men to cross the saddle.

"The hardest thing I had to do, I guess, was lead the charge across the open area on Hill 1,000," said Wilcox. "(Campbell) said, 'I'll lead the charge' and I said, 'No Jim, if I need these guys to follow me for the next six months I'll lead the charge.' So we got about 10 steps out and got blown back into the bomb craters. Sgt. Bort put his hat on a stick and bobbed it along on this deadfall and this machine gun was following it right along and we could not see where it was coming from. Gary Radford went back and he described all these fortifications. We probably could have never dislodged them even though it was prepped with jets and artillery and naval gunfire and gas and ARA (aerial rocket artillery). It went for naught."

The North Vietnamese were anchored to Hill 1,000, pinning down Charlie Company and Delta Company with machine gun fire from well-fortified bunkers, according to the Operational Report – Lessons Learned, 101st Airborne Division (Airmobile) document. A late-morning firefight with small arms fire ensued just before 11 as fire rained down on the companies. An M-72 LAW (light anti-tank weapon) took out one bunker, leaving two NVA positions active.

"Charlie reached the top, Delta didn't," remembered Fred Spaulding, the brigade S3. "There was no way they could have gone across that saddle. There were machine guns covering both sides. It didn't matter which way you came from, you were going to get cut down."

Wilcox's undermanned company of only 30 men reached a spot to the west where it could provide direct support for Rollison's company to the east. Rollison never advanced.

Wilcox, with his battered Charlie Company hunkered down and taking heavy fire, implored Lucas, who was hovering above, to have Delta advance. Lucas wouldn't budge. Campbell and Wilcox were furious.

Charlie Company was taking serious fire and several men noted it was nearly impossible to determine where the fire was coming from bunkers that were so well fortified.

"They (Delta Company) were going up the side of this mountain where they had all these reinforced bunkers," Wilcox said of Delta. "I guess we were just hung out to dry. It's the fog and chaos of war. I think the higher ups did not know we were two platoons going up Hill 1,000, not two companies. They were misrepresenting everything."

Rollison had encouraged his men to avoid any unnecessary action given the depleted nature of the company. Why they didn't advance and why Lucas didn't give the order for an advance remains a mystery.

"We made a two-pronged push with Charlie Company," said McCall, who advanced until his unit too was pinned down. "Somehow I got on top." There he was being peppered, harassed by a North Vietnamese who would throw grenades from a position no further than 12 meters away.

"I would lay down with my helmet pointing toward the grenades," he said. "Then I'd get up and throw a grenade. We had a hand grenade exchange program going. When I came down my platoon sergeant (Radford) was there and had blood streaming down his face."

Spaulding ultimately sent a warning for Charlie Company to get off the hill. It was about to get even uglier. Artillery fire, 250- and 500-pound bombs dropped from the fast-moving F4 Phantoms, napalm, nothing could penetrate the extensive tunnel systems on Hill 1,000. Major Koenigsbauer had adjusted artillery fire to the back side of the hill as the two companies moved toward the saddle. It didn't matter.

"I'm flying above and we looked over the side to see the NVA coming up the back side," said Spaulding. "They looked like ants coming up the back side. We radioed down to tell them to get the hell out of there. I couldn't bring in the gunships on that target line because it would have hit them. They had to get down the hill. It sent them scurrying, dragging their dead and wounded with them."

Wilcox led the men at an angle off the hill.

The battle raged on until around 1 p.m, when Charlie and Delta companies moved off the hill. Two Americans were killed and four wounded in the battle. One of those killed was an unarmed conscientious objector, Rickey Scott, a medic who had been in the field only days before sent into battle. He stood up in the firefight and was killed with a shot to the head.

That incident lives fresh in the mind of Wilcox even today.

"There were a lot of medics who, I learned later, were conscientious objectors, and that was the system fucking with them," said Wilcox. "This kid (Scott) was so willing. I looked at him and asked, 'Where's your weapon?' He said, 'I don't have one; I'm a conscientious objector.' I could think of nothing better to do than keep him near me and then he lasted maybe 36 hours. He went out to help a dead guy. It just infuriates me. He could have been a really willing servant at Walter Reed or Fort Sam Houston in the burn unit, that sort of thing. I think they were punishing him by sending him out to an infantry unit with no awareness."

When Charlie Company got back to the landing zone, Lucas was there to meet with Wilcox. The two men engaged in a heated exchange. Lucas wanted Charlie Company to re-assault the hill. The order left Wilcox fuming as he had left a company of men dog-tired from a heated battle, undermanned and suffering from heat exhaustion and dehydration.

"Jeff got back way before me because we were bringing dead bodies back," said Campbell. "He was taking the wounded back. Jeff met with Lucas way before me. When I got to the perimeter, they sent down for me to come up there. We got into a discussion of things and they wanted to re-assault the hill later that afternoon, by then it was late in the day. We had started at daylight that morning. I lost my medic up there, didn't have a medic, and only had about 20 men that were able to fight and the issue wasn't whether we could attack the hill, it was whether we could do it right then. (It was a) heated exchange. Something was said about the Delta Company commander. I got banished from the TOC. Jeff dealt with it after that."

Campbell had nothing but glowing praise for Wilcox and his leadership of men in the heat of battle. Campbell had been with the company since March and knew the men. Wilcox was a newcomer to Charlie having previously served as a platoon leader with Alpha Company and commanding officer with Echo Company.

"Jeff's a great leader - brave, brave man," he said. "He was the best lieutenant, outstanding lieutenant when he was in Alpha Company before making captain. A leader, he led his men, then he was condemned by the colonel after that day - wrongfully condemned. They placed the blame of the failed attack on him. He did everything he was supposed to do. It was just uncalled for what happened to Jeff Wilcox. It was a mess, terrible."

The severity of battle, the significant discrepancy in troop strength seemed to elude Lucas, according to Wilcox.

"I don't think he ever walked around with a unit in the field; He jumped out of the chopper and he walked over to us and he said, 'When can you be ready to go back up?' remembered Wilcox. "It was just such a disconnect. I thought that I had talked him out of it and that we would go up the next day, rest up overnight, go up the next day, then the whole plan changed. We got shipped to Firebase O'Reilly, some replacements came in. The jauntiness of it pissed me off. His higher-ups thought we were a company and we were a platoon. That never got clear until Campbell set Harrison straight, I think. The thing that got us off the hill was Fred Spaulding radioing down that there's a whole bunch of NVA coming out of bunkers like ants. That's what got us off the hill."

McCall was there as well and remembered the heated exchange between Wilcox and Lucas.

"I remember when Lucas said he wanted us to go back up there and take the hill," said McCall. "That's when Wilcox said it wasn't worth it, that the hill wasn't worth one more life. He was exhausted, fatigued. We wouldn't have said that. Rollison wouldn't have said that. He probably would have taken (Lucas) one on one to discuss it. There would have been little or no bitching about it. That's the kind of leader Rollison was. Lucas asked me my opinion and I told him if we could dig in, make that hill Hill 997, bomb it... I think that made an impression on him because that's what we did."

Hill 1,000 was not going to be relinquished by the NVA. Strategically it was too important. It towered over Ripcord and proved to be the ideal spot from which to mortar the lower-lying firebase.

According to Doug Bonnot, George Davis, a spec 5 Voice Intercept Operator and Translator, advised Lucas during a briefing that at least a reinforced regiment was on Hill 1,000. Lucas, according to statements made by Davis, explained that it was his belief the Vietnamese units were overstated in size and that an NVA regiment was no larger than a United States battalion.

"You normally wouldn't see the enemy stand and fight that long," said McCall. "Most of the soldiers saw the amount of artillery and prep going into that hill and they thought it would just be a matter of marching up and counting bodies. The (NVA) were prepared and would send in reinforcements. We'd eliminate a bunker and start to receive fire from that same bunker."

"Had the division intended to hold Ripcord, removing the threat from Hill 1,000, while not absolutely necessary, would have been a great advantage." – Lt. Robert Layton, Bravo Company, 2nd/501st.

Meanwhile, several kilometers across the valley on Hill 1,000, just west of Ripcord, Alpha and Bravo companies were joined by a Recon unit (2/501st) in another attempt to dislodge the enemy, taking RPG (Rocket Propelled Grenade), small arms and mortar fire. It was just a week after the failed attempt to take the hill by Charlie Company.

Bob Layton (Bravo Company) remembered the withdrawal that day and looking back saw it in clearer context as the overall operation to keep Ripcord open was slipping away.

"In retrospect, I think 2/501st withdrawal from Hill 1,000 foreshadowed the abandonment of Ripcord," said Layton. "We went after 1,000 pretty hard on the 14th and I fully expected we'd return the next day. Instead, we were ordered out. Had the division intended to hold Ripcord, removing the threat from Hill 1,000, while not absolutely necessary, would have been a great advantage. I don't pretend to be a great military tactician, but that's just a thought I've developed from reading and talking with vets."

One American was killed and 20 were wounded. Five NVA dead were found dead during partial sweeps and as the companies withdrew. Artillery was called into the suspected enemy areas.

REMEMBERING FIREBASE RIPCORD

Lt. Col. Otis Livingston was indeed surprised when word came down for the 2nd of the 501st to be extracted from the Ripcord AO (Area of Operation). There would be no more assaults of Hill 1,000 even as Livingston's men spend July 16 working in the area, scouting bunker complexes between 1,000 and Coc Muen Mountain.

Col. Ben Harrison had argued to Gen. Sid Berry that Hills 1,000 and 805 were crucial to securing Ripcord and that additional support was needed to in the Area of Operation.

Fred Spaulding, S3 Air, said the discussion between Harrison and Berry was heated. Berry addressed the casualties, expenditure of artillery resources and aircraft, but did not touch on Harrison's request for additional support, Spaulding said.

Afterward, Spaulding said he sensed it was over when brass was concerned more with how much ammunition was being used versus taking the fight to the enemy. He said Harrison was enraged.

Though he had been on and off Firebase Ripcord throughout the more than four-month campaign to that point, Ben Peters arrived July 17 on the hill as captain of Bravo Company. His journey was a long one, one predicated on hard work and dedication to service.

Peters, from Florida, quit school to join the Navy, then jumped to the Army in hopes of advancing up the ladder. He had been to Germany, served a tour in Vietnam and completed Vietnamese language school stateside prior to ending up with the 101st in January 1970. He was assigned as an S5 and charged with overseeing the pacification programs and the Kit Carson scout program.

"I had some orphanages around Camp Evans that we took care of, helped take care of," said Peters, who was 29 and married with two sons by the time he ended up in I Corps. "As an S5, I had a training team. We'd visit the local villages or hamlets, which had their own little militias. We had a team go around and train them in weapons use. We also had a medical team that would go out in the countryside and around Camp Evans to treat the local people."

While rewarding, aspects of the job were concerning as well. There was no doubt that some of those treated were not friendlies.

"We treated some, surely they were VC (Viet Cong)," said Peters. "We didn't have proof of that, though, and we were to help the local people and we did. When I got there, the Kit Carson scout program was unorganized. The scouts would come into the program and get paid as soon as they joined. Well, they'd get paid and go home. As S5, I was paying them, so if they weren't in the field, I wouldn't pay them. I'd put them on a chopper and send them out in the field. We soon got a pretty good Kit Carson scout program going."

Much of the good work the military did went largely unnoticed in Vietnam, especially post-1968 and after Tet. Peters, however, was a witness to the good work of the Americans. He saw the work, and was part of that good work.

"I liked helping," he said. "The nuns ran the orphanages. Whatever they'd need I'd try to get it to them. It was a poor area and there were many grass hootches with nothing more than dirt floors. Some of them had never been more than a mile from where they were born. When the VC would move in they knew they couldn't beat them so they were friendly to them. When we came in they were friendly to us. They knew we could help them more. Usually the oldest person in the hamlet is the chief. The VC would come in and steal their food stores and if the people didn't meet their demands, the VC would just kill the hamlet chief. After a time of that, I knew that I wouldn't be speaking to the hamlet chief because the people were just afraid to bring them out. You worked with them the best you could."

As much as he enjoyed what he was doing, Peters had his eyes set on being a rifle company commander. Lt. Col. Lucas had promised him the next company that opened up. When that position didn't come, an offer came to get the assignment of his choice and Peters was prepared to take a position further south. Lucas found out and made a deal.

"He said, 'I guarantee you the next company that opens up,' and I shook on it," said Peters. "I declined my orders, went on R&R (rest and recuperation) with my wife in Hawaii. When I got back from Hawaii, I arrived at Camp Evans and the first sergeant came out and said, 'You're Bravo Company commander. I have a rucksack packed and your weapon drawn. There's a chopper ready to take you to Ripcord.'"

Having spent plenty of time at Evans' Tactical Operations Center, Peters was thoroughly familiar with operations throughout the battalion. As headquarters company commander, he had visited Ripcord on numerous occasions.

14

Missing in Action

Lewis Howard Jr. was drafted into the Army shortly after he graduated from high school in Macon, Ga. Tall and lean, he was an excellent basketball player, but excelled in all sports, according to his brother, Ted Howard.

"In my neighborhood, the top-five players of all time would have included my brother," said Ted. "When I developed, around 17 or 18, there was no one in the neighborhood I could not defend. He was the one player I could not stop. He was great in all sports, football, baseball, basketball."

Lewis was more than that though. He was a mentor, a leader and a friend. Those traits also made him a great soldier. While others protested and bickered about walking point, Lewis stepped forward and accepted the duty, without pause, without question. It cost him his life in July 1970 on Hill 1,000.

"He was a great big brother," remembered Ted. "I'd have to say he was the best one of all of us."

There were four children born to Kathryn and Lewis Howard Jr. Lewis

REMEMBERING FIREBASE RIPCORD

Jr. was the oldest, then a sister, and Ted, and the youngest son, Guy.

"With me, even as a kid, if there was some pretty girl around, I might be trying to clown around and act like I'm one of the big boys," said Ted. "Lewis would say, 'Go home.' He'd bust me in my chest and knock me down. There were times I'd get smart with him, but I knew when he meant what he said. He was the smartest one in the family at that time."

Not unlike most American families, the Howards didn't invest much time thinking about the Vietnam War. When Lewis' number was called, he didn't hesitate, Ted said.

"We felt it was all about stopping the spread of communism," he said. "I remember my brother was all for serving his country. He had no qualms, no issues with that. Our father was proud of his son, that he was going to serve his country. My mom, I don't think she wanted him to go. As for me and my sister, I think we were too young to be opinionated about it."

Mother Kathryn wrote often to Lewis and Lewis wrote home. Many in the neighborhood asked about Lewis, as he was well-respected, even revered by some.

Ted still remembers the day the telegram arrived at their Macon, Ga., home.

"I think my sister and I were at the house when they showed up," he said. "The two soldiers came to the house. They came to the door and my sister talked to them."

Lewis was orginally considered Missing In Action, as was Charles Beals, who was on the hill with Lewis, and Stephen Harbor, from Charlie Company, who was killed in action on July 2 at Hill 902.

MISSING IN ACTION

"Just to know he was missing was sad for us," said Ted. "Then the telegrams started coming. I remember I'd just leave home and would go to the playground and sit on the steps because I was so scared one of the telegrams would say he was dead. If I went away, then no telegrams would come. It was so sad. I can recall my mom as she was trying to work with the Red Cross to write letters to the Vietnamese government. The Red Cross would translate the letters into Vietnamese and mail them to the Vietnamese government. In return, the Red Cross required my mom to do volunteer work for them and she did it."

The letter was sent, and some time later, returned. It was covered in stamps and had never made it to its destination. Eventually, Lewis' personal effects made their way back to Macon.

"It was a small suitcase," said Ted. "It was a little bigger than a briefcase. Someone had busted the lock and took anything of value in it. There was a cat-eye ring that had glass stones in the shape of an L. I still have that ring. I liked collecting coins and Lewis had sent me three coins from over there. I didn't want him to die. He was the leader of the family."

Time passed and the family had this emptiness that never seemed to subside. In 1977, Kathryn passed away. Several months later, Lewis Sr., too, passed away. Not too long after that, the remaining Howards learned that Lewis was officially considered Killed in Action.

"Three funerals," said Ted.

Time passed, but questions remained. Then the family heard from Gary Radford, Lewis' sergeant in Vietnam.

"It was a very emotional time," remembered Ted. "I was living in Michigan. Guy was living outside Atlanta. Turns out Gary's mom and sister were going down to Florida and I-75 runs right through Macon. Gary asked if they would stop through and ask around if anyone knew the family. Turns out they found someone who knew Guy. They went back about 100 miles, to Atlanta, and gave a letter from Gary to Guy."

Little did the Howards know that Radford had attempted to track them down even years before. Not long after arriving home, he hopped aboard his motorcycle and took off for Macon, only to arrive and turn around without making contact.

That letter from Radford, addressed to the family of Lewis Howard Jr., was dated March 14, 1989. Radford praised Lewis and discussed the camaraderie and friendship the two shared.

"I remember Lewis when he came into the platoon sometime around October 1969," wrote Radford. "At first he was a rifleman, then he became my RTO (radio telephone operator), a hard job as the radio was very heavy. He was by my side all the time. Lewis carried the radio became he wanted to become my radio man. We were together constantly under extreme conditions, as we were family."

Radford went on to explain the firebase and his company's operations in the area. He also discussed the action of July 6 and 7 and the company's attempts at taking Hill 1,000.

"I did everything possible to get Lewis and Charles (Beals) but just could not do it," Radford wrote to the family. "So did every other man in the platoon.

"After all these years, I am just now able to talk about it. I always thought… I wanted to find the parents of Lewis and tell them about his loyalty to me and the rest of the men in our platoon. We were family."

Soon Ted was communicating with Gary. Questions were many, but answers were few, according to Ted.

"He didn't answer because it was too emotional for him," said Ted.

Soon after making contact with Lewis' family, Radford had kick-started an effort to return to the Ripcord Area of Operations to search for Lewis and Charles. He began writing to Washington and to then-Congressman Tom Ridge, who would serve later as governor of Pennsylvania and as the first secretary of Homeland Security under George W. Bush.

Ridge, in a letter dated March 21, 1994, to Secretary of Defense William Perry, wrote, "This case has been placed in the pending category with no further plans for a field investigation. It is my understanding that this decision was made because of a recommendation of a Joint Investigation Team. The Joint Investigation Team based their recommendation on an aerial reconnaissance flight over the last known location of these two men. However, in the 23 years since these two men have been missing (July 7, 1970), the terrain of the area has most likely changed. Also, it is not expected that the graves of these two valiant soldiers would have been marked. For these reasons, I believe that there should be a recovery party sent in to search for the bodies."

Ridge requested that Radford be permitted to accompany any recovery party sent in, citing the exceptional nature of the case. Given Radford's training and Ranger background, the fact that he earned the Silver Star, Bronze Star and two Purple Hearts, Radford should not be considered a routine citizen making such a request. Radford knew the area, had kept himself in top physical shape and knew exactly where the two men went down.

Ridge himself was a Vietnam veteran and said he believed the government should do everything it could to ensure a full accounting of all POWs and MIAs.

Radford had spent years attempting to get back to the Ripcord area in hopes of finding the two men that had been left behind. He saved money, worked with his employer to accumulate vacation time, and battled the bureaucracy at the Department of Defense, all in an attempt to go back to Hill 1,000 for his fallen comrades.

In October 1994 James W. Wold, deputy assistant secretary of Defense, responded to both Ridge and Congresswoman Barbara Rose-Collins, who represented Michigan's 15th District, which included Detroit, where Ted Lewis lived at the time. He, too, was writing to encourage Radford's participation in any attempt to locate Lewis or Charles. Wold cited Radford's interest as "commendable" but denied his request to take part in a search team.

Radford never let it go, though.

The Army's Division of POW/MIA Affairs issued a letter to Ted dated Dec. 6, 1995, confirming that both Ted and Radford would be allowed to meet with Wold at 2 p.m. Jan. 5, 1996, in the Defense Prison of War/Missing In Action Office, Arlington, Va.

Radford paid for both he and Ted to make the trip.

"When we were in Washington I suggested we go see The Wall and he went into almost a state of panic," said Ted. "He couldn't do it at the time. I hadn't seen it and I knew my brother's name was on The Wall."

I had a big issue with the guys in the Missing In Action-Prisoner of War affairs. They sent me a letter stating they had went back over, 22 or 23 years later, and did a search from a helicopter and saw no visible evidence of remains, from 200 feet above the ground. As for civilians going over at that point? It was not no, it was 'Hell no.'"

Radford and Ted met with Wold with several others, remembered Ted, who also noted a psychiatrist was in the room as well.

"We all wondered about that," said Ted. "Gen. Wold looked at me and said, 'You requested a meeting, what's on your mind?' I lit into him and said I don't think you give a damn about finding anyone over there. Companies here have invested millions over there and I don't think you want to find anybody. He was really upset with me. I was on a real good roll and the fire alarm went off and we had to evacuate the building."

When the group returned, Wold said he had to attend another meeting. Ted said he wouldn't be shortchanged after coming that far. Ted remembered the psychiatrist gazing over Lewis' file as Wold questioned whether maps of the area still existed.

"I told him Gary still has his (maps)," said Ted. "Everything he said, I had a counter for. He said it would be hard to cut a landing zone. I said Gary said it would take about 15 minutes. When the meeting was over they said they'd notify us of their decision.

"Gary wanted to go over. He said he could show them where the remains were."

After the meeting, the two men went to a food court area to eat. As they sat down, the psychiatrist walked up to their table and said she had looked at Lewis' file.

"She said, 'I had to do something,'" remembered Ted. "Because he was from Macon, Ga. She went to school not far from there."

Word arrived in June 1996 that Radford would be accompanying a team from Joint Task Force-Full Accounting on a field investigation in the Socialist Republic of Vietnam. The letter was from the Defense Prisoner of War/Missing In Action Office, requested by Joe Harvey, chief of staff, and approved by Richard J. Conoboy, director, resource management. No one had signed the letter.

"You will need to join the team at Hue, on July 9, 1996 at the Century

Riverside Hotel... You will be responsible for your travel from the United States to the city of Hue, and for any necessary visas or other entry documentation. The United States and the Joint Task Force-Full Accounting do not assume any responsibility for your travel to and from the country of the Socialist Republic of Vietnam and the city of Hue nor for your entry into that country," the letter read in part.

High winds prevented the helicopter from landing on Firebase Ripcord on July 15 and 16, 1996. Then, on July 17, the helicopter was able to land after maneuvering around unexploded ordnance. The team hiked west to Hill 1,000, where Radford led the joint team up to the site where Charles and Lewis were last seen. Radford identified several battlefield landmarks and the team located numerous pieces of equipment including a pair of jungle boots, a single jungle boot, but no human remains. A test pit was dug with negative results, according to the post-mission report, filed by the Joint Task Force.

Along with the boots, sizes 7 and 10, the team found a helmet, Budweiser beer can, remnants of a jungle rucksack, two ponchos, part of a poncho liner and part of a helmet liner. Near the helmet and ponchos the team found the pair of boots, size 10, with no laces and a hole through the sole of one of the boots. Also found were the remainder of the helmet liner, the left and right forearm handguards from an M-16, a butt pack, cloth sandbag, six-quart collapsible canteen, a large bottle of water purification tablets and other pieces of nylon and plastic. This area is where Lewis fell.

The team moved to left about 60 meters, where Charles fell, and found an M-60 with a bent barrel, an M-60 forearm handguard and bipod legs, a rucksack, poncho and right jungle boot, size 7. All the items were found within a 10-meter perimeter. Also nearby was a gas mask.

No burial sites were found.

MISSING IN ACTION

Proceeding up the hill, the team found the remains of a bitterly contested war. On the hilltop and eastern side of the hill the team found artillery ordnance, aircraft bombs, pieces of napalm bomb liners, rifle magazines, canteens, ponchos, U.S. rucksacks, water canisters, light anti-tank weapons (LAWs), grenades, B50 rockets, C-ration cans, heat tabs and more.

"It looked just as it did 26 years ago," Radford told the Pittsburgh Post-Gazette in a story from April 28, 2013. "But, it was peaceful."

While the team moved about the hill, Radford found a nearby tree, knelt and dug a hole, where he removed two copper MIA bracelets from his pocket and covered them with the soil from Hill 1,000. The bracelets bore the names of Charles Beals and Lewis Howard Jr., both of whom had died at age 20 on that hill decades before.

The moment caught on camera, Radford said, "I bury these in their memory. I'd like to say a silent prayer for them, and all the men that were killed on this hill, and the hills around Ripcord, in this Ashau Valley."

Gary called Ted from Vietnam.

"I remember thinking to myself this has gotta be a huge phone bill for him," said Ted. "They had found my brother's boot, which had a bullet hole in it, and his helmet. I was told something about the shoestrings being cut and I remember asking Gary what the significance of that would be. He said a lot of the soldiers would keep their dogtags in their boots. The North Vietnamese would take those. It does make you wonder what happened to the body."

The Joint Task Force surmised the North Vietnamese buried the bodies alongside their own dead for sanitary reasons.

"I feel like Lewis got shot up, got hit with an RPG, things used to stop tanks," said Ted. "I was also told that Lewis was not dead instantly, that they fought for about five or six hours with the enemy. He was crying out for a medic, but they couldn't get to him."

Ted couldn't say enough about Radford's efforts, but still carries regrets.

"My biggest regret is that he didn't make it back," Ted said of Lewis. "But two, my parents died not knowing what happened to their son. There were times I'd hear my mom crying. He was missing in action and she never knew what happened to him. My father, while he was a mean man, there were times I'd hear him crying because he felt if only he could afford to send his son to college he wouldn't have had to go to war. He saw war in World War II, right on the front lines. He knew."

Radford and Lewis, a white man from the Pittsburgh area and a black man from southern Georgia, shared a friendship. Radford has admitted he thinks about Lewis and Charles on a daily basis. Ted thinks there may be more to tell, but it's something Radford can't do.

"We were very thankful to hear from Gary," said Ted. "We got more information from Gary than we did from the military, more pertinent information. We are thankful for all he has done.

"I still miss my brother. I still talk about my brother. I still tell people about my brother."

Some of the artifacts found during the 1996 mission were brought home. The helmet liner and a canteen with a bullet hole in it were given to the Soldiers and Sailors Memorial Hall. The military shipped the M-60 to the hall as well.

A Chinook with a slingload hovers above Firebase Ripcord in July 1970. A Chinook was shot down July 18, something many have pointed to as the beginning of the end for the firebase. Photo provided by Christopher Jensen.

15

The Beginning of the End

Having completed basic training at Fort Campbell, Ky., Terry Stanger attended aviation school in Virginia, where he learned maintenance on the CH-47, better known as the Chinook helicopter, the monster that transported large numbers of troops and supplies in Vietnam.

"On my first day of instruction I was informed that I would crash, burn and die in this type of helicopter in Vietnam," wrote Stanger. "We were taught rotor blades aren't very friendly to humans during a crash or after a crash. 'When you crash, get the hell away from the chopper's blades.' This was pounded into each of us day and night. I had dreams of rotor blades trying to chop me up."

Stanger and crew had attempted a resupply mission July 12 at Ripcord, a place Stanger hadn't heard of, having arrived in country in June.

"We were told it was hot," Stanger wrote. "On our second lift to Ripcord we had just put the load on the ground when I saw an explosion underneath our helicopter, out the left window. I informed the pilot and away we went. A mortar had just missed us and for some reason, I wasn't upset. When you have no experience at war, you don't

THE BEGINNING OF THE END

know what to expect. If the mortar had hit us, I'm sure I would have had a completely different reaction."

The morning of the 18th, it was an early rise for the crew of the Chinook, another trip to Ripcord planned.

"Warrant Officer 1 (Robert) Barrowcliff was inspecting us and reminded us to keep our collars up, visors down and gloves on at all times when flying," said Stanger. "Capt. (Edwin) Grove was quiet and let Barrowcliff do most of the talking. We were now ready to turn and burn. Our first load was going to Ripcord and we were to resupply them all day."

Several Chinooks were taking part in the resupply at Ripcord. After several trips, it was time for lunch and a refuel. Then it was back to Ripcord with a load of 105mm ammunition.

Life on and around Ripcord changed dramatically in the early afternoon hours of July 18. Men on the firebase and in the field had experienced much more contact with the NVA since July 1 and there was a sense that something had changed, there was a shift in the NVA objective. Every chopper in and out of Ripcord faced small-arms fire or worse, 51-caliber fire or mortars.

"After July 18, when the NVA started to shoot 120mmm mortars at us, it was not fun anymore," said Marc Aronson, artillery on Ripcord. "Those made a hell of a noise when they landed and there was nowhere to hide from them. In my opinion, this was the point where the battle turned in favor of the other side."

In what has been described as the beginning of the end for Firebase Ripcord, a Chinook supply chopper was shot down at 1:30 p.m. The massive chopper crashed into the 105mm ammunition storage area, setting of explosions that continued for hours. Fire erupted and men on the firebase attempted to limit the damage and save those that went down with the chopper.

"I was bringing that chopper in with visual hand signals to place a sling load when that 51 opened up from the adjacent hillside," remembered Pathfinder Nick Fotias. "I don't even think the crew was aware (it had been hit). The crew chief was leaning out the belly and he was going to release the slingload when I got him positioned. These tracers went flying over my head and I saw the impact, the rear engine house, waived him off, tried to get his attention. The rear engine housing caught fire and they started getting smoke in the cabin of the aircraft. At that point, they were aware of it. I dove off to the side, was signaling, trying to get them to cut the load. I didn't know if they would be able to fly off at that point or set the ship down on one of the pads. The cut the load and went to hover and tried to lift the ship, then the ship just dropped and it fell right on the sling load of 155s there. Everybody got out but the crew chief."

Sgt. Gary Foster was approaching Ripcord in a Huey when the ship he was riding in came under fire, prompting the pilot to increase elevation and circle above the fire. It was from there that Foster, who was heading in the Ripcord Area of Operations for the first time, saw the massive chopper go down.

"It was me and two others on the chopper, along with the crew," said Foster. "We had some C-rations, some mail, maybe some medical supplies. There were going to try to put us in with our platoon, which was off by itself just below Ripcord. We were flying around and they started shooting at us. You could hear those rounds pop as they flew by us. The pilot took us higher and while we were circling, I looked down and that's when they took that Chinook in. It had a slingload and when it came into the firebase, he started down and it looked like he dropped his slingload. When he tried to lift back off, he didn't have enough power and it settled on its tail then rolled onto its side. It started exploding."

Chuck Holmen enlisted in the Army with his eyes set on aviation. He

THE BEGINNING OF THE END

got it, almost landing a spot with a Huey crew, however he ended up working with Chinooks. Crews rotated as needed, unlike many Huey crews, which would work together most of the time.

"They were big, like a big boxcar with rotors on them," said Holmen, of Wisconsin. "There were five people on a chinook, a pilot, co-pilot, flight engineer, crew chief and door gunner. I was crew chief. I was the second door gunner really. The flight engineer owned the bird basically. Crew chief would help the engineer. The gunner would get his assignment every day. I'd take my place in the doorway, engineer in the back."

Holmen's flight that morning to Ripcord would be his last in Vietnam. They were to transport a load of ammunition to the embattled firebase.

"We took on a full load of fuel, which would have been 1,200 gallons," said Holmen. "We went over and picked up four pallets of ammunition and headed out to Ripcord. I'm watching out the window, we came in, pulled in where we normally dropped off ammo and suddenly there's a guy running down the hill trying to get us to get out of there. I looked back and saw our engines are already on fire."

Stanger, the gunner, remembered being told not to fire without permission from the pilots. Word came in that there were friendlies outside the wire.

"We were making our final approach to Ripcord and were about 300 feet from the top of the mountain when I saw three men outside the wire at the bottom of the mountain pointing something at our helicopter," said Stanger. "I took the safety off my M-60 and pointed my weapon at the three men. Next, I keyed my mic to ask permission to shoot. Suddenly the left engine blew up and started to burn. Fire was coming inside the back of the helicopter from our rotor wash and was flashing us with heat. My helmet visor melted during one of the blasts and heat and flames surrounded my body. The fire was cooking me."

Michael Walker, the final member of the flight crew, released the load of 105mm ammunition so that in the event of a crash, the chopper wouldn't land on the load.

"I was trying to tell the pilots we had been hit and were on fire when all hell broke loose," said Stanger.

"By that time everyone is talking," said Holmen. "There was so much smoke in the cabin I couldn't see the four-by-four hole where the hook was. I learned later from Stanger, he was looking down the hill and saw tracers coming up. We just dropped out of the sky. We were only about 30 feet in the air."

"I was standing in the cockpit screaming, 'We're on fire!' when the fire and smoke suddenly came into the cockpit," said Stanger. "At that same moment we crash landed into the Ripcord ammo dump."

"You could see it was hit," said Ewe Meyer, a member of Bravo Company, which was pulling security detail on Ripcord at the time. "It was floundering like a duck, in a hunt. It wasn't going anywhere, so you could tell it was hit. We were hoping it wouldn't come down on our position so we were watching it, keeping an eyeball on it. It was easy picking. To this day I don't know why they, the Vietnamese, didn't shoot every helicopter down. As a farm kid in Iowa, you go pheasant hunting and shoot them out of the sky, of course they don't shoot back. It seems it would be easy shooting."

"I was headed out on patrol," remembered Lt. Bill Hand, second platoon, Bravo. "The tail rotor went spinning over our heads down the hill. I told everyone to get down."

The moments after impact were confusing and chaotic for those inside the big bird.

"There was a lot of fire," said Holmen. "By the time I got out of the

THE BEGINNING OF THE END

aircraft it was probably 80 percent burned. I would have been in the right door behind the pilots. The flight engineer pushed over my shoulder and jumped out the window. He went over the top of my machine gun. He was the first one out. The rest of us got out when we crash landed. I could hear the rotors smashing into everything outside. It tipped over. I'm sitting there kind of frantic. When I realized it hadn't blown up yet, I calmed down and walked up the radio rack and crawled out. I jumped on the ground. Where my door was it was dirt. I met what turned out to be Col. Lucas as I got out. Then we found my flight engineer (Walker), pinned under the nose. We tried getting him out. Everything was getting messy with the fire, ammunition was blowing up. Lucas was pretty calm. He looked like he'd seen enough stuff, this was just another day on the hill. Stanger was the door gunner. I went back in and grabbed the fire extinguisher. I looked at that thing and looked at the fire and threw it down, there was no way this two-pound extinguisher was going to work."

Stanger smashed into the windshield upon impact.

"I smashed into the center windshield with my helmet and landed on Capt. Grove's lap on the left side of the helicopter," he explained. "Capt. Grove had reached for the door jettison at the same time I reached for the door to get myself off his lap. 'Boom!' Out goes the jettison door with me in tow. I fell down the mountain about 300 feet or more onto some open ammo crates, which had been thrown down the mountain as trash. Lucky for me my helmet was on and the visor closed. I was falling head first down the side of the mountain. My hands hit the ammo crates, followed by my head, shoulders and my flak jacket. I flipped over onto my exposed bak. When I stood up, my flak jacket vest was filled with ammo crates hanging all over it as the nails had become embedded into the metal plate in the front and back of the vest. My eyes were full of blood from the visor cutting into the ridge of my nose. My fingers on my right hand were bent out of place and my right arm felt numb from the long fall. All I could remember thinking is why I didn't feel any pain. Then I remembered what my school instructors always drummed into our heads, 'Rotor blades, rotor blades – get the hell away from the helicopter.'"

Stanger attempted to run, slowed by the crates still clinging to him. He looked up to see the massive chopper roll to the right, away from him. He took his helmet off and shed his flak jacket to rid himself of the crates, then started back up the hill.

"I was worried about the other crew members," he said. "Walker was pinned under the right door face down and the top part of the doorway was on the back section of his legs just below his butt. During the confusion Holmen tried to exit the right door but forgot he was still strapped in. Walker went around Holmen and at that moment the aircraft rolled to the right pinning Walker underneath. We all tried to pull him from the doorway. Holmen even went back inside the burning aircraft to get the fire extinguishers and the escape ax. We tried to cut the metal framework around the top of the door, but there was a huge metal beam around the top of the door. We even discussed cutting Walker's legs off rather than let him burn alive. He kept screaming and begging us to help him. We were beside ourselves. We didn't have any firefighting equipment because we had crashed and destroyed it."

Capt. Philip Michaud and Nicolas Fotias were among those on the firebase who attempted to save Walker, but flames prevented them from freeing the crewmember.

"(Walker) put the gate down and ran out the back and came up the uphill side of the ship," said Fotias. "At that point, the ship teetered over and pinned him under the right side of the tanks. We struggled and struggled trying to get him out, I just couldn't get his legs free. One of the guys from battery came down with extinguishers and held them on us. As long as they held the fire extinguishers directly on us I was able to try to free him. About all I had was the knife and I was using it to try

THE BEGINNING OF THE END

to break up the ground, hoping we could just get him out. Eventually the rounds started cooking off. A couple guys grabbed me and pulled me away. That was about all we could do at that point. Unfortunately I didn't have my sidearm on me at the time or honestly, I think I would have used... I still have nightmares about that part of the episode – the look in that young man's eyes. We made contact and the screams... that was a hell of a way to go. Wasn't much we could do at that point."

"It was right above my position," said Meyer. "I ran up there and helped cut it up, to get the stuff out of there. The helicopter blew up and I tried to get people out of there. Rounds started cooking off. One guy was stuck in there and we tried to get him out of there. It wasn't pretty and everyone was hollering. It was a chaotic moment. We were trying to get (Walker) out and we couldn't."

Walker, surrounded by flames, pleaded for someone to shoot him as work went on around him. Lt. Col. Andre Lucas was among those attempting to rescue Walker. Eventually, the flames, and rounds going off from the ammunition dump, proved too much.

The Chinook had attempted the fourth such delivery of ammunition of the day. When it crashed into the ammo bunker, it sent fuel into the dump setting off the explosions that would last for eight hours. More than 400 rounds of artillery were set off. The Tactical Operations Center and Medical Aid Station on the firebase also suffered damage from the fire.

"I was on a hill east of there bringing supplies," remembered Larry "Crash" Kern, a pilot with the Ghostriders. " We looked over and there it was and it looked like a volcano. Things were exploding and there was fire. One of the guys jumped on my skid and looked in my window and asked, 'Can you get me back over there? I gotta get back to my guys.' I'm looking at him and you want to treat him like a parent. He thinks I can fly him over there. Later I flew over and it was hell. There was one explosion after another. After that they were defenseless. Once they lost those artillery pieces, they lost their ability to defend themselves. There was no roadway to get them out of there, it was stupid. They were stuck out there without aircraft. There was no way they could walk off Ripcord."

Specialist 4 Michael A. Walker, a crew member on the Chinook, died in the crash when he was pinned underneath the massive machine. The rest of the crew, co-pilot Grove, Pilot Barrowcliff, gunner Stanger and crew chief Holman were injured. Holmen and the rest of the crew took cover.

"Rounds were cooking off pretty fast, like popcorn in a popcorn maker," remembered Meyer. "You could really hear them. I got the hell out of there. "

Stanger had taken cover in a bunker, where three privates were also sheltered amidst the chaotic scene.

"We were all scared to death," said Stanger. "I asked the men if they had anything I could use to get the blood out of my eyes. One guy had a Coke and a clean rag, so I washed my eyes with the Coke. That's when I noticed a lot of burning metal flying past the front of our bunker. I asked one of the men to look outside to see what was going on. He reported that the fuel and fire from the helicopter was heading our way."

Stanger inquired which direction they should go and the young privates turned to him as the ranking soldier, seeking guidance. They fled toward another bunker and Stanger got caught in wire, ripping his gloves off.

"That's when the ammo dump blew," he said. "I ripped through the wire and was running down the mountain as fast as I could. Everything around me was exploding. There was fire and smoke. Explosions were

THE BEGINNING OF THE END

knocking me down when suddenly a concussion knocked me to the ground. I blacked out for a several seconds. When I came to I looked up and saw a man standing in a doorway. He was wearing a cross on his helmet and I thought to myself, 'Oh no, I've died and went to Army heaven.' Thank God it was the firebase chaplain. He was standing in the main bunker doorway looking out."

The explosions continued. A medic began working on Stanger's fingers and arm.

"I knew that both the pilots were in the bunker with me and Holmen was in a different bunker," said Stanger. "We had at least two direct hits of 105 or 120 mortar shells on our bunker and the concussion picked up one of the pilots and laid him flat on his back without hurting him."

During the chaos during and following the crash, the perimeter of the firebase remained intact. Artillery attacks from surrounding firebases Barbara, O'Reilly and Rakkasan were ordered, and later from Gladiator to support recovery efforts at Ripcord.

Five 105mm Howitzers were lost in the crash, one damaged. Also destroyed was a counter-mortar radar, two 106mm recoilless rifles and a radio. One soldier was killed and four wounded as incoming mortar continued throughout the day.

"The Chinook burned and rounds just kept cooking off," said Hand. "We hunkered down until everything settled down. When it was safe, we had to clear that area off. They hadn't decided what to do, where to bring another battery in. We were picking up damaged rounds and just waiting for decisions to be made."

CS gas was dropped onto Ripcord, further adding to the chaos and danger for the troops. No one could find their gas masks, said Stanger.

"I was coughing and there was smoke and gas and God knows what else," said Stanger. "About this time I'm praying that someone would come and save us. I'm still sitting near operations when a Huey pilot calls in on the radio. He's going to try to get onto the firebase. He had fire extinguishers and wanted to pick up the wounded and crew members, so down the mountain we ran, trying to avoid the shells exploding around us. All I could think of was getting off that firebase. We all made it to the landing zone and the Huey was on its way to pick us up. I remembered making fun of the Huey crews in school, but after this day I would never make fun of them again. One of the wounded was a pathfinder who was guiding us into the ammo dump. He was injured when our helicopter rolled over and one of the rotor blades broke off and hit him in the leg. I was told later the blade cut off his leg."

Walt Smith was part of a mortar squad with Echo Company, which had been set up on the side of Ripcord and slated for extraction the day the Chinook was shot out of the sky onto Ripcord.

"Our squad was near the chopper pad when the Chinook went down," Smith wrote, "so we took shelter in the heavy bunkers near the pad. It didn't take long for the smell of gas to reach inside the bunkers. Naturally, we didn't carry gas masks, so we ran from the bunkers to one side of the hill to escape the gas. I can remember seeing live artillery shells lying around on the hill that had apparently been blown off the top of the hill where the Chinook had crashed. The smell of the gas had started getting to me and about that time a lieutenant came along and gave me his gas mask. I don't know who he was, but I was extremely happy, for once, to put on one of those masks."

Part of the clean-up for Bravo included clearing as much of the wreckage as possible.

"I had to recover (Walker's) body," said Hand. "It was the hardest thing I had to do there. It was myself and one of the E7s up there. (Walker)

THE BEGINNING OF THE END

still had wires stuck to his chest. He was missing his legs at the bottom. Everything happened so fast. You're just kind of numb to it. You just think about taking care of your people while doing the mission. The most important thing after the mission was to not get people hurt."

Stanger and the wounded flew safely back to Camp Evans.

"All was quiet on the flight back to Camp Evans," he said. "I was crying and my eyes were full of blood again. I felt bad about leaving Walker in the burning Chinook. All I could think about was leaving Walker under that helicopter, begging us to get him out. I also knew Walker's wife was having a baby soon and that was bothering me too."

Back at his company area, Stanger was shocked to see that someone had already taken Walker's personal items from his bunk.

"There was nothing to show he had ever slept above me," said Stanger. "That upset me, but it was 101st policy. Later the battalion commander, Col. George F. Newton, stopped by and asked me to go over what happened that day. We took a walk out to the flight line and began to talk. We didn't talk very much about Ripcord. My first question for him was how someone going into a combat zone can be given an order not to shoot at the enemy without asking permission from the pilot first."

Amidst the wreckage on the firebase, thoughts inevitably turned to the future.

"The concern was how was this going to affect our defenses? Were we clearing the hill for another battery? It wasn't until the 21st that we heard they had other plans."

James Robert Kalsu, pictured here with daughter Jill, was killed atop Firebase Ripcord on July 21, 1970, two days before his only son was to be born stateside. Kalsu was the lone professional athlete killed in Vietnam. Photo provided by Jan Kalsu.

16

From the NFL to the 101st

The firebase suffered a tremendous blow toward dusk July 21 as a mortar landed in the area of the 155s, where Lt. Bob Kalsu, the 1969 Buffalo Bills Rookie of the Year from Oklahoma, was standing with a group of soldiers outside the steps that led down into the Fire Direction Center (FDC).

"I was standing next to Bob, we were talking and he was reading," said Nick Fotias, a pathfinder on Ripcord at the time. "He had just received a letter from his wife about the baby they were expecting. That round came in and landed about five feet back of Bob. He just took the brunt of the blast. We went flying through the opening of the door, down to the FDC, down to the bottom of the steps. He landed on top of me.

"I was stunned from the concussion. I'm laying at the bottom of the steps at the FDC. At first I shook the cobwebs off, then I couldn't see, I had so much dirt and debris in my eyes. That all happened in a matter of seconds and I felt this tremendous weight on me. I kind of rolled him off me to the side and saw he was bleeding from behind his ear. I tried to apply some pressure there, I put my hand over it and there was a hole the size of a silver dollar. I saw brain matter there. For Bob, it was instantaneous. I knew he was gone. At least he didn't feel anything."

REMEMBERING FIREBASE RIPCORD

Kalsu was a mountain of a man and loved by his fellow soldiers.

"He was definitely one of the good guys," said Fotias. "I can't think of another officer that was as loved and looked up to by his men, not just his men but anyone that knew him. He was just that kind of personality. You couldn't help but immediately like him. He was a giant of a guy, but always friendly, outgoing. He'd take his shirt off, jump in and hump ammo, hump rounds with the rest of his men. That's just something you didn't see. He never asked any of his men to do anything he wouldn't do and didn't do."

Also killed in the blast were Roberto Flores, of Bravo Company, second platoon, who had a wife and baby waiting for him in Texas and David Johnson, Alpha, 2-11 artillery. Six others, and Fotias, were wounded.

Lt. Bill Hand was in charge of second platoon, Bravo. Flores was his RTO (radio telephone operator).

"He had just returned from R&R (rest and recuperation), where he had seen his wife and brand new baby," said Hand. "He took one piece of shrapnel in his heart. If he had his flak jacket zipped up he might have lived. I had to recover his body and that was a tough thing."

An All-American at Oklahoma, one of the nation's biggest football schools, James Robert Kalsu was revered as one of the best linemen in the country when he was drafted in 1968 by the Buffalo Bills of the National Football League. His stock soared following his senior season, where in addition to earning All-America honors, he was captain of a Sooners team that turned in a 9-1 record, two seasons removed from a disappointing 3-7 campaign. Before Buffalo snapped Kalsu up in the eighth round, Dallas and Denver, both of which showed prior interest, passed on the big lineman, leery of his military commitment.

Kalsu, in addition to carrying a Division I football and academic load, was a leader in the ROTC (Registered Officer Training Corps) at Oklahoma. He was in line for military service while the most unpopular war in American history raged in Southeast Asia, at a time when the war was heating up in the area Kalsu would eventually end up serving.

Born April 13, 1945, in Oklahoma City, he was an only child, the son of Frank and Leah. His uncle Charles was 6-feet, 6-inches tall and played hoops for the legendary Henry Iba at Oklahoma State. Charles later played pro ball while Frank settled in Del City as a laborer at the Tinker Air Force Base, Del City.

Young Bob was extremely competitive, at everything. He excelled too, playing golf and on the bowling team. It wasn't unusual to hear that Bob had spent the entire day playing golf. Football fit Bob, though. Legendary Coach Bud Wilkinson had recruited young Bob at Del City High and Bob made the easy decision to follow the twice-national-champion ('55, '56) to Norman.

Kalsu was redshirted his freshman season, the same year Wilkinson resigned, following several years of decline. Over the next four seasons, Bob continued along his upward trajectory and became a solid leader of young men, both on the gridiron and through ROTC.

By his junior season, Kalsu was playing for his third different coach, Jim Mackenzie, and had earned a starting spot on a team that finished 6-4. The next spring Mackenzie died of a heart attack and was succeeded by Chuck Fairbanks. The team had a storied season, losing only to Texas by a mere two points.

While Kalsu's collegiate football career had become a myriad of adversity and upheaval, there had developed a calming presence in his personal life. He met Jan Darrow, thanks to a mutual friend who happened to be Kalsu's college roommate, and the two went on their first date Oct. 15, 1966. The chemistry was immediate.

"We gelled," said Jan. "He was Catholic, I was Catholic. We started going out on our own in 1967 and we were married in January 1968."

Bob wanted to play professional football and he knew he'd have the opportunity, Jan said. "Canada wanted him," she remembered. "Bob wanted to play in the United States, though. He was very excited.

"When we came back from our honeymoon, my sister sang, 'Buffalo Bill, won't you come out tonight?' Dallas talked to him and Denver talked to him. The big red flag was ROTC. Later I found out they would have officers come in from the National Guard just to swear the football players in so they wouldn't have to go to Vietnam."

Kalsu wasn't about to back out of a commitment he made, though.

"Bob said, 'I can't back down on what I signed,'" remembered Jan. "I'm no better than anyone else. He did a year at Buffalo, got Rookie of the Year and got his papers to join the Army."

Their relationship continued to progress, as did Bob's career. The excitement was only building, though.

"It moved fast for God's timing," Jan said. "I got pregnant."

His rookie year was an adventure, from the uncertainty surrounding training camp to rookie pranks. "When they'd open up their lockers, if your uniform wasn't there, you had been cut," remembered Jan. "They were always scared to open their lockers. After he'd made the team, they shaved his head. He looked like Mr. Clean," she laughed.

During his year in Buffalo, Kalsu beefed up to 250 pounds, further

FROM THE NFL TO THE 101ST

filling out his 6-foot, 3-inch frame, a good 20 pounds heavier than in his college days. He started the final nine games of the season and impressed teammates, coaches and the front office in Buffalo.

Jan had the couple's first child, a daughter, Jill, in Oklahoma while Bob was in Buffalo. Bob beamed with pride, Jan said. Jill was about a month old when Bob first laid eyes on her.

Bob would soon find himself in a completely different world, though. He was one of just seven professional athletes to serve in Vietnam, six from the gridiron and one bowler. He would serve in one of the worst areas of the war, the outskirts of the A Shau Valley, a place that became synonymous for death with the May 1969 coverage of the 101st Airborne's taking of Hamburger Hill.

Kalsu spent a year at Fort Sill, Okla., before getting his orders for Vietnam.

"When Bob got his orders, his fatigues were soaked with sweat," said Jan. "He did not want to leave Jill or me. He did not know I was pregnant again. We always wanted to have a lot of kids and we were going to use part of Bob's name for one son and part for another one. When he got his orders, I went to the altar before the tabernacle and said, 'Lord, if you need Bob more than I do, please give us a son."

He had a big, booming laugh. His smile could light up a room, literally to hear some explain it. He was like a big kid in a massive, football body.

"His laugh, you could hear it all over," said Jan.

Lt. Bob Kalsu was loved by those he served with. He rarely talked about his successes before his service, the fact that he was an All-American at football powerhouse Oklahoma, or that he was drafted by, and played for, the Buffalo Bills, the team he earned Rookie of the Year honors for in 1968. He never mentioned he started nine games in his rookie season and had the veterans in the trenches worried, all of a sudden concerned about their jobs.

Capt. Robert Anckaitis first met Kalsu while the two served on Firebase Rakkasan, to the east of Ripcord. The young officer didn't know anything about his lieutenant at first, only that he was massive in size.

"Kalsu, he was another officer, but he stood out," said Anckaitis, a first lieutenant before being promoted to captain just days before landing on Firebase Ripcord. "When he came on the base at Rakkasan, even if he wasn't an officer he'd stand out simply because of his size. I remember seeing him at Rakkasan with his shirt off and I was amazed, this big, barrel-chested guy.

"I remember him being a very, very strong guy. He had a smile on his face, a lot. I don't think I ever knew he was an All-American in college, I just knew he played for the Bills. I knew he was an ROTC grad and I knew his wife was pregnant."

Lt. Bill Hand was on the firebase at the same time Kalsu was there. Hand, and Bravo Company, was charged with securing the firebase during those final days.

"We'd talk once in a while when we'd run into each other," said Hand. "I had no clue he was a pro football player or that he'd played at the University of Oklahoma."

Chinooks would re-supply the firebase with ammunition for the artillery companies. When the slingloads arrived, Kalsu would lead the charge to unload the artillery rounds, 100-pound rounds that had to be taken from the helipad to the artillery pit. Kalsu and David Johnson, known by the men as "Big John", would compete to see who could move the most rounds in the shortest amount of time.

FROM THE NFL TO THE 101ST

The two men, known for their immense stature – Kalsu carried a stocky, football build, while Johnson was taller and leaner, still plenty strong – were friends as well as competitors. Kalsu was a white, college-educated Oklahoman while Johnson was poor, black, and from Arkansas. While the two had seemingly little in common, they shared a kind-hearted spirit that endeared them to their fellow soldiers.

Johnson was remembered as a good athlete in school, excelling in basketball and track. Prior to enlisting, Johnson was studying at Philander Smith College in Little Rock, Ark., then put off applying for another student deferment.

Johnson was the only man on that hill in Vietnam who could even come close to meeting the brute strength of Kalsu.

"He used to carry three rounds," said Anckaitis of Bob's strength. "I've told so many people that story. Most guys would carry one, some would carry two. Back in those days, I looked like a P.O.W., I was skinny. Kalsu would get one on each shoulder with the nose plug facing out and the bottom of the projectile behind him, then he'd have someone lay the third one across his shoulders behind his head. I couldn't carry one round. I wasn't strong enough."

Capt. Philip Michaud worked next to Kalsu's 155s in the 105 pit. He remembered talking with Kalsu several times, noting "he died afraid of nothing.

"He was a really, really nice guy. I was devastated when I heard what happened to him."

Fotias explained the trying days of July when the firebase was under near constant bombardment from incoming NVA mortar rounds.

"There's nothing more terrifying and more demoralizing than taking incoming like that," said Fotias. "But honestly, I would rather be in a situation with gooks in the wire and be overrun than be in a situation like Ripcord. In my opinion, to an infantry foot solider, there's nothing more demoralizing than being on top of a hill with nothing to do, nowhere to go and taking constant incoming like that. You just feel so helpless watching your buddies get blown away all around you. I'd rather have something to shoot back at. I've been in both situations too."

Bob never let Jan know how bad things were on the hill. She found out, though, when the two spent time in Hawaii when Bob met she and Jill during his rest and recuperation break.

"Jill and I went when I was seven months pregnant," said Jan. "Bob just loved Jill and I knew it wouldn't be a good R&R without Jill. He looked like a big-old football player coming at us when he first saw us. It scared Jill. She hadn't seen him in about six or seven months. She was about 18 months old. You could see the lump in his throat, thinking she'd forgotten him. We had a wonderful week together."

Bob was tired, though. "He slept a lot. He was exhausted." Then Jan saw first-hand the effects of war on the man.

"We were staying in a hotel where the pool area was in the middle of the complex. While he was sleeping there were fireworks in the pool area and he jumped up, and took off running for cover. He didn't know where he was for a moment. I realized then what he was facing every day."

When it came time to leave - Jan to return to Oklahoma and Bob to Vietnam - neither wanted to utter the word goodbye.

"My plane left first and he's holding my hand there," remembered Jan. "I said, 'Be careful Bob.' He said, 'No, you be careful, you're pregnant with our baby.' He never ever let me know he was in a dangerous spot. The only thing he'd say is, 'I can't wait until monsoon season when it

FROM THE NFL TO THE 101ST

will be quieter.' He was always a man that held presence so that when he told me, 'I'm going to be alright Jan,' I believed him."

Everyone believed in Lt. Kalsu. He was universally loved by his men, and his superiors.

"He was definitely one of the good guys," said Fotias. "I can't think of another officer that was as loved and looked up to by his men, not just his men but anyone that knew him. He just had that kind of personality, you couldn't help but immediately like him. He was a giant of a guy, but always friendly, outgoing. He'd take his shirt off, jump in and hump ammo. He'd hump rounds with the rest of his men. That's just something you didn't see. He never asked any of his men to do anything he wouldn't do and didn't do."

"He was an amazing person," said Ricky Skaggs, who served under Kalsu in the A Battery. "He was the leader who could motivate you without demeaning you, he was a true leader. He would keep you about as good as you could be in those conditions. If you had to be in that position, he'd be the one you'd want to be with."

"He was respected," said Sgt. Al Martin, A Battery. "That's something as an officer if you don't have, you don't need to be there. He wasn't like the rest of the officers sitting on his ass watching us work. The guy he was killed with, Johnson, they were opposite as day and night, but best of friends. They always competed. We carried two rounds apiece, they would carry three, humping 300 pounds from the helipad."

Martin said Kalsu rarely discussed his football days. He was more interested in talking about his family back home.

"He just didn't," said Martin. "We knew about it, but that's where it stayed. He was a common person. You wouldn't know who he was. He was a family man."

His death came just two days before the birth of his son and it sent shockwaves through an already battered firebase.

"That absolutely blew my mind," said Anckaitis, recalling the moment he'd heard Kalsu had been killed. "I knew he was expecting a baby, bit I don't know if I knew how close it was. Just knowing he'd been killed, it was a shock. It was like… this guy is so invincible."

In the late afternoon hours of July 21, 1970, Kalsu was killed by shrapnel from an incoming mortar round outside the fire direction center. The same round killed Johnson and Robert Flores, a member of Bravo Company, which was pulling guard duty on the firebase at the time. Seven others were injured in the mortar attack.

The culmination of a downed Chinook just three days earlier set into motion the wheels of evacuation. Forty-eight hours after Kalsu's death, there would be no one left on the firebase. Everyone was evacuated in the hours after Alpha Company was nearly decimated in the valley to the east of the firebase.

Those 48 hours were hell for those on the firebase, a hell made even worse for the men of A Battery, those who served with, and loved, Kalsu.

"That's probably the worst time, when we lost those guys," remembered Skaggs. "That really freaked me out."

At 12:45 a.m. July 23, in St. Anthony Hospital, Oklahoma City, Okla., Robert Todd Kalsu was born. The family was thrilled with the arrival and everyone knew that Bob would be exuberant over news he'd be the father of a boy. By the afternoon, a young lieutenant had made his way to the Darrow home, where he learned Jan was at a nearby hospital where she had just given birth early that day.

One of Jan's sisters called the hospital to inform the doctor, Philip

Maguire, who had delivered the young Robert. Despite the fact that the young lieutenant did not tell the family why he was there, they knew.

"My doctor came in that afternoon," remembered Jan. "He said, 'Jan, a soldier is coming in to talk to you.' (Maguire) just put his arm around me. Meanwhile, the soldier, he's crying too. I looked at my doctor and told him I don't want to be here, to let me go home."

In those days, new mothers typically stayed in the hospital days after giving birth. Jan wanted only to be home, around family. Her doctor saw that it happened. Jan had one more order of business before she left the hospital.

"Bob and I, we were going to use part of Bob's name for one son and part for another. I asked to see the statistician and asked to change our son's name to Bob's name."

Jan admitted being in shock for some time after hearing her husband had been killed a world away. When he returned home, she was asked if she wanted to see the body. She didn't. She couldn't.

"His uncle went because his parents couldn't go," said Jan. "Later, in the mail, I got his suitcase, his regular clothes and his wedding band. I cried when I saw the wedding band. It was then I knew how hard he had been working. His band had been worn smooth. I just cried."

17

Nowhere to Go

Lt. John Smith was a career-minded offer from the ROTC (Reserve Officer Training Corps) program at Tennessee Technological University in Cookeville, east of Nashville, halfway to Knoxville along I-40. He ended up in Vietnam in May 1970, assigned to Delta Company, 1st/506th, which operated in the area of Firebase Kathryn, east of Ripcord.

"I was an eager 23-year-old first lieutenant when I was sent to Ripcord," said Smith. "Eagerness has a way of disappearing when the lead starts flying, but you quickly learn to function."

Smith and the rest of Delta Company, under the command of Capt. Don Workman, aka Ranger, would soon be tested. He discussed the tremendous responsibility that came with leading young men into combat.

"I took being a leader very serious," said Smith. "I did not think I was better than any of my guys, and I felt totally responsible for their well-being. I worked hard to bond with them; not in the sense of being their buddy, I was never anyone's buddy, but in the sense of making sure they knew I shared every hardship and discomfort they did. I dug holes, I humped a full ruck, I went on patrols, I did everything they did. However, my first obligation was to lead men in combat. In that role, I did have to be tougher than was natural for me. They were my primary personal weapon. They had to clean their weapons. They had to pull guard duty – without going to sleep. They had to be quiet, both in our NDP (night defensive position) and during movement. I could, by virtue of my rank, insist that they do things they did not want to do on occasion. By the same token, I felt I had to lead within certain boundaries. Simply saying 'do thus and so' wouldn't always get desired results. Occasionally I was challenged."

Just a day or so earlier, Smith showed his leadership.

"I took a patrol out and down a hill from the company patrol base," he remembered. "The vegetation was very thick and the terrain was very rough and steep. At the base of the hillside we suddenly came to a clearing. Across the clearing was an entrance to a cave. I knew the company would be staying on the ridgeline above the cave that night, and I simply could not in good faith just ignore the possibility that the cave was occupied. At the same time, I was not willing to send any of my guys across that rocky open area to check out the cave. After some soul searching I pointed out our location to my RTO (Radio Telephone Operator) and a few others. I said, 'Here is where we are. I am going to go inside the entrance to that cave. If there is anyone in there I am dead. If that happens, don't worry about me; I'd be past saving. Call Ranger and tell him where you are so he can send someone to get you out of here.'

"With that, I pulled the pin on a grenade and held the spoon in place with my right hand, flipped my M-16 on rock n' roll (fully automatic), and started across the clearing. Fortunately there were no live dinks in there, at least none that wished to make their presence known. There were two dead ones just inside the entrance so I figured that if they were there in that shape there wasn't likely to be anyone else inside, so I replaced the pin and waved the rest of the patrol on over. In hindsight, that was an utterly stupid thing to do. My demise would have caused all kinds of problems for them, but it did get their attention."

He would need it over the next few days.

The men of Delta Company, 1st/506th, awoke the morning of July 20 in the area of Triple Hill to a bright sun fueling a hot day. A scheduled re-supply was to be accompanied by a move east, toward Hill 805. During the re-supply, Smith got word that, back home, his wife was pregnant. With little time to celebrate or ponder the future, soon, it was simply back to work.

"The helicopters came in and lifted first platoon out to be transported to the new ridgeline. The scheme was for first platoon to secure the south side of the LZ (Landing Zone) and second and third platoons would secure the north side of the LZ. The contrast in temperature was amazing as we lifted off. The air was cool; a very welcome respite from the suffocating temps on the ground.

"We were unaware that first platoon had already made contact at the new LZ, but as we approached, the door gunners suddenly alerted and started firing up the area. A quick look at the left gunner's face told me this was the real deal. Suddenly I felt very vulnerable as I sat in the doorway. I stuck my head out and took a look at the LZ as we approached and had the sensation of being drawn like a magnet. It was almost surreal as I realized that I was going into a hot LZ and there was nothing I could do about it. In my head I knew I was not much of a target moving at the speed we were going and from a few feet away you could not really distinguish an individual riding inside the bird, but my heart told me I was 10 feet tall and a very large target. Then the training takes over and you do what you have to do.

"Once on the ground we moved to the north side of the LZ to establish security for the CP (Command Post) and third platoon."

Smith soon realized his platoon sergeant was not on the ground even though all the choppers had landed. Later it was realized the final chopper in was hit and had turned back toward Evans rather than risk landing, or crashing on the landing zone.

"He later described watching 51-caliber tracers coming at them, which looked like baseballs," said Smith. "The point being that getting shot at has a way of getting your attention."

The remainder of the company did arrive and the landing zone was secured.

"What happened next was totally unbelievable to me," said Smith. "During the remainder of the insertion, the gunships were escorting the lift birds, the door gunners were firing, and we on the ground were firing suppressive fire as the birds approached. I would think that everybody within five klicks would know we were there. However, three dinks apparently did not get the word. We were getting organized in preparation of moving up the ridgeline to the north when these three guys actually walked into our perimeter. They were carrying two AKs and a hoe-like digging tool on their shoulders. They were totally oblivious to our presence. Fortunately one of our machine gun crews was watching the trail where it entered the perimeter and saw them coming. The gunner was standing up and yelling 'Dinks!' as he opened fire. He held the trigger and fired about 150 rounds of M-60 ammo into them at point-blank range. I turned around as I was diving for the ground and saw them literally 'dancing' in the air as they fell to the ground in a mangled heap. They were dead before they hit the ground, and the damage to the human body caused by 100 or so rounds of 7.62mm ammunition is truly amazing. They were the first people I actually saw die in combat."

Smith expressed amazement at his total lack of feeling for them, despite their apparent youthful age. His reaction came as a shock, he'd later write.

"I wasn't angry, I wasn't happy, I wasn't sad," he said. "I was just nothing."

Later that night, the company set up a night defensive position while first platoon, under Lt. Randall Thompson, moved off the LZ to the south and immediately ran into contact. Part of the routine for setting up a night defensive position was to patrol around the potential site in a cloverleaf pattern while some stayed within the perimeter to prepare holes for fighting positions.

"All of us were well into our preparations in the late afternoon when all of a sudden we heard gunfire from the first platoon area," said Smith. "They were setting up approximately one kilometer from the rest of the company and encountered an established enemy position very near their NDP (Night Defensive Position). A brief firefight ensued and I started getting my mind geared up for the possibility of going to their rescue. I cannot tell you what actually happened at their site, but they took heavy casualties and had to pull back as evening was rapidly approaching. Medevacs were called and Capt. Workman (Ranger) sent me and a squad down to the LZ to secure it as the wounded were brought down.

"After consulting with Lt. Thompson, Ranger decided to bring the remainder of first platoon back to the company position consisting of second and third platoons and the remnants of first platoon. I was struck by the subdued appearance of first platoon as they came off their hill."

Smith said the gravity of the moment was clearly evident as he saw his fellow troopers.

"A few hours earlier they were typical GIs, horsing around and in a reasonably good mood. Now my friend, Lt. Thompson, was totally changed. He had gone from a cocky, colorful stud to total disbelief at the turn of events; troubled by the fact that so many of his men, including himself, were now wounded, but moreso by the fact that they had been unable to retrieve their buddies when they left. Personally I felt for him and his guys, but professionally I knew where we would be going the next morning, and I dreaded it."

The North Vietnamese knew too, as troops from the 101st Airborne Division did not leave their dead behind. The NVA would be watching and waiting, and Delta Company knew it.

Once the casualties from first platoon were evacuated, Smith took the rest of the men and the squad that had been sent to secure the landing zone back up the hill to the company position. With 10 extra men and a hard, rocky ground within the position, preparations weren't as strong as the men would have liked. It was time to rest in preparation for the next day's mission.

"Despite a sense of foreboding regarding the next day's mission of recovering our dead... I was surprised at how easy it was to go to sleep that night due to the exhaustion of the day of close combat in stifling heat," Smith said. "In fact, it was difficult to stay awake while pulling guard duty. What we did not realize at the time was that the dinks knew exactly where we were and they had their own agenda for us, which did not include us coming back to their position to retrieve our comrades. They intended to kill us."

Listening posts reported movement outside the perimeter during the night and the thought was an NVA attack was imminent, but no such attack materialized.

Delta Gets Out

At first light, the men from Delta Company packed up and prepared to break camp. Workman had yet to call regarding the day's plans, but everyone knew what was ahead.

"Suddenly I heard some mortar tubes begin to pop," said Lt. John

Smith. "As a cherry lieutenant, I wasn't sure I knew what I was hearing, but in a few seconds I hear three rounds explode in the vicinity of the LZ (Landing Zone) we had come in on (July 20). As I started toward the CP (Command Post), I saw Ranger already calling in counter mortar fire. That was all the confirmation I needed to start alerting my guys to take cover. The next rounds hit approximately halfway up the hill and I knew the next adjustment would be on us. I had experienced some mortar fire previously, but none of it was controlled and it was of very limited duration. I expected that this time as well. Boy was I wrong. The tubes started popping and it seemed they would never stop. I could not believe it. Then the rounds started falling on us. That is at once horrifying and frustrating. You know they are coming. You have no idea where they are going to hit but you imagine they might actually hit directly on you, and it's frustrating because there is not one thing you can do about it except hope and pray."

Delta was hit hard and took numerous casualties. Two were killed, including Smith's medic.

"To say the scene was chaotic is a gross understatement," Smith wrote, "but we finally moved off the hill even though the mortars were still falling, including some rounds containing CS gas. Once we returned to the LZ we started evacuating the wounded once again."

The day continued with at least three more ground attacks, according to Smith, which were broken up by Cobra gunship support as well as some F-4 Phantoms, the fast movers. The company took few additional casualties, however several choppers were damaged as ammunition was brought in and men flown out. A medevac was shot down by an RPG (Rocket-Propelled Grenade) and partially blocked the landing zone to further traffic.

"Both Ranger and myself had been hit but neither of us seriously so," said Smith. "Neither of us were inclined to leave the battlefield under our own power."

Reinforcements from Delta Company, 2nd/506th, arrived midday, noted Smith, "a welcome sight indeed."

"Again, not being privy to everything going on in the command post, and for what reason I don't know, we spent the rest of the afternoon digging in to prepare for another night in a place that every dink this side of Hanoi knew we were. At that point I was not optimistic about surviving this battle," wrote Smith. "Suddenly there was a radio call that told us to prepare to evacuate. I speculate here, but I suspect that was in reaction to the decision at a much higher level to evacuate and close Ripcord and the AO (Area of Operations) surrounding it. Needless to say, we were glad to get out of there despite the gnawing at our conscience of leaving three bodies on the south side of the battle area. Ranger assigned me to the first lift, and I was very happy to oblige. I ran across the LZ and dove into the bird and was up and away, totally oblivious to the fact that I would never see Capt. Workman again. When I last saw him he was standing tall and erect on the edge of the LZ directing traffic as the birds came in."

A string of helicopters approached as the bird Smith rode out on departed. Subsequent choppers took fire from another 51-caliber, one of which crashed onto the landing zone. It was the fifth chopper in and the Huey took fire and began to sway and flipped onto its side. A rotor sliced Workman in half, his head and shoulders landing under the machine while his legs fell to the earth. For his actions those two days, he was posthumously awarded the Silver Star.

Larry Kern was piloting the bird that crashed. Despite the crash, his actions in the bird saved lives, avoiding a crash onto numerous troops gathered at the landing zone. A veteran pilot with the A/158th Ghostriders, a group that flew throughout the A Shau, Kern had been under fire and shot down several times while flying in support of Ripcord since March. July 21 proved to be a day that still lives in his mind, though. He and his crew left early that morning on what was explained as a rescue mission.

"My co-pilot was James 'Weasel' Sanders, an active admiral's son and one of my best friends," Kern would remember. "Door gunner was Specialist 5 'Mac' William McFarland. I had not flown with McFarland but a few times before that day. I believe he was in the second platoon and I was in the first. Crew chief was Specialist 5 Ned Epps, a really nice kid who was always upbeat and seemed to be very good at his job."

Delta was pinned down and under fire on and around a small, cleared saddleback on a ridgeline to the south and below Hill 605, across the valley, east and below Hill 805. The Ghostriders, accompanied by Cobras, flew reinforcements in and out under heavy fire and no one had been shot down, remembered Kern.

"Those reinforcements had to be put in on the hot LZ on Hill 605 because the saddleback LZ was actually much more dangerous to land on than 605," said Kern. "The plan was for the elements of the 2/506th, which now had been inserted on 605, to move to the south, down the ridgeline. Then, with the help of air support, the new troops would reinforce and rescue the troops that had been decimated the previous night. We would then return to pick up all remaining soldiers from the area after the mission was accomplished."

The pilots returned to Camp Evans after the insertion and were riding an adrenaline high.

"After being scared shitless and dodging the big one, young guys get a natural high," said Kern, who earned the nickname "Crash" for the number of times he had gone down in Vietnam.

As the pilots awaited a call to return, Kern learned his position was

NOWHERE TO GO

changed from Chalk 4 to Chalk 2, or lead aircraft. Crash, who had just turned 21 the month prior, questioned the move.

"I keyed my mic and said, 'Hey guys, I don't think I'm ready to lead a mission. What say you?' Irish (Capt. William Glennon) agreed. 'Yes Crash, it's too soon,' Irish said. "

Crash elevated his chopper, hovered to the left and fell back into position, a violation of pilot superstition he remembered. "You never switch your luck," he said.

Now flying Chalk 4 (fourth in line) among nearly a dozen choppers, the crew began to tune to the frequency of the troops on the ground amassing at the appropriate landing zone.

Intense enemy fire erupted from the west side of the landing zone. A medevac chopper had already been shot down and instructions were to go in low, then fly east off the landing zone, under the next aircraft in. The men on the ground were surrounded. Chopper crew chiefs were ordered to check their weapons.

"I gave them the green light to check their weapons," said Kern. "That meant that they were able to fire a number of rounds from their M-60s to confirm they were in firing order. Both McFarland and Epps opened up for about five to 10 seconds. The sound of the weapons clattering stopped, but the increasing sound of our heartbeats began as we approached the mountain ridgelines.

"Due to the LZ site and the fact that a major portion of the LZ was blocked by the downed medevac, we could land only one aircraft at a time. And needing to fly out 180 degrees back to the east… we were forced to approach the landing zone single file (not uncommon in I Corps because we regularly landed on similar LZs under fire on mountaintops and ridgelines). As we neared the LZ, I remember looking at the aircraft in line in front of me and thinking how beautiful the sight was. The green mountains in the distance framing the Hueys in a way that was very peaceful. We came in with a little over 200 yards of spacing.

"As Irish approached the opening on the ridge, he radioed 'Chalk 1 LZ cold!' As he said that, I saw large green tracers coming at him from his 12 o'clock, originating from the ridgeline to the west of the landing zone, midway up the slope of Hill 805. I radioed to him 'No Chalk, you're taking fire from your 12!' At that time he did his pedal turn and radioed that he was taking fire. I could see the mortar rounds were hitting the LZ as well. Chalk 1 flew east underneath Chalk 2 as instructed.

Kern recommended McFarland resist firing as aircraft would be flying underneath. Chalk 2 began to take fire as well. Tracers were coming toward the Huey from both sides, prompting Kern to change his mind.

"Open up when you're ready," said Kern, "just be careful of our guys."

Chalk 3 took fire from the tracers of 51-caliber enemy fire from Hill 805 but escaped damage. The noise was ramping up, Kern noted, and AK-47 fire could now be heard as communications continued between the pilots and the men on the ground.

"At this point my aircraft started receiving heavy small arms fire from left, right and below," said Kern. "My crew began firing their M-60s furiously. The noise was deafening. Weasel said, 'Shit Crash, this is bad.' I looked at him and said, 'Let's get in and out fast, shadow the controls, OK?' He clicked his mic twice, meaning yes, and I tried to get into a numbing zone. I had to concentrate on the LZ so it was up to Weasel to watch the instruments and pay attention to everything around us while I focused on flying. He shadowed the controls meaning he put his hands lightly on the controls. He had to be ready to take over if I was hit."

NOWHERE TO GO

Kern's Huey was taking fire. Chalk 3 was on the landing zone, delayed as troops apparently panicked in an attempt to board the chopper, packing too many on the bird to fly. That forced Kern to slow, and fire on the chopper to increase.

"I heard some rounds strike the aircraft," said Kern. "An RPG flew past us and detonated late."

Crash keyed his mic and asked if he should rotate to the rear. Just then, Chalk 3 lifted and turned to leave the landing zone. Time slowed, Kern explained, as the events that would play out over the next few minutes seemingly happened in slow motion, feeling like hours.

"I saw the guys on the ground in trouble and knew I had to nose the aircraft toward the landing zone. Just as I nosed forward we were hit with a barrage of many rounds. It sounded like someone had thrown handfuls of stones on a tin roof, only it wasn't a roof, my gunner 'Mac' started screaming, 'Oh God I'm hit! Oh God I'm hit!' Things got worse quickly. I felt the hits and suddenly we took a hail of hits all at once. I turned to see McFarland in the right crew well. His M-60 was gone, totally blown away by an RPG. He looked like he was in shock as he held his hands, covered in blood, in front of his face. His helmet was badly damaged and he continued to scream. I knew we were in bad shape. We were too slow, too high and now the enemy had us zeroed in. I still had no place to move forward to because the men on the LZ were clustered where my aircraft needed to land."

Kern's chopper continued to take hits. Troops on the ground began to crouch as the feet approached 100 feet. Ground troops occasionally fired into the trees and mortars were landing to the left of the incoming chopper. Another round of 51-caliber fire rained in on the chopper.

"To our 12 o'clock they started hitting our aircraft with the force of sledgehammer-like hits," said Kern. "We needed to move out of the kill zone. I had to abort. I keyed my mic and said, 'Fuck this shit, Chalk 4, we are hit and taking more, our crew is wounded, I'm peeling off!' I turned the aircraft to the left to get out of the kill zone and head back to Camp Evans."

Kern banked left and took more 51-caliber hits. As he leveled off, Irish came over the radio and yelled, "Crash! You're on fire, you're on fire. Crash! You're 3 o'clock."

"I looked to my right rear and saw my worst fear," said Kern. "Fire. I looked and could see McFarland, who was still screaming, and behind him coming from the right side of the engine well was a steady flow of flames and smoke. Other pilots in my flight began yelling 'Crash, you're on fire, go back to the LZ!'"

That was the last thing Kern wanted to do. Chaos had erupted as McFarland couldn't communicate with Kern. He pondered turning off the fuel as he gazed west at the miles between him and Camp Evans.

"Now with fire involved, our only chance was to get down as fast as possible," said Kern. "I had no choice but to return to the only LZ that was within reach, so I kept turning to the left, making a circle. As we turned we were approximately 200 yards out and started receiving the same type of enemy fire as on our first run, only this time the 51-caliber was right on target. Rounds started to hit my windshield, spraying us with plexiglass and many of the instruments on my control panel actually began to explode, popping in little bursts of fire."

Weasel keyed his mic and notified Kern that they were losing power. Fuel was being lost. Kern told Weasel to kill the fuel and battery switches as the chopper touched down, hoping the fire would extinguish. Meanwhile, the aircraft was still taking hits.

"We were shocked to see the troops on the ground, not realizing our situation and frantic, were still waiting to be rescued on the spot where we needed to land," said Kern. "They started to scramble as we approached. By this time I would not have been able to stop if I tried.

NOWHERE TO GO

My hands were full. Weasel saw the troops were in danger and began waving his hands, trying to get them to move away."

As the chopper fell, just short of the apex of the hill, it took an RPG to the rotor system and a rotor was lost, hurling the machine to the right and onto the ground. What was left of the rotor continued to spin and sliced Workman in half. Amazingly, no one else on the ground was injured.

Dust and smoke filled the cockpit. The noise and commotion of radio traffic was now replaced by explosions on the ground, small-arms fire and McFarland, still screaming.

"I looked toward my co-pilot and could not see him," said Kern. "I thought he had disappeared, been vaporized or thrown out somehow."

The 51-caliber shots continued to hit the aircraft. Kern, who was hanging over Weasel, yelled to his co-pilot to get out.

"I looked out what was left of my windscreen and... the damn 51s are still firing at us," said Kern. "I released my seatbelt and fell into Weasel's seat. I crawled to the back of the aircraft, which was filled with smoke and dust, but no one was there. The small of my back was hurting and as I climbed up the floor of the chopper, which was now a wall, I thought I must have been shot in the back. I got out the top of the aircraft, what was really the left side of the aircraft, and found that I was perched on top in plain sight of everyone in Northern I Corps with a weapon. My back was in extreme pain. I had to get off that aircraft. I scrambled over the skids and dropped to the ground approximately seven to eight feet. My legs collapsed and I fell to the ground in a yoga position. My chicken plate (chest armor) was forced up into my chin from my waist and I was knocked into a dazed state."

Kern thought he had been paralyzed. Dazed, he could hear but couldn't feel anything below his neck. He was propped upright by the armor, sitting at the top of the rise of the landing zone, facing the same direction as the nose of his downed chopper. The 51s were still firing toward him and he could hear them going by his head and see the rounds ripping up the dirt around him.

"I could still see the green 51-caliber tracers coming at me and I knew I would die at any second," said Kern. "I had accepted it as my fate. It was very peaceful. I was ready. It felt good. It was over."

The trance Kern found himself in was broken with shouts of "Crash! Crash! Get down Crash!"

"I could start to move again and I fell forward to the ground and began to feel my body again," said Kern. "The voice belonged to Weasel, who was below me on the hill. 'Get off the top of the rise, they're shooting at you!' I rolled away from the rise and started crawling toward him. I got behind the body of a soldier for cover. I pulled out my mighty Smith and Wesson .38 and knew we were dead. At that point I noticed again the LZ was covered with dead. We looked around and there were no live ground soldiers that we could see. Epps, who had gotten out the other side of the aircraft, joined us from behind the tail of the aircraft and he had an M-16."

At that point Kern realized his face was covered in blood. He couldn't feel his nose. "They'll sew it back on," he told Weasel, who had noticed the blood. "'Where is Mac?' I asked. Weasel and Epps shrugged their shoulders."

The men were then approached by a soldier who crawled from the tree line on the south end of the landing zone. "Follow me, we have to get away from the aircraft," the soldier told the crew. "We need to find our gunner," Kern told the soldier. "He is crushed under the aircraft," the soldier said. "I am sorry sir, but he died. The men on the other side of the LZ told us he is dead."

The brave young soldier corralled the men and led them off the landing zone, advising each to grab a weapon and a steel pot (helmet) from a downed soldier. Kern froze and began to shake.

"McFarland was dead," said Kern. "This was the first guy I had lost. He was my responsibility. I failed. I felt like I was supposed to do something but had no idea what that could be."

The crew was now infantry and followed the lead of the grunt that came to save them. He was their lifeline. They crawled nose to heel with Sanders (Weasel) behind the soldier, then Kern, then Epps. Each grabbed weapons and protection from dead soldiers on the LZ as they approached a tree.

"I couldn't take his helmet," Kern said. "I didn't want to see his face. I could not look at the dead. It was too much for me to absorb. I felt odd taking his weapon and I tried to keep from looking directly at him. It was all so overwhelming. I was flying minutes before and now I was crawling among the dead and knew I was probably soon to be dead as well."

Once they reached a tree line, Kern saw eight to 10 other soldiers in foxholes. Several waved frantically urging the flight crew to press on. The hole was about four feet square and about four feet deep. Kern was still in shock and, now, amazed to be alive.

"You were shot down sir," the soldier told Kern. "You have some wounds but you're going to be fine. I am sorry you got shot down trying to get us sir. We appreciate it."

"This kid was sorry we got shot down," Kern said. "I felt like shit. I failed. I must have fucked up. A better pilot would have done something different. I asked him how bad our situation was."

"Very bad," he said to Kern. "We lost a lot of guys since yesterday and we probably won't get out, we could be overrun at any time."

The men were in NVA bunkers. Crawl holes extended from the bottom of the bunkers into underground systems. Cobras fired from above and smoke remained thick in the air.

"There was smoke in the air and a smell that was a mix of explosives and the smell of blood," said Kern. "There was small arms fire just below us in the trees. The mortars had stopped. I looked at the kid and said, 'It seems to have gotten quieter.' He said, 'Yea. It gets hot while you guys come in. They really start hitting us when the choppers come in. You guys got the hell shot out of you. We really thank you sir.'"

A specialist 5 then grabbed Kern and told him command and control wanted to speak with him. He grabbed the radio and identified himself and his aircraft. Kern glanced at what was left of his aircraft as the man at the other end of the line said he thought the entire crew had been killed. Kern told him the location of the 51s and soon the Air Force was dropping napalm on the positions

"An Air Force jet fell out of the sky and dropped napalm on the targets," said Kern, "lighting them up with huge balls of fire. Then a second jet did the same, followed by a third. For a few seconds I was delighted at the thought of killing the bastards that had played a big part in shooting us down and killing my crew chief. I hoped they didn't die. I hoped they were wandering around burned to crisp but not dead."

Cobra fire was called in on top of Delta's positions after which the men were to cross the landing zone. All the preparatory fire worked as they crossed without being fired upon. As Kern crossed, he caught a glimpse of McFarland. He was wounded, but alive. The aircraft had fallen on him, however soldiers had freed him and prepped him for departure by placing him on a litter.

"I was told by ground troops that my aircraft had killed an officer who was rushing to get on my aircraft, not knowing we were crashing," said Kern. "He was about to go home in days. His name was Capt. Workman 'Ranger'. With its one remaining rotor blade, my aircraft decapitated him as it flung on its side, killing the captain instantly. He was going to leave the unit in six days and go home in three weeks. To this day I am still haunted by that fact."

NOWHERE TO GO

Capt. Charlie Lieb (Charlie Company) was a roommate of Workman at West Point, both members of the lacrosse team prior to leaving for Vietnam. "He was a very good lacrosse goalie, I think All-America. He was a regimental commander, one of the top-five positions at West Point. I had a lot of respect for Donnie Workman."

Smith and elements of Delta Company had made it back without knowing what had happened at the LZ they had just left.

"I rode blissfully to the rear in Camp Evans," said Smith. "When I stepped off the bird, the first sergeant approached me and said, 'Ranger didn't make it.' I was totally dumbfounded. Not fifteen minutes earlier we were elated to be getting out of there and he was completing his last mission in Vietnam and all was well, then I am told he is dead? I was simply stunned, too stunned to really react. I was disappointed at the death of my medic, but was emotionally prepared to deal with such losses. But Ranger's death was so totally unexpected that I simply had no mechanism in my being to deal with that."

Delta arrived two days earlier with about 95 people, Smith estimated, a nearly full company for that time in the 101st Airborne Division. Twenty-five were extracted on July 21.

"I believe we lost seven KIA (killed in action), but we had a ton wounded."

Kern was in awe at the bravery of the men of Delta Company.

"At least half a dozen times during the ordeal some of the guys thanked me for coming into the LZ to try to pull them out and two of them actually said they were sorry we had to try to get them," said Kern. "The men knew we were fish out of water and did their best to take care of us."

Once they reached the landing zone, Kern was approached by a young soldier carrying his chicken plate, which had been discarded earlier.

"He came up to me and asked me if I wanted my armor plate and handed it to me," remembered Kern. "'Thanks for trying to help us, sir. I'm sorry your pilot got hurt.' He had carried that 20-pound object all the way from the saddleback LZ while we were under attack and in danger of being killed. I was overwhelmed that he would do that for me.

Maj. Gen. Ben Harrison (retired) is pictured at the Ripcord Association reunion of 2014 at Myrtle Beach, S.C. Photo provided by Chris Brady.

Two weeks after the evacuation of Firebase Ripcord, Col. Ben Harrison ordered the Brigade Reconnaissance Platoon to fly in and recover those

Delta Company soldiers that had been killed in action July 21. After some resistance to the mission, Harrison himself ordered the sergeant questioning the mission to the helipad where Harrison ordered him in and flew him to the area near 805 to explain how the bodies would be recovered.

Upon returning to Evans, a platoon was gathered and flew back to the area, accompanied by two Cobras, went in and recovered the bodies. Harrison's slick took most of the bodies, which included Workman. The smell was explained as simply horrible and it was hard for the men to not get sick, Harrison noted.

"I could not believe we were leaving first platoon's KIAs (Killed In Action) behind when the order came down for us to leave the LZ (Landing Zone) where all the action had taken place," said Smith. "We had two or three KIAs on the north side of the LZ that were going to be extracted with us, however all that changed too when the final aircraft was shot down and Ranger was killed. Of course, by that time, I had no knowledge of what was happening as my bird was heading toward Evans. Upon returning to the rear I was told what had happened and that all of our bodies had to be left behind for retrieval at a later date.

"I felt a double sense of depression knowing we had left bodies behind (in addition to losing Ranger), and I also knew that we would have to go back in there to get them and that place was crawling with dinks who would be waiting for us to return. Of course, at that moment I had no idea that I would go to Charlie Med and be forwarded to the Evac hospital, making the exercise a moot issue for me. I still felt that we had failed them when I woke up in Phu Bai and that feeling did not leave for several days. Dammit, that still hurts."

Escalating Danger

Lt. William Pahissa radioed Capt. Chuck Hawkins with word that a high-speed trail and communication wire had been discovered by

Alpha One. It ran at the base of Hill 805 and was tapped so that a Kit Carson Scout attached to Hawkins' company could listen in. It was around 3 p.m. July 20.

The wire ran from a mortar unit firing upon Ripcord from the Hill 805 area to an enemy division headquarters in the area of Hill 902. The Kit Carson relayed to Hawkins that Ripcord was effectively surrounded by as many as four regiments. It was information that was not entirely shocking, but the realization that so many NVA were in the area

Hawkins and the rest of Alpha Company, armed with information gleaned from the wiretap, were on the move. Lt. Col. Andre Lucas had informed Hawkins in a secure radio conversation that he wanted Alpha Company to take a prisoner. Lucas wanted further confirmation of the NVA numbers.

"Division apparently had some reservations about the veracity of the wiretap information," Hawkins wrote. "I was flabbergasted, but I gave him a WILCO (will comply).

"I led with third platoon. They were doing OK with their E-5 platoon leader. I placed my CP (Command Post) directly behind third. I think (Lt. William) Pahissa and first were next and (Lt. Lee) Widjeskog and second pulled drag. We had not gone more than 200 meters in the direction we'd been the day prior when the point team for third platoon jumped three enemy, wounding one severely, and maybe wounding the two that got away. The wounded enemy didn't make it."

Blood trails led to no enemy bodies, and the one found had been wounded severely, with brain matter leaking from his skull and his breaths sporadic. Therefore the decision was made to put the enemy out of his misery.

"I held the company in place while I tried to figure out options," said

Hawkins. "I didn't want to move to link up with (Capt. Don) Workman and D-1/506. That mission of several days ago had long been overcome by events. I felt it would be too risky; too many potential enemy. The low ground in the vicinity of the wiretap bothered me. I had a nice, long debate with myself while the rest of the company maintained a secure posture."

Hawkins would continue his thoughts: "The enemy situation was unclear to a large extent, but I did have some firm ideas about his posture: There was considerable enemy strength on the backside (southeast and east) of Hill 805. From the wiretap we knew there was a suspected enemy mortar regiment in that area and was probably protected by a couple battalions of infantry – battalions that had probably committed forces to the successive nighttime battles for Hill 805. We also knew the general path of the commo wire and high-speed trail, and that it very likely terminated at the enemy's division HQ (headquarters) farther up the lower part of the Coc Muen ridgeline to our west. How was the division HQ defended? With a battalion? Maybe. A company, at least. I thought, seriously, about moving toward the division HQ. We'd have to move cross compartment to get to the ridge and then move uphill. I wasn't too keen on that notion, but did consider that I could achieve the element of surprise.

"But what if we did tangle with enemy units around a division HQ? Who would come to our aid if we needed it? And we certainly would have. I knew that the battalion was spread thinly in the AO (area of operations); that the 2/501 had been withdrawn. Only Workman and I were in the field, and Bravo Company on Ripcord. Could brigade or division provide reinforcing units to assist if I got in trouble? If they could, where would they find an LZ (landing zone) to go in? A lot had been written about 'pile on tactics' occasionally used in Vietnam, but at this point, there weren't a lot of places to pile on to, LZ-wise. Brer Rabbit and the Tar Baby came to mind, and we were the Tar Baby.

"Finally I called a leadership council and gave my instructions for the day. We would keep to what high ground there was in the valley we'd entered, but would move a few hundred meters west of the previous day's line of march. Then we'd hole up in a daytime defensive posture, put out LP/OPs (listening post/observation post) to try to entice the enemy to come to us. Better to be on defense at this point, I thought."

As the day wore on, Hawkins chose to hold the daytime defensive position. A team from first platoon would be sent out before dark to scout and secure a night defensive position. The company would later move into place. "I was satisfied with the plan and company leaders bought into it," noted Hawkins.

Robert Journell and Russell Walker engaged a pair of enemy soldiers in the afternoon hours of July 21, killing one with a head shot and possibly wounding the other, Hawkins said. Journell reported that the dead enemy's head just "exploded like hitting a watermelon." The surviving soldier escaped, but members of Alpha Company found documents, including a courier pouch with detailed map and communication from the North Vietnamese Army headquarters.

"I felt that nailing an enemy courier team and the captured documents and map satisfied Lucas' desire to get a prisoner," said Hawkins.

A secure radio conference call with Lucas that night and other battalion elements was revealing to Hawkins.

"(The call) hinted at possible withdrawal from the AO (area of operations), but there were no specific instructions at that time," he said. "I figured that the next day, July 22, I would continue to move the company west-northwest to the next ridge and then ease up the ridge to be near a (landing zone) I knew about.

"The night of the 21st we were quiet, didn't dig in, made as little noise as possible. Our collective gut knew that too many enemy soldiers had gotten away when we'd had our sharp, one-sided fights with them. We knew the enemy had to be looking for us. But we were ghosts and they hadn't found us yet. Could we stay that way?"

That night and into the early morning hours, an answer came as enemy scouts tripped a grenade booby trap left behind in the prior day's daytime defensive position.

"(William) Baldwin and Jody Smith had put a grenade inside an empty C-ration can, attached a trip wire and pulled the pin," said Hawkins. "The can kept the spoon from flying off until it was pulled from the can by someone hitting the trip wire. We knew with certitude that the enemy was looking for us, and in the middle of the night they had to be serious."

Alpha Two was with the rest of the company in the valley below Hill 805 to the southwest.

"We stayed there until it got almost dark then sent some guys to the next knoll and abandoned the original knoll. We did something we weren't supposed to do. They booby-trapped the dead body and left him back on the other knoll. When we moved over to the second knoll, it was a couple hours after dark, we were trying to keep quiet. We heard that grenade go off and you could see the flash and explosion. We really didn't see or hear anything else the rest of the night."

A Decision Is Made

Gen. Sid Berry decided to evacuate Ripcord, a decision he seemingly was trying to justify just after 5 a.m. July 22 in a letter he had written to his wife. Citing mounting casualties and a need to do something different, he stopped short of affirming the evacuation. That would come later in the day, though he acknowledged in a subsequent letter that he had made the decision that morning.

REMEMBERING FIREBASE RIPCORD

At 9:30 p.m. Berry wrote, "Must get some rest, get up at 4 AM, and be in the air by 5 tomorrow to oversee tomorrow's operation – extraction from RIPCORD. This morning I made the most difficult professional decision of my life: to get out of RIPCORD as quickly as possible. Easier said than done."

Lt. John Fox piloted Berry in the command and control chopper throughout July and respected the general immensely. The decision to leave Ripcord weighed heavily on the general, as did the mounting casualties.

"You never used the word retreat around him," said Fox, who pulled three tours in Vietnam, dating back to the days when Americans were still referred to as advisors. "He wanted to stay but he realized it was an untenable situation and we had to pull back, move or do it another way. We were not in position to support this thing. We didn't have enough protection.

"He made the decision to go ahead and pull out of Ripcord. It was the toughest decision I think he ever made, but he knew it was the right decision. It was bad it had to be that way. There was no harshness between (Col. Ben) Harrison and Berry. Both agreed it had to be done. The mood was – (Berry) hated to do this. It was against his grain. He was a warrior."

While Berry knew extraction was necessary, his letters clearly indicated he had concerns.

Berry would years later, in the June 1986 edition of the "Ripcord Report" would write, "The shooting down of the artillery ammunition resupply Chinook helicopter the early afternoon of 18 July and the resulting destruction of guns and ammunition supplies set in motion our re-evaluation of the situation at Ripcord which resulted in my decision to withdraw from Fire Support Base Ripcord.

NOWHERE TO GO

"The decision to withdraw from, on and around Ripcord was the most difficult decision I have ever made. No soldier, least of all a commander of the 101st Airborne Division, ever wants to withdraw or retreat. That goes against our nature – and should. Yet, all things considered, I made what I believed to be the correct decision; and I believe the subsequent events confirmed the soundness of my decision."

Berry detailed the chain of events that led to his decision in a speech to the Ripcord Association in 1985.

"The total casualties during the period 13 March and 23 July, in the Ripcord area, were 68 killed, 443 wounded… Sixty-eight dead, 443 wounded… When does it become no longer worthwhile to stay in the Ripcord area? That's a lot of casualties. For what? Well, the long or the medium term – intermediate term – 'for what' is that the division is pulling out pretty soon. So that makes casualties which are dear by an measure ever dearer – if you know you're going to take casualties and then you're pulling out.

"On the 15th of July, I became the acting division commander for about the next three weeks because Gen. Jack Hennessey – having been in Vietnam for over a year with that division, and he'd been on a previous tour – was going back (for the marriage of his daughter). So he left, leaving me with instructions to continue planning for the offensive out toward the A Shau."

Berry noted that July 7-8 the 2nd Battalion, 17 Cavalry discovered another North Vietnamese regiment in the area of Khe Sanh moving from Laos toward Ripcord. That movement diverted the attention of division and produced the joint operation of the 101st and 1st ARVN (Army of the Republic of Vietnam) Division.

"And then – really the turning point in my mind – this was three days after I took acting command of the division on the 15th – most of us, many of us saw this. I happened to be flying in the area when I saw it."

He, of course, was referencing the Chinook being shot down.

"That was really the beginning of the end of our being on Ripcord," Berry said. "We lost six guns. We lost two 106mm recoilless rifles. We lost a lot of other equipment there, and we lost some people…That raised the question: Should we continue staying on Ripcord? Remember, we lost six of 12 guns, and we lost the guns that could fire closest to our infantry that were out around in the jungle. Now there was a very quick reaction to that. The brigade commander, then Harrison, both of us in the air – he contacted me by radio and said, 'We've got to open a new firebase.'"

Plans for the evacuation came together quickly and confidence grew as the hours passed.

"We had asked for five battalions to be OPCON (operational command) to us so we could take the fight to the enemy," said S3 Fred Spaulding of the meeting he attended with Berry and Harrison where Berry first mentioned extraction. "Berry told Col. Harrison, 'You're not getting five battalions.' There's a bit of difference as to what was said next," admitted Spaulding. "I was the briefing officer, standing right there. I am told not to leave until the commander tells me to leave. The briefing officer is supposed to stay there, listen to everything. I'm standing behind Berry; Berry wasn't looking at me he was looking at Harrison. (Berry) said, 'No, you're not getting your five battalions,' so Col. Harrison says we need to pull them out. (Berry said) 'You're going to withdraw under fire, while surrounded?' Harrison says, 'Yes sir, that's exactly what we intend to do.' Berry said, 'Impossible!' That's when Col. Harrison looked and me and said 'Fred, get on it.' He'd never called me by my first name before. Berry spun around because he didn't know anyone was standing there. He didn't know there was a witness standing there. I'm on my way out the door and Berry said, 'Captain!' I said, 'Yes sir.' (Berry said) You mean to tell me you're going to withdraw from four different locations while under fire?' I said, 'Yes sir, but it's only three locations.' He said, 'Impossible!'"

NOWHERE TO GO

Plans were already in place, according to Spaulding. Those plans were tweaked a bit to have aircraft go in empty so as to pick up rather than insert. "We already had the fireplans for all the gunships, the routes, we had it all," said Spaulding. "It was done."

As plans to evacuate Firebase Ripcord were being made, the men of Alpha Company were themselves attempting to get out of the area of the valley southeast of Ripcord and southwest of Hill 805, which had been so deadly for the enemy over the course of the previous two weeks.

Capt. Chuck Hawkins was the lone member of the company who knew an evacuation had been discussed.

"As far as I knew we were going to an LZ (landing zone) for a re-supply," said Lt. Lee Widjeskog. "I knew nothing about being evacuated. Hawkins knew about it but if he transmitted it, I didn't pick up on it. It wasn't necessary for me to know. All I needed to know was where we were going. We started out with the intent of going southeast of Ripcord. Chuck had already started first platoon out headed that way because we always wanted to get off our NDP (night defensive position) before 9 o'clock in the morning."

Ron Janezic, a member of Alpha's first platoon, remembers those hours before heading out that morning.

"I remember that day very vividly," said Janezic, from Brooklyn. He had recently been issued a new pair of boots and recalled the smell of death that accompanied the footwear. "I smelled them and threw them away. I honestly smelled death on them. It was eerie, hard to explain. I just had this feeling they weren't intended for me.

"That night we set up and didn't hear a thing. It was dark and you couldn't see three feet in front of you. The next day the companies started pulling out."

REMEMBERING FIREBASE RIPCORD

That day still haunts Hawkins.

"I wish to God that I could do this day over," he would write. "I wish I had thought about things with the same deliberation I had the two days prior. But I didn't. My mind was fixed on getting to the next ridge and moving near the LZ up the ridge. I figured it would be as good a place as any for us to be extracted, something I felt certain would be ordered in the very near future. Looking back on it, I should have moved out before dawn. But I hadn't planned that, hadn't given any instructions for such a move.

"We had stand to before dawn, after which we got ready to move. Pahissa (and first platoon) would lead, followed by third, followed by second. We uncoiled and moved out about 0930 (9:30 a.m.)"

By 10 a.m., the platoon was headed toward the southwest landing zone.

"Things got fucked up pretty quickly," said Hawkins. "After Pahissa's intramural firefight, by which time he'd crossed the small stream and valley leading to the ridge to the west, I received a secure set transmission from Lucas directing me to the LZ just east of Ripcord."

Dale Lane, who had previously served as radio operator with Alpha Company, was at the time manning the secure set for Lucas at the time on Firebase Ripcord.

"Lucas came into the TOC (tactical operations center) and had me contact Alpha Company," remembered Lane. "I think that's when they decided that they were getting off the firebase so I called Capt. Hawkins on the secure set, so Lucas could tell him that he had to get to a spot where he could get them out. It just so happened the secure set went down. So Lucas told me to shackle up an order to reverse course and go back the way they came. Hawkins, when he got that, about 15 minutes later, called me back – I was his RTO (radio telephone operator) for quite a while before I went to Ripcord – so he called me back and as RTOs do sometimes they'll frequence up to a frequency nobody's using and you just talk plain. His first words were, 'What the fuck? We can't backtrack, we'll run into problems.' I said, 'Hey you need to talk to the man, I'm just the messenger.' He said, 'Put him on.' I told him he's already left for the night, went back to Camp Evans."

With that, it was time to reverse course.

"There was confusion," said Widjeskog. "Suddenly the colonel said no, he didn't feel he could support that LZ from Ripcord. I guess he was trying to get a place he could support with direct fire. We were about one-and-a-half kliks (1.5 kilometers) away from Ripcord. Lucas had bailed out of the TOC and was in his helicopter. At any rate, the captain was told to go the other way and he couldn't change it. He called (me) and said go north to the other LZ. We had to wait for first platoon to get back, so by the time they got back it was about 1 o'clock, way later than it was supposed to be."

The 22nd happened to be Widjeskog's birthday. He had gotten up that morning expecting at some point during the day to receive some packages. "I got them," he would say of what lay ahead.

"I called first platoon back, moved Widjeskog to the head of the company column and we prepared to move to the LZ east of Ripcord," Hawkins said. "Third would follow second; (Lt. William) Pahissa would bring up the rear. This was my second mistake. We should not have backtracked. I knew better. I thought about it. I could have ignored orders and gone ahead to the LZ I had in mind. I didn't."

For Hawkins to have reached Lucas with a message, it would have required code, according to Lane, which was a time-consuming process and not always effective.

"We no longer had a company perimeter," Hawkins wrote. "The platoons were uncoiled and in a linear formation getting ready to move.

This accident of posture saved the company from the initial enemy onslaught. We were facing the enemy's direction of attack linearly, and not in a perimeter. We had the maximum number of weapons available to bring to bear against the enemy attack when it occurred."

Janezic remembered hearing mortar rounds going off, setting off what would become unbelievable hell for the men of Alpha Company.

Widjeskog and second platoon moved out at 1:30 p.m. Pahissa and Staff Sgt. Gerald Singleton were at the command post while Forward Observer Steve Olson was to the north with Radio Operator Floyd Alexander and Hawkins' secure set operator, Bill Wagnon.

"Widjeskog's drag team had disappeared into the brush," remembered Hawkins. "It was time for third to begin moving. At 1330 (1:30 p.m.) I heard M-16 fire from second platoon's position. My initial reaction was, 'Damn, we've jumped some more enemy.' I felt elated, very proud of my men. The feeling didn't last a moment. Fire intensified from Widjeskog's location and included the sharp whip-crack of RPGs and the rapid fire of RPD machine guns. Almost simultaneously I heard the hollow 'thonk, thonk' of enemy 82mm mortars firing from the east. I turned that way and as mortar bombs began bursting around us I could see enemy soldiers coming at us; running, crouched over, firing, some blue helmets here and there, perhaps identifying leaders directing the mass attack. My stomach tightened in a knot. The familiar tingly feeling rushed through my body – adrenalin pumping through the bloodstream. I knew we were in deep trouble."

Widjeskog and his men had a sense something wasn't right as they got no farther than 100 or so meters down the trail. It was a sense he and the men had long before they had left their night defensive position.

"We could smell NVA, but we weren't certain it was them," said Widjeskog. "We had killed a bunch of them in the last couple of days and we had their equipment on board."

NOWHERE TO GO

Medic Martin Glennon had a premonition the day before, and he, too, noted the smell as they headed into the brush.

"The day before I went out (away from the perimeter) to go to the bathroom and when I was out there, there was like a voice that said your company is going to be wiped out," said Glennon. "I looked around and there was no one. It was a weird premonition-type thing. That morning (July 22), I was on guard duty and I smelled the NVA. They are not very far, they are right out there. I'd been out there seven months, I knew. It was a fishy smell, rice and fish. They eat that and the smell on them. They were close."

Doug McVay, second platoon's point man, walked up on mortar guys setting up shop on the trail.

"He jumps back and says, 'There's someone up there,'" remembered Widjeskog. "I said, 'You didn't shoot?' 'No, I thought they were our guys.' I told him there's nobody up there."

Robert Journell and Russ Walker then took point. Tony Galindo manned the machine gun as second platoon moved forward. They didn't get far.

"I was last, about 30-40 yards behind the point," said Sgt. Gary Foster. "Word came back to get down, the point man had seen something. The RPG went off and there were all kinds of rounds being fired. The shit hit the fan up at the point. I look back down the trail behind us and a North Vietnamese came up and I shot him. After that, there was no end to the fight going on. It just opened up everywhere. I started taking rounds, there was shooting everywhere."

"The NVA opened up with machine gun and RPGs," said Widjeskog. "They blew this tree down 20 feet in front of us. Everybody dropped and started to shoot. My radio man got hit. We heard them dropping mortar rounds, hitting (the company night defensive position) with tear gas and high explosives. Guys on the hill later said the NVA were pushing so fast, some of them were hit by their own mortars. They pushed the company off the hill and ended up being on the back side of the hill. They didn't press their advantage.

"We were getting hit from all sides of the trail. We were cut off. We dragged Mulvey back, dropped his ruck. I wasn't going to get his radio, there were too many NVA there. I was thinking, 'I had two more radios, of course one was down and one with the platoon sergeant (John Brown). As soon as the shooting started, (Brown) got shot, took a round through the face."

Glennon was there to aid Brown, admittedly terrified, but intent on helping his platoon mates.

"He was shot through the mouth," said Glennon. "It came through one side of the cheek and out the other. I was able to put an IV through him."

"All he could do was keep his head down so he didn't drown in his own blood," said Widjeskog of the gory injury. "It took out part of his tongue, part of his jaw."

"It blew his jawbone out," remembered Foster. "John was up on his knees and elbows trying to keep from choking to death. Doc got an IV started and probably saved John's life. Man that had to hurt."

Casualties had started to mount. "There were so many being wounded, I had to take care of everyone being wounded," remembered Glennon. "Journell was behind a stump, in a firefight. We got an RPG, some guys got shrapnel. (Russell) Walker got wounded in the leg. Tony Galindo got hit with friendly fire, it went through his face, opened up his cheek. It wasn't as bad as it looked, but it certainly looked bad. I couldn't even put a bandage around his face.

"This was the worst time, it was pandemonium. We couldn't stand up because they were waiting for us to stand up. Mulvey was close to me. He was the radio man for the platoon sergeant, Squad Leader (Thomas) Schultz was on the perimeter."

Mulvey, Widjeskog said, was a non-combatant. "I don't think he fired his gun," noted Widjeskog. "He simply couldn't."

At the tail end, Widjeskog's platoon was effectively being protected by Foster, new to the platoon.

"Every time I'd look down that trail, there'd be another soldier there," said Foster. "I had 400 rounds they'd given me when I started. I loaded, about 17 rounds per clip, 23-24 clips. As fast as I could shoot these guys they were stepping out there or I could see the bushes moving. In that thick undergrowth I could see that someone would shake a bush. I'd put half a clip into the base of that bush. I know that I was killing these guys. They were sneaking through there and I'd bust their ass. There was a tree near that was big enough to get behind. They were shooting at me and I had about seven hand grenades.

"If I couldn't get them with an M-16, I'd throw a grenade. I threw every grenade I could get. I ended up shooting every clip I had that afternoon, and I didn't waste ammunition. I got to where I was pulling grenades out of Brown's rucksack."

Glennon began to panic with Schultz dropped back from the perimeter to attempt to provide some comfort during the horrific battle.

"I remember Schultzy coming to me from the perimeter and saying, 'We're going to make it through this,'" said Glennon. "It gave me confidence. He went back to the perimeter and they shot him."

Foster's action at the rear saved lives. Still the new guy, many didn't even know his name.

"He said he looked down the trail, an NVA soldier came out on the trail, looked the wrong way, 'Pop!' there he dropped," said Widjeskog. "He said, 'That's the only guy I saw all day. Now I saw guns pointed at me and shooting. There were guys shooting, but that was the only guy I saw all day.' (Foster) just started shooting people. Somebody'd fire and he'd shoot at them and they'd stop firing. Pretty soon they were firing from behind the trees. Foster started throwing grenades. They didn't fire anymore. That's good. Eventually, he threw all his grenades, he threw all Brown's grenades. He said he probably threw a dozen grenades. They were throwing satchel charges and grenades at him. He had one go off, it blew his shirt off, burned his shoulder and blew out his eardrums. Another hit him with shrapnel in the leg, the arm. It takes a tremendous amount of courage to aim and shoot at someone. He did it because he had no choice. After 15-20 minutes, he managed to get Mulvey and Brown back to the rest of the platoon, so we weren't strung out so far."

"They were throwing plastic explosives," remembered Foster. "Some of them would go off, some wouldn't. I know one of them I watched came in and landed right in front of Brown, about 15 feet from me. It bounced and landed underneath his head; he was looking straight down on it."

"It didn't go off," said Widjeskog. "Brown was on his knees with his head down so he wouldn't choke on his blood. He saw it land. Brown was lucky as could be because it would've killed him, probably taken his head off."

Another satchel charge landed near Foster.

"I rolled forward enough to get a tree between my head and that explosion," he said. "It went off and burnt my uniform off from about my knee on my left side up to my belt. It blew it off up to my armpit. It blew dirt and whatever else. My eardrums had been blown. It couldn't have been more than three feet from me. You couldn't quit fighting at the time."

"We continued walking around," said Frank Marshall, a veteran member of Alpha One having been there for the insertion of troops in March. "At that time we were going to go down in the valley a little deeper… They hit us with mortars, RPGs, everything they could think of."

Hawkins and third platoon were taking fire as well. The adrenalin was pumping in the heat of the day. "You get out of trouble by killing the bad guys," he said. "My first thought was to focus on killing. I had raised my M-16, was taking aim, drawing a bead and logic kicked in. Dick Ames' admonition from the first of June burned in the back of my mind, reminding me that my job was on the radios, calling for support, taking command of the situation.

"Instinctively I knew that if I started shooting bad guys it wouldn't stop until I was out of ammo or dead. There were too many. I needed a more secure place to set up with the CP (command post), and the base of the ironwood would become a focal point for enemy activity. I ran. 'CP, follow me!' I hollered. 'Rally point, 75-meters west!' We headed for a small rise in the ground beyond which it dropped off to an intermittent stream bed. The brush was thick there. We could at least have some concealment. RTOs Witt and Vic ran with me, loyal and sticking to me like glue. No one else from the CP followed. We slid over the edge of a small rise. RPG and small arms fire followed us. Commo (communication) sucked. Vic popped up the long pole antenna. More RPG fire. We moved a few meters. Vic struggled with the long pole. 'Damn it,' he cursed, 'stay in one fuckin' place!' We hunkered down, crap flying through the air everywhere."

Hawkins credited the RTOs for being calm under fire. Witt got battalion on the line and Hawkins made contact with Widjeskog, only to hear a sentence before the lieutenant's radio went dead. Hawkins then told battalion at the tactical operations center, now staffed entirely by NCOs as the officers were in the rear planning the extraction and withdrawal, that he needed cobras and close-air support.

"I hoped that Olson was cranking up mortars on Ripcord and artillery from other firebases in range," said Hawkins, unaware that Olson was dead and that first platoon had already lost several men.

Floyd Alexander was a 20-year-old radio operator from field artillery assigned to Lt. Steve Olson, who was working with Alpha Company, moving with first platoon. Olson lost his life immediately as the ambush began.

Artillery and mortars would have to wait.

"I pulled him down," remembered Alexander. "They were all over us. I got him down and said, 'Stay down Steve,' and he started to get back up. I grabbed him by the shirt, he pulled away and took a direct hit. The guy on the other side of me got hit bad and I thought both of them were dead. I was getting ready to pull back to see if I could find any more survivors. When I started pulling back, I heard one of the soldiers screaming for help. I went back to get him because there's no way I'd ever leave a guy. When I went back to get him, I heard the NVA coming so I just told him to be still and I laid over him. I saw five of them bunched up and, I hate to tell this story, I shot them and all five of them fell. Then off to my right… I saw two more coming and I shot both of them."

Alexander covered a fellow soldier who had been blinded by a satchel charge, encouraging him to keep quiet as the NVA approached. The injured trooper, who proved to be Hawkins' secure set carrier/operator, soon passed out under the weight of Alexander.

Mark Draper was a medic with Alpha Company. He lost his life July 22, 1970, along with more than a dozen others from Alpha Company. Photo provided by Bruce Brady.

"You could hear the NVA chirping, so I covered (him) and told him not to say anything," said Alexander. "I saw one of the NVA go up to our medic (Mark Draper), who was already shot up. The NVA soldier finished him off. I couldn't do anything to help him because if I were to give up my position they would have killed both of us. Last thing I remember they started working toward us and I remember seeing their feet and all of a sudden everything went blank. It's like I went to sleep."

He had. The NVA had kicked Alexander in the head and fled without shooting. The kick rendered him unconscious. They assumed he was dead as he was covered with the blood of two other soldiers and the tissue of Olson as he was ripped apart by an RPG.

"I don't know how long I was out," said Alexander. "When I came to the guys told me one of the NVA soldiers kicked me in the head. They were on a mission and they wanted to kill us all. They got off to a good start."

Hawkins, in late May after assuming command, had established a procedure that the forward observer would handle all the indirect fire while he handled cobras and fast movers. It was a good division of labor, he noted. "Besides, I had developed a passion for air support," said Hawkins. "A couple gunships came on station in a matter of a few minutes. That was the second thing that saved us.

"I had a very good sense of where members, elements of the company were. I just knew. Cobras began gun runs. The enemy began keeping his head down. I established contact with Widjeskog. Main thing I wanted was for him to pop smoke to clearly identify friendlies. We did the same. Gun runs came close and then closer, as close as 15 feet, Widjeskog reported later. In the time it took this to occur – five, 10 minutes perhaps – I had time to assess the situation. One possibility: Break up the company, escape and evade, hope to make it somewhere to safety - the lowlands, perhaps. But I didn't have an answer to what happened after giving such an order. I refused to contemplate it further. We were in a fight and that's what we would have to do. I calmed them down, got serious."

Second platoon and Widjeskog were still fighting to survive. They were in a very narrow perimeter with enemy on all sides and because of the undergrowth, visibility was poor.

"The bushes would move, though," said Widjeskog. "Anything that moved we shot at because we were lying on the ground, firing pretty low, which meant we probably hit people. You'd see movement, then you'd shoot and there wouldn't be any movement."

The firefight continued and the NVA seems intent on eliminating the entire company. Satchel charges and hand grenades are lobbed at second platoon, which is still stationed along a small bit of high ground. "We were pretty narrow," remembered Widjeskog. "Some are landing in on us and some are going past us. We're shooting back so the air is getting black with explosives. It was at that point I was up on my knees directing fire, checking things out, when a grenade landed about 10 feet away. That goes off, it was a Chicom grenade luckily, not a very good grenade. I got minor shrapnel, flesh wounds in my shoulder, thigh, neck, nothing deep. Another piece of that shrapnel hit my machine gunner (Galindo) in the cheek, closing his eye. He ended up with tunnel vision as a result of that explosion. Foster said he thought it was the same grenade that went off and hit Journell, who was killed. It could have been, we were close enough. Journell was probably 20-25 feet from the grenade, but that's close enough if you get hit with the right piece. That's how things are, just chaotic. It's luck."

"Journell he got wounded - it went in his back and into his internal organs," remembered Glennon. "He was shaking and talking fast. I couldn't save him. He died in front of all of us. He was probably going into shock. I was trying to get the morphine out, he got the morphine, not too long after that he passed in front of us all."

Everyone was on edge.

"There was a low place where we set up," said Foster. "You could hear a command or two in Vietnamese, then you could hear them dropping a round in a mortar tube. There's no defense from that unless you're in a bunker. That was terrifying when you could hear them dropping rounds in the tubes. They knew where we were. There was not as much fire, but every once in a while one would drop out from behind a tree and shoot at us. They were more shooting at sound than what they could see."

Alpha was inflicting heavy casualties on the NVA as well. Widjeskog figured as many as 40 NVA were killed in a matter of a half hour, but there was no official body count. "They went down, we didn't care, so long as they weren't shooting at us," he said.

Radio contact between Hawkins and Widjeskog soon resumed and the two coordinated incoming fire.

"I remember first radio contact with Hawkins," said Widjeskog. "He said, 'Man I thought you were dead.' I said, 'No, we just hadn't been able to get the radio back up.' He asked how we were doing and I said I had lost a pair, Schultz and Journell. I asked, 'How about you guys?' He said, 'A basketball team.' He knew he had lost five, but he wasn't sure."

First platoon had been nearly cut down in a mortar attack followed by machine gun fire.

"Don (Severson) and I looked at each other and ran forward, away from the company, and there were these huge trees you could almost fit into and be protected on the sides," said Janezic. "We were about 50 feet in front of everyone else. Don was 15 yards over from me. Mortar rounds were popping five feet in front of us. We were protected by these trees. I have a little shrapnel in my stomach. We pulled back and everyone had left the hillside. We could hear firing going on. We got set up, pulled back about 25-30 feet and Don was by one side of the tree. I was on his western side and next to me about seven feet was Lt. Pahissa, next to him Sgt. (Gerald) Singleton. Next to lieutenant was (Robert) Brown, who got hit by a mortar round."

Medic Danny Fries was also killed in the gunfire that followed the mortar round. Of the three medics assigned to Alpha's three platoons, two were dead.

"Fries was a great guy, great personality," said Janezic, still emotional when discussing the morning of July 22.

The platoon had been lined up, each facing up the hill.

"All of a sudden I look over and a machine gun went off and I looked next to me and the sergeant had a hole right in his head. It was near Brown. I looked down at the sergeant and the cigarette was burning through his hand. He was dead. I see Don and I just don't know how the bullets missed me. The machine gun just tore everyone apart. I don't know how it missed me."

Janezic ran down the hillside and eventually linked up with other members of Alpha including Tommy Webster.

"We were off the hilltop in very thick vegetation," remembered Janezic. "You couldn't see through it. When we were being fired upon, the only one I could see is Don. I dove down in the vegetation. We didn't know what the hell was going on."

Death surrounded the young men.

"I would hear people yell out 'Curahee!' and we'd yell back," said Janezic. We thought maybe we were being Caraheed by the NVA, and probably were. We were shell-shocked and prepared to die. How are we going to get out of this? I was thinking. We didn't know how many were after us, but we knew we were in trouble. Some guy next to us, I don't know who, he picked up an M-60 and at this point the Cobras were coming in and shooting into the hillside. They took out one of our machine gunners."

Severson, the gunner, was killed the exchange. His wife gave birth to a baby girl the next day.

As grim as things looked, Hawkins had trained his men well. The captain was confident in the positioning of the NVA, east, northeast and southeast of the company. He knew where the mortars were. Reports indicated there were three enemy companies surrounding Alpha.

"Then Maj. Skip Little came on station in his OV-10 pusher-puller forward air control plane and announced that he had a set of fast movers on the way," said Hawkins of the Air Force pilot. "Together, we went to work.

"The first set of F4 Phantoms had 1,000-pound bombs, too big for CAS. I gave Skip the coordinates for where I thought the enemy division HQ might be. He sent the F4s in hot on the first strike and reported secondary explosions. We didn't have time to celebrate. I needed more jets, small bombs, napalm. When the next Phantoms came on station I moved the Cobras to the other side of the air corridor. I wanted the F4s to make their passes. The Cobras could keep firing; they just had to stay out of the line of attack of the jets. Still no artillery or mortars, so I realized Olson was out of action, but I couldn't think about that."

Hawkins realized without radio contact and no Pahissa, no Singleton, that troops were scattered into pockets and involved in individual fights. Firing was everywhere. Gunships, jets, rockets, mini-guns, M-16s, M-60s and grenades screamed from the American side while the NVA fired mortars, RPGs, AK-47s, RPDs and satchel charges.

"I had been wounded in the initial mortar barrage, but not badly," said Hawkins. "I knew it, but I didn't really feel it. It took time, maybe 30 minutes and things began to stabilize along the 'front,' such as it was. The Cobras and Phantoms we redoing what I needed: Killing the enemy and suppressing his fire... keeping his head down. I had good commo with the battalion TOC, the Cobras and Skip Little and I could holler back and forth with members of first and third platoon and with Widjeskog."

Hawkins teamed with Little and took over the battle. "Jets and gunships started queuing like barbershop customers taking a number," he said. "They all wanted in on the fight. I had settled into a groove less afraid now and getting angrier, determined to fight the battle my way and not the way the enemy commander wanted. He had thrown his best punch and we were still standing. Now it was our turn to throw punches, and I had a lot of punch at my disposal."

Thought then turned to artillery and how best to use support from Ripcord. Hawkins wanted to pin the enemy into position and block any additional enemy movement into or out of the battlefield. He ordered fire along a northwest-southeast line several hundred meters east of Alpha's position along a stream between the company position and Hill 805.

"Artillery and mortars would be the anvil," wrote Hawkins. "Skip Little and his fast movers and the gunships would be the hammer. Now, all my soldiers had to do was keep from being overrun."

"We were just trying to get rid of the NVA," said Widjeskog.

It was a scramble from there. Hawkins was calling in airstrikes while his men were humping it to the top of the hill. Casualties mounted. Hawkins remained cool under pressure.

"He handled it well," remembered William Baldwin, who was carrying the radio. "I was right by his side the entire time. He had artillery, Cobras and jets coming in. He brought them in different ways so that none of them would be in each other's way. He was calm. He was a rock. He certainly helped save my life."

Marshall, battling up the hill, came to the aid of a medic only to be hit with an NVA satchel charge.

"It exploded and hit the back of the medic and burnt my face and gave me a slight concussion," said Marshall. "I rolled down the hill. As I'm rolling down, someone picked up my helmet, put my helmet back on my head, slapped my face a few times and got me to go back up to the top of the hill."

Baldwin too got knocked down the hill from an explosion. "I got up and everything still moved," he said. "I had pain in my back and I reached back and had blood on my hand. I went back up to where my radio was." Communication was fuzzy so Baldwin opted to use the long pole. "I don't know if they could see the son of a bitch, but that's when they shot the RPG in at us."

Hawkins continued rallying his men and Marshall, who was still carrying his M-79, was handed an M-16 as he trekked up the hill. The idea, according to Hawkins, was to consolidate the men at a Night Defensive Position, a small bit of high ground that may offer better defense. Night was approaching, and casualties continued to mount.

"That's when I got hit again in my arm," said Marshall. "An RPG went off real close and I got it in my arm, sliced my arm open and I went down at that time. My arm was sliced open to the bone, but I was OK."

With his arm bandaged, he continued up when he was hit by shrapnel from an RPG. "I got a big chunk in my ankle bone and I went down again."

Hawkins' airstrikes were coming in and word spread up the hill that the Phantoms would be depositing the 250-pounders near the unit – danger close.

The bombs fell into the jungle as Americans continued to scramble for safety.

"Skip's Phantoms finally did the trick," said Hawkins, "dropping 250-pound high drags practically right on top of our position. The enemy started to flee."

Hawkins and the pilot were in communication throughout this time, with Hawkins relaying instructions and both men working together to make corrections. Runs by the Phantoms included 20mm cannon fire in addition to the bombing runs as the cannon fire could be brought closer to the American troops.

"(Hawkins) came over and said 'We've got them coming in so get your guys down,'" remembered Widjeskog. "They are not supposed to drop them within 200 meters of friendly troops and I did not know at that time if he was calling them in closer than that. It doesn't matter if he intentionally called them in close or it was an accident. There were two bombs as I remember, one of them landed up on the company hill on the lower slope and did not go off. The other one landed northeast of my position, within what I felt was about 75 meters and that is where the enemy was. When that went off I remember the concussion; the sky turned black, the smoke, everything was black. When the smoke cleared I don't think there was a tree that I could see that was higher than eight feet. After that, every time a jet would come over, the NVA would jump out and head out of there. That's when I saw my first NVA."

"I thought hell opened up," said Alexander. "Things just disappeared when those things hit."

"Chuck Hawkins directed it almost on top of us, said it was our only way out," said Marshall. "We took cover and the 250-pound bomb went off right on top of us. We all lifted off the ground a little bit with the explosion. At that point it was dark, it was cloudy, smoke was all around and the NVA just took off."

What was left of Alpha Company got to the top of the hill, cleared it and set up positions, unsure of what was next.

"We finally got the NDP back," said Hawkins. "It cost Sgt. (John) Kreckel his life and I got shot through the neck by a molten jet from an RPG. I thought it was a kill shot, but it wasn't. God's grace. Widjeskog and his men finally beat back the enemy trying to overrun them and rejoined the makeshift company perimeter."

Alexander had linked up with Hawkins. At Hawkins' feet, an ARVN bleeding to death and a severely wounded Kit Carson scout.

"He was hit in the throat," remembered Alexander of seeing Hawkins. "Our Kit Carson scout (ARVN Sgt. 1st Class Pham Van Long) was bleeding real bad. I tried to stop the bleeding. I didn't have enough fingers to plug the holes. He had so many holes in him I couldn't help him. I sat there and talked to him until he finally died. He had a hold of my hand. If there ever was a death grip, he had one."

Long had been attached to Alpha Company and served as an interpreter. Hawkins remembered that Long enjoyed working with the Americans and never went back to his parent ARVN unit.

Widjeskog and Alpha Two gathered the wounded and dead and joined the command post.

"We started going through rucksacks and looking for water," said Widjeskog. "We had been fighting for six hours and the thirst was incredible. I remember the water I tasted. It was just the most delicious water I had ever tasted. There really wasn't a whole lot of water so we passed it around. I remember seeing the bodies of the first platoon leader (Pahissa), he had a bandage on his head, he had been shot in the head from the beginning, but the medic had time to put a bandage on him. The medic (Draper) was there with him. His platoon sergeant (Singleton) was there, so was his RTO and machine gunner, assistant gunner. Their whole command structure had been killed from one end to the other. There were a few dead NVA soldiers that I didn't pay attention to. We got organized for the night, thinking we were going to get hit. You couldn't dig in anywhere there were so many big trees, roots. We just hunkered in and waited for the attack. You're trying to stay awake. All night long flares were dropped around our position. When it was light (to those flying) they flew away, leaving us in the darkness of the thick jungle. It wasn't too long before I collapsed, couldn't stay awake any longer. Just about everyone else was asleep. I awoke about a half hour later as the sun was getting brighter."

"We had 76 men in the company, there were 14 dead and 56 wounded," said Marshall. "We set up NDP and we waited there all night long. The ships in the ocean there were shooting flares all night long, so we had light all night long from the flares and the canisters were popping down, falling down on top of us. We stayed there all night long. I was scared as hell because all they had to do was come back and they would have wiped us out completely. At that point, I was up all night long and I was terrified."

In addition to Pahissa, Singleton, Schultz, Olson, Journell, Severson, Draper and Fries, Alpha Company that day lost John Babich, a radio operator; gunner Virgil Bixby, Ovell Spruill, Robert Brown Jr. and Stanley Diehl.

In addition to the "basketball" illumination flares from Chinooks, Cobras circled around a strobe Hawkins had mounted on a pole.

"We were in tough shape but prepared for any resumed enemy attack," said Hawkins. "I moved around the perimeter checking on wounded men and making sure those who could still fight knew their sectors of fire. I succumbed to fatigue early in the morning (July 23) and slept until first light. My RTO Witt grabbed me and put me down; Said he'd watch the radios, that I needed sleep."

18

Delta Makes a Daring Rescue

'I really got real with the possibility of dying.' – Fred Gilbert, Delta Company

When it came time to tap a company to rescue Alpha Company, Delta Company, under the command of hard-charging Rollison was selected. Charlie Company was depleted, having never really recovered from the July 2 battle on Hill 902, then incurring more casualties at Hill 1,000 less than a week later. Bravo Company was still pulling security on Ripcord and would be evacuated by midday, so it was up to Delta to answer the call and answer the call they did.

"It's gotta be Delta, Rollison," remembered Spaulding. "We told Rollison the story and he said, 'Fred, my guys are shot up too.' We went over to the barracks, where they had about 15 medics in there working on them, patching them up, changing bandages. Capt. Rollison said, 'Gentlemen, I need your attention. Alpha Company is trapped and they are shot so full of holes they can't get on the choppers. We gotta go out there and get them."

Lt. John Flaherty was among those aboard the choppers that morning with a mission to rescue Alpha Company. He knew Rollison well.

"First of all, he had a great, big personality," said Flaherty. "He was on his second tour, and he had experience. Plus, he grew up in northern Georgia, where he was an outdoors guy. He was so confident. He came in with this agenda that we were going to absolutely be the best. I can remember in the beginning around Firebase Jack (east of the mountains in the flatlands near Camp Evans), he really taught me how to be a platoon leader. I thought I knew how to lead troops and what it took, but he brought it to a whole new level. He was extremely demanding, not only of the men but especially the officers. He expected them to set the example, to check the troops and make sure they were doing all the things they needed to do to survive. He made everyone shave every day. He said if you look good, you feel good. He made sure there was light discipline and noise discipline. I became, based on what he taught me, a very good platoon leader. I think I owe my life to him because he was demanding. Beyond that, he became my friend."

Knowing that, there was no question the men of Delta were ready and willing to accept the mission.

"These guys didn't know Alpha Company from Adam, but yet they're Currahees," said Spaulding. "They got up, grabbed their shirts, grabbed their gear – every one of them had bandages on. Rollison is telling this one 'No, you're too injured, you're too bad.' They all wanted to go. When you have men like that you can be outnumbered 100 to 1 and they're not going to do a damn thing to you. You're going to kick their ass every time. They cared about their fellow soldiers. That's the kind of men we had."

Being part of aviation, House was naturally part of the planning that went into getting Alpha Company out and he knew it would be difficult. That was not going to stop the men from getting in and making the attempt to save their fellow Screaming Eagles.

Kenneth Mayberry, call sign Phoenix 50, was an aircraft commander

DELTA MAKES A DARING RESCUE

with C/158 Aviation Battalion. He was part of the 10-aircraft combat assault team that flew Delta Company into the landing zone for the rescue and evacuation of Alpha Company. The mission started before daylight.

"We were cautioned not to use our landing or searchlights, which should tell you how dark it was at that time of the morning," said Mayberry.

Before sun-up July 23, the airships were on their way. By 5:45 a.m., Delta Company was on the ground.

"Alpha Company, wherever they got hit on that ridge there was no pickup zone around and there were so many wounded they couldn't get their wounded out," remembered House. "They had more wounded than not. The decision was made early in the morning. Rollison, who got one Silver Star, should've gotten 10 - he was really a warrior. They are putting in Delta Company to fight through the bad guys, link up with Alpha Company and carry the wounded back to the LZ (landing zone), where we dropped them in. We put them in before daylight. Flying in the mountains at night, you've gotta remember there was no CavNav, no night-vision goggles. If you turned on the light and there were any bad guys - that was their aiming point. You're going into these things and we flew the area so much, we got a feeling for it. It was hairy putting in Delta Company that morning to go get Alpha Company. We weren't medevac-type aircraft, we were just slicks no doors, no seats except for the pilot and co-pilot, crew chief and gunner. It was just slinging these guys on board that were all shot up. "

Hawkins awoke to see in front of him the face of a North Vietnamese Army (NVA) soldier he had killed the day before. "No emotion," he said of the moment. "Tired. I knew I had to get up to do my job, whatever that job would be for this day. I know Rollison and Delta Company were coming sooner or later. I hoped we didn't get hit again. I was weary, but alert."

Members of Alpha Company under Hawkins could hear the choppers, though they were unsure where they were headed or what the mission was.

"This was a tough day and you put in day after day of this intensity. It was a mission and the mission was to put Delta Company in to save Alpha Company and damn it, the fact it was dark - we were going to do it," said House.

"They landed about 500 meters over," said Marshall. "They got attacked when they landed and they took a couple of wounded in the beginning, on the hot LZ."

"Between Rollison and myself, we knew Chuck Hawkins," said Flaherty. "They were another company, but they were our buddies. We knew they'd come help us if we needed it.

"When we landed, Rollison said to me, 'Jack, I want you to haul ass down there, we're going to get them and fuck everything else.' So that's exactly what we did."

Flaherty was charged with blowing the landing zone. Sgt. Mark Skinner exited his chopper from the right side along with his radio operator and immediately moved away from the landing zone. Skinner heard the machine gunner ripping into the woods, then yelled for more ammo. He gathered his ammo and that of his radio operator and charged across the landing zone. He dropped red smoke, indicating a hot landing zone, got down and was informed there is a 51-caliber machine gun position just off the landing zone.

"So we had a quick exchange," remembered Skinner. "I tossed a frag, he tossed a frag. We no longer had any fire coming from that bunker, but I was wounded."

Eliminating the position, though, allowed the remaining birds to drop in.

DELTA MAKES A DARING RESCUE

"The second and third birds came in," said Skinner. "I went to get up and my leg wasn't working."

Fred Gilbert had just turned 20 a little more than a month prior to Delta's mission. A self-described country boy from Perryville, Md., Gilbert enjoyed hunting and readily accepted the job of walking point. He had done it for much of his time in the Ripcord Area of Operations, along with his buddy, John Carr, with whom he'd operated as a point-slack team.

"We lived in the jungle," said Gilbert. "We were one with the jungle and that was a good thing for me as a point man, because I was a country man, a deer hunter. You can't be a city boy and walk point. You're gonna die quick."

Gilbert and Delta had been turned away the night before and he recalled the feeling of flying over the area, knowing Alpha Company was there, somewhere, clinging to life.

"We went round and round," he said. "Where the LZ was to go to get Alpha Company was on fire. I remember sitting on that chopper looking down and saying, 'Wow. Those poor sons of bitches. We can't get to the ground to even help them.' We fly back to the Currahee pad and sat right there. I remember me and John Carr sitting there saying those poor bastards are going to get slaughtered tonight. Think what a cold feeling that must have been to hear all that going on, then hear the choppers fading away. That had to be gut-wrenching. In my heart, the chances of finding anyone alive was terrible, bad. I was pretty close."

Morning came and the choppers arrived. Gilbert remembered feeling it would be his last day in the jungles of Vietnam, his last day on Earth.

"This time I really got real with the possibility of dying," said Gilbert. "You couldn't get to the ground the last time and it's probably not going to be much better this time and I was right on the money. I look down there and what do I see? Red smoke. They came out from under the ground, and got on their guns. Skinner was on that first bird that came down. He's out there fighting near hand to hand to with them. They throw a grenade, he throws it back. They shoot him in the leg. What a battle that guy fought. You gotta keep the men coming. Skinner fought so valiantly and he saw to it they kept coming."

Everyone got in and Gilbert and Carr took off along the trail, headed for Alpha's position.

"We start moving," remembered Gilbert. "I was moving very fast, 'cause I figured if I was moving fast, I'd be a harder target. There was nothing between me and A Company but the enemy and God. I knew damn well the longer I stumble along that trail, the more blood and death, that's all I'm thinking. This is it, this is where I'm going to die, but I gotta get to them boys. Walking point is like stalking deer, but not this time, it was like a jog.

"The world's being shot up. I jumped over a lot of dead Americans and a lot of dead NVA. I never will forget it – stone dead."

While Gilbert and Carr are snaking their way along the path toward Alpha Company, Fred Spaulding is coasting above to support and help assist the men along the way.

"I'm still moving," said Gilbert. "Carr's seeing every bit of it with me. I knelt down and said 'You better call these boys and let them know the next thing that shakes a bush is their rescue and not the enemy.' They stacked so many dead people up I knew they'd be trigger happy. Even in all that duress, I was thinking."

Meanwhile, Spaulding is still in the loach above, soaring along at treetop level, dropping grenades to the left and right of the trail, taking fire the entire time.

DELTA MAKES A DARING RESCUE

"I take off and we're still looking for 51s," said Spaulding. "We fly over Alpha and tell them they have guys coming in, that Delta's coming in to get them. 'Roger, we're here.' About this time the radio is going crazy. We're flying right above them. The enemy is not dumb. They already had Alpha surrounded like they're in the middle of a doughnut, so they're branching out and trying to cut in between both of them so they can envelope Delta too. I'm throwing grenades out and about the time we break left, they walk in on the edge of Alpha Company."

Gilbert still credits Spaulding with guiding the way and getting him to Alpha safely.

"He was rolling hand grenades out of that loach and hitting them in the head," said Gilbert. "I remember telling Carr, 'I don't know who that son of a bitch is over top, it's God himself, but he can see more than me. I know now it was Fred Spaulding. His skid was touching the triple canopy. It's a wonder it didn't hook something and come down in the bush with me."

As they broke through the perimeter and saw the men of Alpha Company, the severity of the situation settled even deeper.

"I could smell the blood on the ground," said Gilbert. "It was a terrible, terrible scene. They'd been pushed right to the end. I went right through the perimeter, then I saw Hawkins. He'd been shot in the neck. Everybody's got a gun and they are sitting ass to ass. There was no infantry company I had ever been involved with that looked like that. It was a terrible sight."

"Delta walked in and said they found all these bodies as they came in," said Widjeskog. "According to them, they found 60 bodies. We had obviously done them a lot of damage because they didn't hit us that night. A lot of that damage was done by artillery. We hit them hard enough that they couldn't regroup that night."

REMEMBERING FIREBASE RIPCORD

Another landing zone had to be prepped to get the dead and wounded out. Rollison was blowing trees up himself, firing at the bases of the trees, lopping them off in order to allow the choppers room to maneuver.

"The company moved over to us, came up the hill to us and my position was right where they were walking through," remembered Marshall. "They were handing us candy and water. It was like a scene from a movie, it was just horrible. They start cutting the LZ right away and they were blowing up trees so the helicopters could come in to us. As as they were blowing up trees, there was one was in the middle that wouldn't go down. The captain of Delta Company (Rollison) took an LAW (light anti-tank weapon) and shot the tree down. Randy House brought the helicopters in to rescue us, and Delta Company started throwing all the wounded from Alpha Company into the helicopters. The helicopters had to come straight down because the clearing wasn't big enough for them to come in and out. They had to come in straight up and down."

Widjeskog noted there were no less than 12 litter cases, further illuminating the severity of the attack on Alpha. Everyone was stable at that point, good for the crews attempting to land and leave in a tough situation.

"They threw me on the helicopter and at that point I think was the scariest time of my time in Vietnam," said Marshall. "Getting on that helicopter and knowing all they had to do was shoot that one helicopter down and they could have come down and got us all. As soon as that helicopter lifted and got above the tree tops, it just sped off at that point and I was relieved. I knew I was going to a hospital."

Many thought this was the end of the line for them on this planet.

"Capt. Hawkins had done a good job," said Flaherty. "He had a nice perimeter. They were in tough shape. We put the dead and wounded

DELTA MAKES A DARING RESCUE

on choppers and by the time it got to us, there were probably 10 of us left on the ground. I was really happy to get out of there because I didn't think I would. I thought we'd be attacked and I was amazed we got out alive. It was a hover LZ so the choppers were exposed for a long period of time, just stationary going up and down."

"My birthday was July 24 and I never thought I was going to see it," said House. "I said 'This is it,' because of all the activity going on."

Fourteen members of Alpha Company had been killed. Fifty-one were wounded.

19

Evacuating the Firebase

At Camp Evans Pathfinders Cpl. Jim Howton and William Kohr had made the trip to the mess hall when they received word that two fellow pathfinders had been shot on Ripcord.

"Within 15 minutes we were on a chopper," said Howton, who had been on firebases throughout the I Corps area and knew the dangers that awaited on Ripcord. "You always have the juices flowing, you never knew what was going to happen. We knew all the other pathfinders, eight or 10 of them, 25 percent of our whole group were wounded or killed. We had the feeling that you go out there and you're not coming back in one piece."

The night of July 21, Howton met with Lucas and several other officers at Ripcord, a meeting Howton recalled with vivid clarity.

"I'll never forget it," he said. "Lucas said, 'We're staying, we're going to continue the mission.' He said, and these were his exact words, 'The good ship of Ripcord will not go down.' I'm going, 'Oh my gosh, we're going down.' We were so zoned in, they had us dialed in. Nothing could touch them. They were 10 feet underground and they'd just sneak back into the mountain. We were in a precarious position to say

EVACUATING THE FIREBASE

the least. I was surprised at that point there was no mention of extracting from that hill. It all changed the next night."

As is routine for pathfinders, someone had to be on the radio at all times. For Howton and Kohr, known as Hardcore, there were no breaks, there was no sleep.

"We didn't sleep for a couple of nights there," said Howton. "I know Hardcore didn't sleep. I wasn't having a good feeling about this whole thing."

Organized Chaos, Casualties at Firebase Ripcord

Lt. Col. Andre Lucas is pictured outside the Tactical Operations Center atop Firebase Ripcord in early July 1970. You can see his call sign "Black Spade" on his helmet. Lucas received the Medal of Honor posthumously for his actions in evacuating the firebase. Photo provided by Chris Jensen.

"I think of all the sacrifices people made out there, the risks they took. The one thing that I think that I've learned from being through that battle is I

have more insight into people's mindsets when you read about battles. You can command respect, but you can't demand it. You have to earn it. If you work hard enough, you'll earn it." – Capt. Dr. James Harris.

At Ripcord, it was complete chaos. Plans were in place if things got out of hand, though.

"This wasn't our first rodeo," said House. "We'd been in some other pretty good, chaotic fights, so we had some pretty good contingency plans in this mission we'd planned. We planned it for two nights, the 21st and 22nd."

Charlie Company, down to only about 30 men, was airlifted on the 22nd. Bravo, under Capt. Ben Peters, remained at Ripcord, along with Artillery 1/319. Delta was evacked that night.

Lt. Bill Hand had taken over second platoon, Bravo Company. Only in country days at this point, he had learned quickly.

"I broke my cherry at Ripcord," he said. "We had all kinds of defensive positions set up. It was a steep hill. You're listening to the radio and what was happening with all the companies in the field."

It was chaotic, and the mission started before daybreak.

"We were briefed the night before," said Dale Ireland, a Chinook pilot tasked with arriving at the firebase during the initial wave to remove artillery and any other supplies deemed too important to leave behind. "We picked out the pilots who were going to fly. We knew there was a likelihood we were going to lose a couple birds. We had people hit, but we didn't lose anyone in our company.

"I wasn't afraid that morning, I just knew we had to pull those guys out because there was a real threat of being run over. Going before first light, we had three rallying points set up in the dark. We had

EVACUATING THE FIREBASE

three companies marrying up until you had to go in. I was more afraid of that, having choppers run into each other in the dark, than the mission."

That would change later, though.

The initial move surprised the North Vietnamese, perhaps taking them by surprise. Soon, though, strikes on the firebase increased.

"The evacuation started as scheduled, but the enemy increased their attack with thousands of artillery rounds hitting Ripcord," said Capt. Isabelino Vazquez-Rodriguez.

Vazquez-Rodriguez was tapped by Lucas to develop plans to evacuate men and equipment from Ripcord. He and Lt. Gabino Caballero flew into Ripcord as plans and schedules were developed. Commanders were briefed and the reality that the firebase would be evacuated in just hours began to set in. Word trickled out to the troops as well.

"I had people say 'bring 'em on,'" said Peters. "I had some troops saying, 'bring 'em on.'" We didn't know how many people were out there at that time. There were more enemy troops than at Hamburger Hill. As far as holding them off, maybe we could, maybe we couldn't. It was a wise decision to get us off."

Some 24 hours after declaring the good ship of Ripcord would not go down, Lucas again headed a meeting in the TOC at Ripcord, only this time plans for extraction were being formed.

"We had the briefing that night," said Howton. "That's when they told us we were going to extract the next day. Then (Lucas) gave me the shock of my life. He told me that the pathfinders were not going to be needed, they (the officers) were going to handle it. I thought, 'You gotta be kidding me.' Lucas decided they were going to run the show. He evidently didn't like us. I was shocked, had never heard of this.

REMEMBERING FIREBASE RIPCORD

I remember calling back to the rear and saying we got pulled. That night I told Hardcore we just got pulled, that we're not doing anything tomorrow. He was shocked. We didn't think it was going to go well."

Peters said that with cutbacks, the decision to evacuate was the only logical way to go.

"Everyone was kind of excited because they were going to be getting the hell out of there," he said. "After you've been on top of that hill, after a month of being on top of a hill and having mortars coming in, you're ready to go."

Capt. William A. Glennon had been busy flying combat assaults July 22, including several missions around Hill 805. Upon returning to Camp Evans, Glennon began shutting down when he got a call to report to battalion headquarters for a mission brief for the following day.

"I was very tired and asked if someone else could go instead, at which point our company commander, Maj. Richter came on the radio and informed me that the battalion commander, Lt. Col. Stenehjem had designated the order of battle for the evacuation of Ripcord in the morning, and he wanted all his flight leads present for the briefing, and furthermore, the briefing would not start until I got there.

"Once I arrived, the briefing started and followed the usual five paragraph 'field order' format. Key to me was the flight lineup which was as follows: First in would be C Company (Phoenix) led by Phoenix 16 (House), followed immediately by A Company (Ghostriders) led by yours truly, Ghostrider 16, followed by B Company (Kingsmen). The rest of the division's aircraft would follow in order. This flight order made the most sense as House and I were the most experienced flight leads in the battalion at that time and both of us had been involved in all the combat assaults in and around Ripcord for the entire period of the operation since it was opened.

EVACUATING THE FIREBASE

"The briefing was relatively straight forward and simple. From my perspective, it was simply knowing the critical timed events, such as airstrikes start and end, artillery suppression start and end, aerial rocket artillery times, escorting gunship flight routes, direction of break, our own flight route in and out, the usual details in other words. Deep in our hearts, we all knew that this carefully planned sequence of events was unlikely to survive past the first life, but it was the plan nonetheless."

Morning greeted the firebase as troops hustled to prepare for extraction even as the choppers were en route from Evans.

"July 23 dawned bright and beautiful with clear blue skies and just a few puffy, white clouds," remembered Glennon. "It was picture-perfect flying weather. After I got my 10 aircraft lined up and ready for take-off, I tried to get an update on command frequency, to no avail. It was being 'jammed' by the NVA. I did manage to get in touch with Capt. House on the aviation frequency and he confirmed that everything was still a go and that the NVA were jamming the radios. He confirmed that the overall air mission commander's aircraft was not airborne, and he was filling in as air mission commander, controlling the flight operation at that point while the rest of his flight was inbound to the hill."

Howton and Hardcore were still dazed by the decision not to use pathfinders during extraction activities. That daze lasted only a few hours.

"The next morning started, I don't remember how long it was, maybe 15 minutes, I don't know if we had even brought in a chopper when Lucas was killed," said Howton. "That's when we took over. It was chaotic with all the incoming we received as the choppers were coming in. I did virtually all the radio transmissions from that point to the very end. Hardcore and myself, we're bringing traffic in and at times we'd go out and grab the wounded, bring them back, we were running around like crazy. Caballero would at times run out and physically bring in choppers because it got to the point where we tried to bring these choppers in to different locations because they'd have one zoned in, so I'd move them over to another helipad. We had the CH-47 burning behind us. The TOC was on that upper hill and the CH-47 (Chinook) that got blown up was about 50 yards from where we were."

Between July 22-23 massive artillery and air strikes were conducted in the Ripcord area at known and suspected enemy locations. More than 2,200 rounds of mixed-caliber artillery ammunition were fired in support of the extraction of 2/506th. Orders were to expend all ammunition, leave nothing behind. Beginning at 5:45 a.m., fourteen CH-47s were used to extract 22 sorties, which included six 155mm howitzers, two M-405 bulldozers, communications equipment and an M55 machine gun. Only one of the Chinooks was shot down. Eight others were hit, four of which were later deemed not fit to fly.

Spaulding remembers vividly the sight that morning as the sun began to come up and the American airpower began to mount, ready to take on the largest rescue mission in Army aviation history.

"The China Sea is behind us, the sun's coming up and it's black out in front of you, but as the sun is coming up it's hitting the top of the mountains and it was really beautiful," said Spaulding. "You're somewhat in awe when you're looking at that. At that point, the radios start popping, all the different outfits are calling and telling me they're on their way. I turn south and it was the most awesome sight you ever saw. It looked like thousands of helicopters with the sun reflecting off the plexiglass. Outside is the gunships, inside are the Loaches, then inside are the Hueys, they're all lined up. As far as I can see there are these helicopters coming, with their radios popping. I thought, 'My God, what an awesome sight. And, I'm part of it.' It made you so proud to be an American. Everyone in all those choppers, they were all there for the same reason, to get those guys out."

EVACUATING THE FIREBASE

Glennon and the Hueys made their way westward.

"We took off and headed to our initial checkpoint just to the west of Firebase Jack," said Glennon. "I could see the aircraft making their passes and the flaming napalm strikes going in around the hill – all according to plan. Just then I got a call from Capt. House that his flight was taking heavy fire on approach and some of his aircraft had to break off, but that they would circle around and get in just in front of my flight. He also briefed me on the best route in and where the most fire was coming from. His final comment was 'I hate to keep this damn thing going but you're cleared in.'

Ireland arrived at Ripcord to remove a 155 howitzer. As he brought the bird in, he knew this was a different mission.

"The 23rd is the only day we got hit so bad I didn't know if we'd actually make it back," said Ireland. "We'd taken fire coming in, but often we were never touched, or it just produced small holes. Actually, as a pilot, you're just concentrating on your job, you ignore it. It sounds crazy. You ignore everything around you, the bullets, the artillery explosions. You have to ignore it.

"As we were pulling the 155 out, the whole area lit up with artillery explosions. When we were hooking up we had a round land in front of us, blowing holes through the aircraft, through the plexiglass, through the rotors. As we picked up, we picked up on an angle to our right and mortars landed right where we had been. They just missed us. They had bracketed us and would have hit us had we not pulled out."

When Ireland landed his chopper at Evans, there were holes in the rotors "you could put your arms through," he said. The chopper's hydraulics had also been knocked out.

Kenneth Mayberry had flown Delta Company in to extract Alpha Company prior to returning to Ripcord for the evacuation mission.

REMEMBERING FIREBASE RIPCORD

"We refueled and joined the largest number of airborne aircraft I had ever seen," said Mayberry, an aircraft commander who carried the call sign Phoenix 50. "Every aviation asset the 101st had was airborne. All three lift companies from the 101st and 158th battalions were orbiting in the flatlands. You need to picture in your mind six flights of 10, all flying individual formations nose to tail, orbiting in close proximity to each other. On top of that, groups of Cobras, Loaches, Chinooks and Rangers were everywhere. It was a perfect setting for complete chaos."

Steve Pullen was with 2/17 Cavalry. After breakfast and before sunrise, his captain asked if he'd like to see the evacuation.

"I said, 'Sure,'" he remembered. "I will never forget the sight I saw from a distance. Jets and artillery were hitting the hills. I saw a couple of CH-47s bringing out the artillery. After the CH-47s departed we saw Hueys in a trail formation. The ridges and Ripcord were full of smoke and dust. Despite the smoke, I could clearly see the NVA .51-caliber fire from the surrounding hills and mortar rounds impacting on the firebase. I hated to think we were giving up Ripcord, but never was I so proud to be an Army aviator."

Bravo Company Sgt. Phil Tolson had learned of the extraction the night before as he and his men continued to pull security on the firebase.

"I was told I was going to be the last squad to leave," remembered Tolson. "I didn't like that information." Tolson's day would be hectic, harrowing and death-defying. He wouldn't be alone in the experience.

Tom Chase, a door gunner, flew with the 163rd Aviation Battalion. He described the mood the morning of the 23rd as one of disbelief.

"We took off that morning for Ripcord about 4 a.m.," said Chase. "It was a lovely sunrise coming up over the South China Sea. Disbelief we were going to be pulling an extraction like that under fire – in that terrain – and as quickly as possible."

EVACUATING THE FIREBASE

Lucas hovered high above the firebase in his command chopper as Chinooks lined up to remove the 105s and 155s, something Gen. Sid Berry had ordered. Extraction of equipment began at 6:30 a.m. and all six Chinooks got out, several damaged extensively as 51-caliber fire rained upon the big birds as they hovered into position to hook up the equipment.

Lt. John Fox, a three-tour veteran of Vietnam, explained the "Stairsteps of altitude" at Ripcord, which rose 2,000 feet in elevation. "Recovery helicopters worked from the ground up to maybe 3,000 feet," said Fox. "Four thousand feet was for support aircraft such as support gunships and Cobras. 4,000 up to 5,000 feet was command and control airships, such as those for Harrison and Berry."

Twenty-four loads would be needed to evacuate all the equipment from the firebase. Eight more Chinooks sustained damage and one shot down in the area once manned by the 105s. It was about an hour into the extraction when the big bird crash landed.

"They decided the best thing to do was to pull us out of there," remembered Hand. "We got word we were going to be moved out. We got things ready to move and plans were for us to expend all our ammunition. Artillery was supposed to fire all their rounds before they got slingloaded out."

Troops began loading slicks around 8:30 a.m. Lucas, Harrison and Berry were all stacked up above the firebase having already returned to Evans to refuel. Soon confusion set in as slicks stacked up eastward toward Firebase Jack. House, the steady-handed pilot took over as air mission commander and order returned.

"The command and control bird – flight lead, which was probably the 3rd Brigade Commander Ben Harrison had commo problems," wrote Mayberry, piloting with the C/158th Battalion and House. "Every time he tried to give us an order his radio would break up and we'd hear nothing but the noise of squelch. Fortunately for us our flight lead,

REMEMBERING FIREBASE RIPCORD

Phoenix 16, Capt. Randy House, recognized the gravity of the situation and took over."

House recalled the difficulty in communications with pilots and those on Ripcord during the evacuation. Amidst the chaos, the pilots had to maintain clarity given everything that was happening around that hill.

"Because of communication problems we had, the amount of fire going into Ripcord was knocking antennas and snapping antennas," said House. "It was really bad (communication) and if you can imagine a Huey, there's two FM radios, UHF radio, VHF radio and then your intercom and there's four people on the intercom. The infantry is on FM, the artillery is on FM, the Air Force is on UHF, the gunships are on VHF and all of this is going into your helmet at the same time. You learn to listen to four radios and to listen to your crew chief and gunner and what they are seeing and making sure you don't run into helicopters or run into F4s coming in. When you can read the name of a pilot on his helmet when he's coming in at 3 or 4 or 500 miles an hour dropping, that's close-air support buddy. When your guns are shooting and your machine guns are shooting and they cue the mike, and you're talking to guys on the ground and there's explosion after explosion on the ground from incoming rounds. You can tell what an M-16 is and what an AK is It's almost surreal and what's happening in that little cockpit, plus you have to fly a helicopter."

The pilots never wavered.

"I think there were 63 slicks flying that day," said House. "I was just a little young guy and just in charge of my own company. Someone else was in charge, but then when the chaos happened and the communications got bad all of a sudden I could see nobody was going in to get the infantry off this firebase that was about to be overrun. That's when someone had to take charge. I took charge and everyone just saluted, they were just glad to have someone giving them directions.

EVACUATING THE FIREBASE

That's when we came up with the three pads. (We would) come over the falls to the east, come in a flight of three, I'd be talking to the pathfinder and he'd be telling me the intensity of the fire on the three pads, I at the last minute would call out Pad 2 and that would mean chop 2 would go in and the other two would act as if they'd go in but they would continue on, so we were getting one in at a time, and we're alternating between 1,2 and 3."

Mayberry remembered the plan.

"There were three helipads that they were concentrating on," he said. "Capt. House and the Ripcord pathfinder realized (the NVA) were concentrating on one pad at a time. In other words, pad one would be bombarded, then they would move to pad two to bombard it and then shift to pad three. Capt. House attempted to bring in the aircraft to the pad as soon as the bombardment shifted to the next pad. He immediately organized the flights and had them each individually fly over a prominent waterfall in the area and then would inform each aircraft which pad on Ripcord to land on."

That strategy paid dividends, and saved lives, as the enemy gunners had to shift their fire. Going into all three pads at once meant those choppers would all take fire.

"The emotion was we had a mission to be done. Lives were at stake," said House. "The enemy was strong. It was one of those things that had to be done. I don't remember being stirred up, excited, it was just 'Damn it, we've gotta do this.'"

The first flight of 10 Hueys made go arounds and the Phoenix choppers, with Mayberry and House, were in the second flight of 10.

"I was probably chalk two or three," said Mayberry, referring to position in line. "After reporting falls inbound, I picked my pad and I saw mortars impacting ahead of me – Boom, boom, boom, boom! I counted about four or five mortars impacting and had planned to make a go around when they suddenly stopped. I could see the guys I was supposed to pick up so I immediately elected to go in. Then, as I flared and prepared to land, another mortar impacted and it knocked all the troopers flat, like bowling pins. My left leg burned, like it had been stuck with a hot poker, and I knew I had been hit by shrapnel. Over the intercom someone said, 'Go around' and I said, 'No, get these guys first. I felt responsible and instead of making a go around, I landed.

"Before my skids touched down I saw a flash of my crew chief (John Ackerman) running past the left window and the door gunner (Wayne Wasilk) running past the right window. They carried those wounded soldiers back to my aircraft. I was witness to the greatest act of heroism I had ever seen. One more mortar and they were dead. Because we were on the ground so long I had numerous people calling asking if I was OK or what was wrong. I couldn't answer. I was staring straight ahead at the surreal scene unfolding before me and I was afraid to break the spell for fear another mortar would splash down. After they loaded all the wounded soldiers we departed."

Another Phoenix chopper flew alongside Mayberry's bird to check for battle damage, escorting the crew back to Camp Evans, where Mayberry touched down at Charlie Med, the medical facility.

"My crew tried to help the wounded soldiers using our emergency medical kits," said Mayberry. "These guys were wounded bad, so there was little we could do other than apply compression bandages. I learned that blood has a distinctive odor."

There were two men on the firebase that had been there with Alpha Company March 12, the day of the insertion, and were standing on the firebase the day it was evacuated – Bill Heath, who was by then with Headquarters Company and Dale Lane, the battalion RTO (radio telephone operator).

EVACUATING THE FIREBASE

"We were going around and getting everything in slings," said Heath. "We'd get Chinooks in and get everything out. We had to do that under constant mortar fire. Some guys got hurt, some were killed. At first light choppers started coming in and you're standing there with rigs. It was organized chaos. All of the Kit Carsons were detained. As more and more rockets came in there were fewer places to land. There was smoke, fire, you couldn't land. Some of the equipment couldn't get hauled out. Troops are getting extracted."

It was 9:15 a.m. when a mortar round landed at the feet of Lucas, blowing the legs off the lieutenant colonel and killing Maj. Kenneth Tanner.

"I was standing right next to him," said Lane, battalion radio operator for Alpha, recounting the moment the explosion went off. "There were four of us, me, Lucas, Maj. Tanner and another RTO. As near as I could tell the mortar round landed right in the middle of us, about two feet from any of us. I got blown back into the TOC and had shrapnel wounds on my chest and face and I was kind of blinded. I couldn't see very well. By the time I shook off what happened I might have been out 30 seconds, a minute, but when I came to they had dragged Lucas back into the TOC and I could see well enough to see he was badly wounded. I looked out and saw Maj. Tanner - I had only met him about three hours before that, but he had been blown into some concertina wire, kind of draped in the concertina wire."

Private Gus Allen, who happened to be in the wrong place at the wrong time, walking past, was also killed in the blast.

Heath was prepared to jump on a chopper he and his men were assigned to when he saw Lucas and Tanner go down.

"There was a little pathway across the hill to where we were going to catch our ride," said Heath. "We were to stand on a bunker and jump in the chopper as it came in. I had this horrible feeling that this is not our chopper. Then, 'Boom!' this round came down and it sent Lucas and Tanner up in the air. I could tell the major was dead; he was twitching messed up. We got up and ran over there. Looking at him I thought he died right there. I thought, 'This is really getting serious.' Another chopper came in and it was our time to go. As we are leaving they were telling us to shoot. You could see bad guys off the hill. We got some air and distance from Ripcord and the chopper lost altitude, just dropped. At that point, I'm not ready to go back to war, I'm just ready to get the fuck out of dodge. They are flicking dials and switches. He tilts the chopper and starts going to a hilltop in the distance. He limps it over that hilltop and the hilltops get smaller. He got us to Evans, and dropped the chopper on the pad. It was full of holes. I don't know how many trips he'd made. It was trashed. There were fluids coming out. I was so thankful to make it back. Everyone was kind of in a daze."

As for Lucas, Capt. James Harris, the battalion surgeon, worked frantically to address the lieutenant colonel's lower limbs. Harris was considered a hero on the firebase. Medic James Crawford was assigned senior battalion medical assistant to Harris and said he was "a tremendous guy, very heroic guy. He got the Silver Star. I personally dug shrapnel out of him. He was not afraid of anything."

Harris recalled the incident that ultimately claimed Lucas' life.

"He met up with Maj. Tanner down a little bit from the 155 TOC," said Harris. "They were between there and the gun pits. Somebody said the colonel got hit and I went out the back door to see what happened. There was someone dead. It was Tanner. I grabbed Lucas underneath the armpits and dragged him on his back into the 155 TOC. We got him up on a stretcher. He looked a lot older than he really was. I kept thinking who we have on this firebase that old. Before he came to, someone unzipped his flak jacket and the first thing that popped out was his collar with the cluster and someone said, 'Oh my God, it's Col. Lucas.' That's how we figured out who

EVACUATING THE FIREBASE

it was. We had a couple guys put him on the stretcher and took him down to the lower pad.

"He was definitely not dead when he left the TOC. My assessment at the time was he would likely have both legs amputated. He checked his genitalia and they were intact. There was one point where he said, 'We've gotta stop this bleeding.'"

"When they called me and told me the colonel had been hit, I was to report to the TOC (Tactical Operations Center)," said Capt. Peters. "Doc Harris had him on a stretcher and I was talking to Col. Lucas and that's when he gave me his map and said, 'Well Ben, I guess you got it.' I said, 'Yes sir, I can handle it' and he said, 'I know you can.' I said 'You're going to be alright. We get you out of here and you'll be fine.' The chopper came in for him and I just took it from there."

"Just my humble opinion, I thought he was a goner," said Lane. "He was pretty well shredded up. They said he died on the helicopter going back. I thought he might have died before he left the firebase."

Communication continued to be difficult.

"We were having a hard time getting accountability," said House. "Is everyone off the firebase? That was my question after a while. Is everybody off and once the pathfinders were off I just didn't have good comm(unication)s or any comms so we weren't about to stop this operation. If there was one wounded guy or one guy in a trench, so I was trying to get confirmation from the 506, do we have everyone off? That's when Col. Lucas decided he had to go in and that's when he got killed. The rest of your life you live with the fact I'm communicating with Col. Lucas, I'm calling him, 'Sir I can't keep sending these people in and nobody's getting on my aircraft because every time we go in we get the dickens shot at us.' I don't mind going in but nobody's getting on our aircraft. So Col. Lucas goes in and that's when he dies. A phone call between me and a captain and a lieutenant colonel and the lieutenant colonel ends up dying. I thought about that afterward because I didn't know he had died until the next day, there was so much going on."

When word came that Lucas had been hit, House knew it was he that would be tasked with picking up the wounded lieutenant colonel.

"Getting in and getting out, it was an art form," said House. "I'd done it so many times. I had been talking to him and told him I can't keep sending my guys in if your guys aren't going to get on our aircraft and he says 'I'll take care of it Phoenix 16.' So he goes in and the next thing I know Pathfinder tells me as soon as he jumped off the helicopter a mortar hit and killed him. I couldn't send anybody else in there to get him. It was my job. He died because I asked for his help. I didn't even think about asking anybody else to do the mission. We were orbiting and you could imagine 63 Huey helicopters, I'm not sure how many Chinooks, I'm not sure how many Cobras, I'm not sure how many F4s, but this was a busy place and this is all in a very small area, all this stuff flying around. The guys that loaded his body also got on my aircraft, there wasn't anybody else around.

"The comms were so bad, they said he was down. This was no place for a medevac. They are heavy, they don't have door gunners, so I knew I could get him to Jack or one of the firebases where we could get medical support to him quickly. I knew I could get in there and get him better than anyone else. There was no discussion, this was just done. It was just what had to be done."

House choppered Lucas off Ripcord and delivered his body to Camp Jack, just east of the mountain range in the flatlands, a little over halfway back to Camp Evans. He did so in order to return to Ripcord so he could continue evacuating troops.

Berry was flying over the extraction mission in his command and control chopper, piloted by Lt. John Fox. Word that Lucas had been killed hit the general hard.

EVACUATING THE FIREBASE

"He reached up and touched me on the arm and said Col. Lucas was just killed," remembered Fox. "We were flying right over the top of Ripcord at the time. (Berry) was in the back (of the chopper). He knew Lucas personally. Lucas had been his instructor at Ranger School. He was very saddened, shocked. I knew then he was really upset by it."

Much of Bravo Company was extracted by 9:35 a.m., nearly two hours later than expected due to heavy enemy fire aimed at Ripcord. Hueys were inserted one at a time to extract soldiers.

"I knew everything had to be evacuated before me," said Peters. "I was the kind that does what has to be done, whether it's my job or not. We were calling in the choppers to pick people up. The pathfinders took care of getting artillery and equipment off. Then I still had all my people to get off the firebase."

With mortars falling like raindrops, casualties continued to pile up on the firebase. Many received shrapnel wounds and continued to fight.

"It was like 10:30, 11 o'clock," said Tolson, describing the mortar attack that hit him. "I saw it hit, which was amazing. The way these bunkers were built, you had a fighting position like a foxhole, but it was a rectangular foxhole, big enough for a couple guys to get into, deeper than waist deep but not shoulder deep. I was sitting in the doorway in the bottom of the fighting position. Bombs are falling all over the place and you kind of had to keep your head down. That was the only day I wore a flak jacket and steel pot. The rest of the time it was too damn hot. The flak jackets were too cumbersome and the steel pots were heavy, nobody wanted to wear none of that stuff. I looked up and remember seeing a big orange ball, then it was nighttime. I went from bright sunlight to I'm sound asleep and it's darker than hell. I hear people yell, they got him, he's dead. I thought, 'Oh shit, somebody else got killed.' I eventually opened my eyes. The guys in my bunker said, 'He's not dead.' I'm still kind of goofy and trying to sit up. I didn't even know I got hit. I sat up and looked and I got metal sticking out of my leg, blood running down my arm, but nothing hurts. I'm trying to pull this metal out of my leg and it won't come out. Finally it dawned on me, I got hit. I had no pain, zero, zip."

Lt. Bill Hand got hit with a mortar fragment before he was able to get aboard a chopper. The lieutenant in charge of second platoon just wanted to see his men off safely.

"You feel the responsibility to them and you don't want to let them down," he said. "The survival instinct keeps you going."

"When the choppers would come in the mortars would start hitting the hill," said Peters. "We were having trouble getting people loaded. You would have to scramble to get off the hill. Choppers would stay on a second or two, then take off. As soon as they would take off there would be more rounds hitting."

Bravo Company had been evacuated, as had any remaining artillery.

"We weren't taking anything with us," remembered Hand. "They put termite grenades in those 105s that had been damaged. As soon as the last rounds were fired from the 155s, they were extracted. The helicopters were coming into their firing pits to extract those guys. They would come in and I would get real irritated, that (artillery) would hesitate and those helicopters would have to take off. A number came through and took off empty."

Hand remembered the scene well.

"It was a lot of smoke and people scurrying around," he said. "I was looking to see where the rounds were hitting. If the (NVA) had been more accurate, they could have done a lot more damage. We kept it hush-hush enough that I don't think they realized there was an extraction until it was half over. It was organized chaos."

EVACUATING THE FIREBASE

"Around Ripcord it looked like the World War II movies," said House, noting the shear of incoming fire against the morning sky. The pilots would not be deterred, though. "I had 10 hueys, 20 pilots, and I was the only commissioned officer at times. The rest of them are 18-, 19-, 20-year-old kids right out of high school, unbelievably bright. Maybe they'd spent a year, six months in college. These guys were fearless. 18 year olds just don't think they're going to die. I remember thinking these guys are unbelievable. Nobody wanted to make a go around. A go around meant it was too bad to land and so I was having to force people to make go arounds. They just wouldn't do it. And it was all the pilots."

Bravo's Carl Wyrosdick remembered hearing that choppers wouldn't attempt to land for fear of being shot down.

"It really pisses me off to this day," said Wyrosdick. "They were going to leave us. They ordered the helicopters to abandon us because the incoming was too heavy. Then a helicopter pilot said, 'Screw you, we're going to get our guys off,' and they got us off."

On the firebase, a Chinook was shot down on top of an ammo dump, causing additional chaos.

"The situation went from bad to worse very quickly when a CH-47 was shot down on top of the ammunition storage," said Vazquez-Rodriguez. "The evacuation became very difficult because of the artillery fire and the enemy use of anti-aircraft guns to prevent easy access into the base. While I was monitoring the battalion network I heard that (Lucas) and the operation officers were severely wounded. "

At that point, Vazquez-Rodriguez wanted to return to Ripcord to assist in the evacuation, however attacks on the firebase had intensified.

"I felt that perhaps the company commander providing security for the firebase was not familiar with all the defensive systems I had established when I was there. My pilot got me into Ripcord by maneuvering very low and making several turns. When I landed, there were numerous wounded personnel throughout the area that needed evacuation. It was a very difficult situation for the evacuation pilots

and they were doing their best under the difficult and dangerous situation. The upper (helicopter) area of the base was being used for the extractions. I loaded as many wounded personnel as I could and sent the helicopter back to Camp Evans."

Meanwhile, Vazquez-Rodriguez noticed the southern slope was not well protected so he gathered the walking wounded, those capable of firing their weapons, and put them in position to protect the slope in case of an enemy assault.

Vazquez-Rodriguez recalled the evacuation's final hours and the scramble to get everyone off before the bombers were to come in.

"We continued to load the wounded as the helicopters were available and eventually got everybody out including the dead soldiers," he said. "Lt. Caballero got all the equipment removed and the brigade commander called the B52 bombers to blow the top of Fire Support Base Ripcord to prevent the enemy from using it."

Communication issues, confusion on the firebase and mortars raining in on the firebase meant several men were left isolated, wondering when or if choppers would return to pick them up.

Men from Bravo Company manned bunkers and fought off the North Vietnamese as the crept closer and closer to the firebase. Tolson was ordering his men up from the lower section of the northern side of the base, just below the TOC. He took note of the mortar round sequencing. "I noticed they were coming in three at a time at that point," he said. "Three and a pause, three and a pause." He had the young men run to walkway toward the top of the mountain, then left to the TOC.

EVACUATING THE FIREBASE

Men from Bravo leapfrogged from position to position before making the final trek up the hill to awaiting birds.

"After the third round had hit, I'd send them and they got out," said Tolson.

Andre Rice took the stairs instead of the pathway and lost his leg when a mortar round landed, Tolson said. "I remember he got hit and everybody was yelling and screaming that he was down. Chris Hinman got up and got Rice out of there. I eventually saw Rice at the TOC with his leg blown almost all off. You could see up inside his leg. You could see the veins, the fat and the bone, just a horrible sight."

"I could hear tubes popping everywhere," said Wyrosdick. "You knew the rounds were coming in. There was nothing you could do. I was in a bunker and Capt. (Peters) hollered and said we needed to get those 51s off our ass. He needed a volunteer. I figured I was dead anyway so I went out and asked where he wanted them. Chip and I went out and had a couple LAWs and fired. The helicopter pilot asked us to get one more (51). I just did what I was supposed to do, I kept firing until they quit. Then they opened up on me. Captain said, 'Get your ass out of there!' and I rolled right. Everything's moving slow but your brain is moving fast, do this, do this, do this. You can think clearly. I couldn't even hear anything. All the fire stopped, the noise – kind of like training kick in I guess."

Tolson and Ewe Meyer stripped the M-60 machine gun off one of the downed choppers, collected ammunition, grabbed an asbestos glove and hit Tolson's bunker as the NVA continued to creep closer.

"The gooks are trying to come up the mountain after us," said Tolson. "Ewe and I are taking turns shooting this machine gun down the mountain, one guy holding it with the asbestos glove so you didn't burn your hand and the other guy hitting the triggers. When the barrel got hot, we'd hose it down with LSA. We're just going nuts with that."

Peters ordered the men to prepare for evacuation as the birds started coming in. Rounds continued to rain on the firebase as the brave chopper pilots swooped in and departed as quickly as they arrived.

"They said, 'Go!' and I ran as fast as I could go," remembered Wyrosdick. "I heard rounds hitting the door, the dirt. How they missed me I have no idea. As I jumped in, the floor had blood all over it and I slid all the way to the other side. The door gunner grabbed me and jerked me back in. The bird was already gone. I looked down and it was like ants coming out of an anthill, they were just all over the place."

Tolson eventually noticed no one was around.

"I took off to the TOC," he recounted. "Before long a bird or two comes and everyone is gone but me and a couple of my guys. There's like three or four of us left. I had no contact with anybody, didn't see anybody, didn't hear anybody firing any rounds, no one yelling. I thought we were alone then a couple guys came out and I have no idea who they were or who they were with."

Those two were Pathfinders Howton and Caballero.

"As the day went on, I didn't think we were ever going to get off this hill," said Howton. "We would go around checking bunkers to see if anybody was left. We'd fire some rounds down the hill every now and again."

The men gathered to gameplan as the NVA continued to attempt to break the perimeter.

"I may not get out of here but there's going to be a pile of those little bastards in front of here before I'm gone," Tolson remembered telling the men. He then suggested the men scatter, fire rounds from time to time to give the impression there were more Americans on the hill than there were in hopes to keeping them at bay until another chopper could get in."

EVACUATING THE FIREBASE

It is unclear who was on the last chopper out. It could have been Caballero and Howton, it could have been Tolson and Wopperer. Each made it back safely, though. Capt. Peters said he and two others were the last off.

"The whole time I thought if there's any way we get out of here in one piece, it will be a miracle, it will be God's miracle," said Howton. "I got a little shrapnel in my left arm that I didn't bother with. I was praying. I was hoping it wouldn't take another mortar round, jumped on the helicopter and waited to get hit. It was brutal, so many guys were screwed up. The adrenaline was going for hours and hours and hours. I got off there and was just wiped out."

Peters said he remembered everyone had vacated the firebase when he and three others were left.

"When we got down to the last chopper it was Lt. Wallace, myself and an RTO," the captain said. "Everything just went quiet. It was just nothing. We waited for what seemed like 20 minutes, but it was probably more like five minutes, for the chopper to pick us up. We jumped on and it took off. They went high and we looked back at the firebase. When we did that, it was like you had been carrying a 200-pound sack on your back and someone had just lifted it off. Relief.

"There were a lot of people that said they saw people coming up the hill. I didn't see anything like that. Ben Harrison asked me if I saw anyone coming up. I said no. He said he didn't see anything either. When everything was going on, you're thinking about how to get everything done, accomplishing everything that's gotta be done. You don't have time to get scared. I was really concerned about people getting hit. When we were the last ones off the hill, Lt. (Bill) Hand, when I got back to the rear, was among some that thought I had been left behind. Lt. Hand was trying to get a group together to go back to get me. I got back and they wanted to go get something to eat. I said, 'Let's go down here and pray for the ones that didn't make it.'"

REMEMBERING FIREBASE RIPCORD

Tolson's account differed a bit, but nonetheless was just as convincing.

"I'm on the radio in the TOC by the doorway at this point and I'm starting to think I don't want to do any running," said Tolson. "My leg doesn't hurt, it's just stiff from the shrapnel. They were out there moving and firing, then they were gone. I don't know where they went. I got a hold of one of the pilots and told them I was still at the TOC and I needed a ride. They came back and said they aren't coming, there's too much incoming. With that I gave them a piece of my mind. I remember telling them, 'Don't come back then, or I'll shoot your ass down.' I was pissed. Then a guy called me and said he was Phoenix 16 (House), said he was coming in, wasn't landing, would pass in front of the TOC slowly and I needed to jump on. Soon after that, this helicopter came in from Impact Rock. I jumped on the helicopter. I'm laying face down on the floor and all of a sudden this guy lands on top of me. I have no idea who he is.

"This helicopter, I swear to God it was vertical, nose down, going down the side of that mountain 9,000 miles an hour. He just went off across the top of the mountain and dove straight toward the ground. I thought we were dying."

When he realized all was well, Tolson sat up, realized he had a pack of peanut M&Ms in his pocket, opened them and shared them with the pilot.

"I guess he liked them too," said Tolson. "We ate them all the way back to Camp Evans."

Kenneth Mayberry's chopper departed Charlie Med and limped back to the Phoenix Nest, its home base. Mayberry's chopper had inserted Delta Company early the morning of July 23 so that the young troopers could evacuate the bloodied remnants of Alpha Company, then took part in the extraction of troops from Ripcord.

EVACUATING THE FIREBASE

His Huey landed approached the firebase amid a barrage of mortar rounds and immediately turned medevac, rescuing several wounded troops. Soon it rose again and took off for Camp Evans.

Once it landed at its home base, it was immediately grounded.

"I had over 40 holes," said Mayberry of his bird. "The floor of our aircraft looked like someone had taken a five-gallon bucket of blood and dumped it on the floor. The bird's next flight would be under the belly of a Chinook slingloaded to Da Nang for repair."

Mayberry had taken shrapnel in his leg during the rescue mission, but refused to be treated throughout the day.

"My battalion called twice asking if I had been wounded," he said. "They had seen my aircraft. I lied and said no. By the time I got in that night my leg was really hurting so I got a beer and went to our medical hooch and had the shrapnel extracted."

The heroism of his door gunner, Wayne Wasilk, and crew chief, John Ackerman, did not go unnoticed.

"I tried to put them in for medals," said Mayberry. "I thought Silver Stars were appropriate but my platoon leader told me he would have to put me in for a higher award, so I dropped it. Medals were not a high priority then. I regret that now."

Air Force pilots also played a huge role in the successful evacuation of Firebase Ripcord, soaring in and around the firebase dropping 250- and 500-pound bombs as well as napalm.

In the days following the evacuation, fast movers revisited Ripcord, dropping bombs on remaining bunkers and anything the NVA could have used.

REMEMBERING FIREBASE RIPCORD

Gen. John Hennessey, on July 31, sent the following correspondence to the commander of the Seventh Air Force:

"Because of the extreme enemy pressure on the firebase the extraction could not have been successful accomplished without your assistance. The attack against hostile positions in the Ripcord area by your aircraft before, during and after the operation insured that friendly losses were held to a minimum. No one appreciates your support more than the infantrymen and artillerymen who were on the ground."

Of those final days, Jim Fairhall wrote in a Ripcord Report, "Flying in support of Firebase Ripcord wasn't one of the Air Force's better-known jobs. It wasn't as glamorous as hitting a bridge in North Vietnam. But many of the pilots of the 366th Tactical Fighter Wing knew that something bad was going on in the mountains overlooking the A Shau Valley and did their best to help the troops on a battered hill called Ripcord and the jungle around it."

Bruce Brady, a member of Alpha Company, is the father of the author, Chris Brady. Wounded in July 1970, Bruce was hospitalized aboard the USS Sanctuary, then in Japan before being shipped home to serve the remainder of his duty at Fort Carson, Colo., where Chris was born June 8, 1971. Photo provided by Chris Brady.

Acknowledgments

Telling the story of combat is near impossible, just ask any veteran who has seen real combat. With bullets flying, jets screaming overhead, choppers rumbling in the distance, fellow soldiers screaming in pain, it's an experience only those who have been there can adequately communicate and even then, accounts of the same action can vary dramatically. Quite simply, the reality of war is incomprehensible to anyone who hasn't lived it first-hand. Attempting to tell the story of a four-and-a-half month battle that raged in the triple-canopied jungles of the A Shau Valley in the northern most reaches of South Vietnam is tough, but not nearly as tough as the men you read about in the pages of this book.

To be able to tell their story is the single greatest privilege I've been given in my career as a journalist and writer. It's a humbling task and I've taken great care in telling their stories. This is their story, first-hand accounts of what it was like to live in conditions most cannot fathom, fight in a kill-or-be-killed theater in a time where GIs throughout the rest of the country were being cycled homeward.

Thanks first goes to Frank Marshall, who graciously allowed me into his home when I first had questions about what happened at Firebase

Ripcord in 1970. Marshall was there from day one in March 1970 through the siege throughout July and wounded prior to the final extraction July 23. His dedication to the men who fought at Firebase Ripcord through the Ripcord Association is absolute and worthy of tremendous respect.

It is thanks to Marshall that I was able to reach out to hundreds of veterans of the Battle of Firebase Ripcord. He and Lee Widjeskog, who himself dedicates so much time and effort to the Ripcord Association, have been nothing but welcoming and helpful. Each was willing to assist me with every question I've had over the course of the year-plus I spent researching the battle. For that I'm eternally grateful.

Thanks to Marshall and Widjeskog, I was able to spend considerable time with veterans of Ripcord who shared incredible stories, experiences that have lived with them through decades, experiences some had not shared with anyone in their own families. There were tears shed and bonds created. Several of those interviewed were connected with men who had not spoken to one another in 45 years, despite the fact each lived in the other's mind near daily.

Most importantly, the lens of war was opened through the men who had lived it.

I must also thank Chuck Hawkins, who provided me with so much information about the battle, both in terms of background and personal insight. He always made himself available, no matter what corner of the globe he may have been in at the time, and for that I'm thankful. As an officer on the ground, Hawkins' commentary on the battle and the men who were there proved invaluable. To have gleaned information from such a respected officer left me humbled.

Likewise, thanks to Ben Harrison, retired Major General, who himself authored a book about the battle, "Hell On A Hilltop", required reading for anyone interested in the history of the Vietnam War and the Battle For Firebase Ripcord. Gen. Harrison made himself available whenever I had questions and meeting him was a true honor.

Ken Miller, who served with the 3rd Brigade Air Cavalry, was of great help. He opened his home and allowed me in to take part in serious discussion of the war, pre-Ripcord dating back to Hamburger Hill and through Ripcord. His openness allowed me insight into the war from battling in the triple-canopied jungles to the battles that continued in life postwar for these men. Other conversations and correspondence with Ripcord veterans like Steve Matsumoto and Leonard Moore and veterans from the 101st such as Wilburn Wall, Ronald Hudson and Arthur Wiknik Jr. proved invaluable as well.

Thanks also to Dr. James Smither, who heads up the Veterans History Project at Grand Valley State University. Dr. Smither graciously agreed to read numerous drafts, as did Hawkins, Marshall and Widjeskog, to ensure accuracy. Smither's work with the Veterans History Project at GVSU is to be admired and will forever serve to remind us what so many sacrificed to ensure the quality of life so many take for granted today in the United States.

An enormous thank you goes out to all the men who agreed to speak with me. Whether thirty minutes or hours on end, the conversations with the men who fought at Firebase Ripcord left me further driven to dig deeper and keep going. Telling their stories was an honor.

It is through the stories of these men that one can begin to understand what combat in I Corps of South Vietnam was like. No one, other than those who were there, will fully encapsulate the chaos that is war. Two men fighting just an arm's length apart, scanning the thick jungle before them saw two vastly different landscapes, vastly different outcomes as a result of fighting the North Vietnamese.

War is confusing, no matter how much training a soldier goes through. Throw in the fact it's 110 degrees, you've spent the entire morning humping a 90-pound rucksack up a mountain and you haven't had a warm meal or shower in over a month, and you understand how events can become lost in a myriad of experiences that are rarely marked by times, dates or calendars.

I must also thank my father, Bruce Brady. It took many years to fully understand what indeed he lived through during his time in South Vietnam and in hindsight, it's clear to me why he withheld information for so many years. His story is similar to most who spoke with me, yet completely unique in its own way. Being able to speak with the fraternity of veterans from the 101st Airborne Division has allowed me to better understand my own father and thus strengthened our bond.

For that, I'm forever indebted.

It again comes back to the reality of having been a combat soldier. How do you tell someone what it's like to see your buddy ripped apart by a rocket-propelled grenade? How do you explain having to make the decision to kill or be killed? How do you explain what your emotions are like when you are charged with stripping the clothes off a member of your platoon that was killed in action, and placing his body, or what was left of it, in a body bag? How do you explain what it's like to live through a firefight, then have to sleep that night having not eaten and with the realization that your dead friends are laying on the ground near you awaiting the next helicopter out?

"In a sense, some of it is contempt," said Bob Layton, who served as a lieutenant with Bravo Company, 2/501. "I don't feel I need to explain myself to you because you were back here going to frat parties and getting laid and I was in Vietnam doing what I had to do. That could be part of it. Part of it could be that silent John Wayne stuff. My dad and their dads were in World War II and they didn't talk about it. Every now and again you'd try with someone you trust. You realize you can't explain it. You can't explain combat to someone who has not been in combat."

That is why the Ripcord Association serves such an integral role in the ability of these men to lead normal lives even 45 years after their engagement in the jungles of Vietnam. Many have held on to their memories for decades, scared to share for fear of what may happen if the truth is deemed too outrageous to be believed by someone they love. It was only after attending a Ripcord Association reunion, or meeting individually with others who served in the Area of Operations, that they were able to release the memories and pain of those days in combat. While these men may not have served in same foxholes, they fought the same enemy and endured the same hell on earth over those months in the jungles and mountains of I Corps.

"That's why I'm comfortable here," said Layton, while attending the 2014 reunion in Myrtle Beach, S.C. "There are no questions here. We all understand each other on that basic level. I'd just be frustrated because I couldn't explain it the way that person would understand. You can't explain getting shot at and seeing dead bodies."

The stories of these men need to be heard, deserve to be heard.

Thanks to the dozens of Vietnam veterans from Central Pennsylvania – Marines and those from the Air Force and Navy – that sat down with me for interviews, further providing me background for this project. There was no good area in Vietnam and those who fought from the Me Kong Delta to the Central Highlands to the Demilitarized Zone deserve this nation's gratitude.

Special thanks too to Greg Maresca (Marine Corps, retired) for invaluable input throughout this process.

It is through the Standard Journal Newspaper, Milton, Pennsylvania, and Publisher Amy Moyer that I was afforded the opportunity to interview so many and glean so much additional information about the Vietnam War, from 1963 through the early 1970s.

Lastly, thanks to my family: My wife, Kay, and my son and daughter, Justis and Katlyn. This has been a long, and at times, trying process. Having this war on my mind for this length of time has certainly filtered into my family life and it's had its trying moments.

The following list includes the names of those men killed in the Ripcord Area of Operation under the command of Lt. Col. Andre Lucas.

March 12, 1970

Daniel Heather, Alpha Company, 2/506
Dudley Davis, Alpha Company, 2/506
Gerald Shanor, Charlie Company, 2/506

March 16, 1970

James Stanley, Charlie Company, 2/506

March 26, 1970

Marvin Shell, Bravo Company, 2/506

March 31, 1970

Harry Hayes, Bravo Company, 2/506
Newton Tapp, Bravo Company, 2/506
Thomas Shriner, Bravo Company, 2/506

April 1, 1970

Milton Swain, 326th Engineers
William Wall III, B-319th Artillery
Terry Ratcliff, Bravo Company, 2/506
Donald Ragsdale, Bravo Company, 2/506

Don Heimark, Bravo Company, 2/506
George Underdown, Bravo Company, 2/506
Carl Barnett, Bravo Company, 2/506
James Miller, C-319 Artillery

April 3, 1970

John Wilson, Bravo Company, 2/506.

April 6, 1970

Steve Steward, Charlie Company, 2/506
Carl Goodson, Charlie Company, 2/506
Lawrence Christman, Charlie Company, 2/506.

April 8, 1970

Lynn Osborn, Delta Company, 2/506

April 9, 1970

Charles Selman, Bravo Company, 2/501
LeRoy Nelson, Bravo Company, 2/501
James Mace, Bravo Company, 2/501
Herman Clay Jr., Bravo Company, 2/501

April 10, 1970

Donald Sistrunk, Bravo Company, 2/501

April 15, 1970

Dean Dafler, Alpha Company, 2/506
Charles Steffler, Alpha Company, 2/506
Bobby Young, Alpha Company, 2/506

April 16, 1970

Dennis Heinz, Charlie Company, 2/506

April 17, 1970

Norman Peery, Bravo Company, 2/501

April 18, 1970

Michael Vagnone, Alpha Company, 2/501
Robert Dangberg, Alpha Company, 2/501

April 19, 1970

Dean Frey, Alpha Company, 2/501
Jeffrey Joseph, Bravo Company, 2/501
James Jarrett, Bravo Company, 2/501

April 23, 1970

Garry Worley, Alpha Company, 2/501
Benjamin Nicks III, Echo Company, 2/501

April 28, 1970

Raymond Susi, Echo Company, 2/506

April 29, 1970

Edgar Berner, Headquarters Company
Jeffrey Klaves, Headquarters Company

April 30, 1970

David Staton, B Troop, 2/17 Cavalry

John Sensing, B Troop, 2/17 Cavalry
Robert Masseth, B Troop, 2/17 Cavalry

May 8, 1970

David Huberty, Headquarters Company

May 11, 1970

Albert Milburn, Delta Company, 2/506

May 14, 1970

Robert Lowe, Alpha Company, 2/506

May 16, 1970

Gerald Mauney, Alpha Company, 2/506

May 18, 1970

Nicholas Saunders, Charlie Company, 158th AHB
Robert Cole, Charlie Company, 158th AHB
Carlton Gray, Charlie Company, 158th AHB
Harry Stone, Headquarters Company
John Darling Jr., Headquarters Company

May 26, 1970

David Johnson, 326th Medical, Eagle Dust Off
William Hawkins, 326th Medical, Eagle Dust Off
Edward O'Brien, 326th Medical, Eagle Dust Off
Bruce Graham, 326th Medical, Eagle Dust Off

June 3, 1970

Wieland Norris, Alpha Company, 2/506

June 5, 1970

Charles Richardson, B Troop, 2/17 Cavalry
Vernon Hovey III, B Troop, 2/17 Cavalry

June 8, 1970

Winfred Smith, Alpha Company, 2/506

July 2, 1970

Robert Radcliff Jr., Charlie Company, 2/506
Stephen Harber, Charlie Company, 2/506
Robert Zoller III, Charlie Company, 2/506
Lee Lenz, Charlie Company, 2/506
Thomas Hewitt, Charlie Company, 2/506
Thomas Herndon, Charlie Company, 2/506
Roger Sumrall, Charlie Company, 2/506
Richard Conrardy, Charlie Company, 2/506

July 3, 1970

Robert Utecht, Bravo Company, 2/506

July 4, 1970

William Ray, 58th Infantry Scout Dogs
William Sullivan, Charlie Company, 2/501
Jimmie Robinson, Charlie Company, 2/501
Carl Mickens, Charlie Company, 2/501
Gary Thaden, Charlie Company, 2/501

July 5, 1970

Michael Waymire, Headquarters Company

July 6, 1970

Sandy Porter, Bravo Company, 1/506

July 7, 1970

Gerald Risinger, Charlie Company, 2/506
Lewis Howard Jr., Delta Company, 2/506
Michael Grimm, Delta Company, 2/506
Charlies Beals, Delta Company, 2/506

July 8, 1970

Rickey Scott, Charlie Company, 2/506
James Hupp, Charlie Company, 2/506

July 9, 1970

Terry Williams, Echo Company, 2/501

July 10, 1970

Frederick Raymond Jr., Alpha Company, 2-11 Artillery
Victor De Foor, Bravo Company, 2/506
Roy Johnson, Echo Company, 2/506
Patrick Bohan, Headquarters Company

July 14, 1970

Dennis Huffine, Bravo Company, 2/501
Terry Palm, Delta Company, 2/501

Paul Guimond, Delta Company, 2/501
Gary Schneider, Delta Company, 2/501
Keith Utter, Delta Company, 2/501
William Jones, Delta Company, 2/501
James Hembree, Delta Company, 2/501
John Keister, Delta Company, 2/501

July 16, 1970

Richard Timmons, Alpha Company, 2/501
Michael Walker, Alpha Company, 159th AHB
Burke Miller, Alpha Company, 2-11 Artillery
David Beyl, Delta Company, 2/501
William Rollason, Delta Company, 2/501

July 20, 1970

Larry Plett, Bravo Company, 2-319th Artillery
Dennis Fisher, Bravo Company, 326th Engineers
Durl Calhoun, Bravo Company, 326th Engineers
John Knott, Delta Company, 1/506
Bill Browning, Delta Company, 1/506
Patrick De Wulf, Delta Company, 1/506
Eloy Valle, Delta Company, 1/506

July 21, 1970

Brent Law, 326th Medical, Eagle Dust Off
David Johnson, Alpha Company, 2-11 Artillery
James Kalsu, Alpha Company, 2-11 Artillery
Larry McDowell, Bravo Company, 2/506
Roberto Flores, Bravo Company, 2/506
Francis Maune, Bravo Company, 2/506
Ronald Schultz, Delta Company, 1/506
Donald Workman, Delta Company, 1/506

Robert Hays, Delta Company, 1/506
Frank Asher, Delta Company, 1/506
Peter Huk, Delta Company, 1/506

July 22, 1970

Danny Fries, Alpha Company, 2/506
Ovell Spruill, Alpha Company, 2/506
Robert Journell III, Alpha Company, 2/506
Virgil Bixby, Alpha Company, 2/506
Mark Draper, Alpha Company, 2/506
William Pahissa, Alpha Company, 2/506
Thomas Schultz, Alpha Company, 2/506
Gerald Singleton, Alpha Company, 2/506
John Kreckel, Alpha Company, 2/506
Robert Brown Jr., Alpha Company, 2/506
John Babich, Alpha Company, 2/506
Donald Severson, Alpha Company, 2/506
Steven Olson, Bravo Company, 2-319 Artillery
Stanley Diehl, Delta Company, 2/506

July 23, 1970

Harvey Neal, Alpha Company, 2/506
Gus Allen, Alpha Company, 2/506
Wilfred Warner Jr., Delta Company, 2/501
Kenneth Tanner, Headquarters Company
Andre Lucas, Headquarters Company

The following is a list of names of those men killed from 3rd Brigade, 101st Airborne Division during the Ripcord battle. These names include those killed at firebases surrounding the Ripcord Area of Operation as well.

March 12, 1970

1st Lt. Dudley Davis, Alpha Company, 2/506; Spc. 4 Daniel Heater, Alpha Company, 2/506; Cpt. Gerald Shanor, Alpha Company, 2/506.

March 13, 1970

Spc. 4 Robert Goosen, Alpha Company, 2/501; Spc. 4 Benjamin Jackson, Echo Company, 2/501.

March 14, 1970

Spc. 4 Cecil Dobson, Alpha Company, 1/506; 1st Lt. Gerald Hauswirth, Alpha Company, 1/506.

March 15, 1970

Sgt. Paul Carson, Alpha Company, 2/501.

March 16, 1970

Spec. 4 James Stanley, Charlie Company, 2/506.

March 17, 1970

Spec. 4 Carl Gilbertson, Delta Company, 1/506.

March 20, 1970

PFC Dale Blake, Charlie Company, 1/506; Sgt. James Davis, Charlie Company, 1/506; Spec. 4 Harold Harris, Charlie Company, 1/506; Cpl. Philip Knieper, Charlie Company, 1/506; Spec. 4 James Kurth, Charlie Company, 1/506; Spec. 4 Ronald Leonard, Charlie Company, 1/506; Spec. 4 Rudolph Lovato, Charlie Company, 1/506; PFC Michael McGuire, Charlie Company, 1/506; Spec. 4 Gary Stacey, Charlie Company, 1/506; Spec. 4 Willie Walker Jr., Charlie Company,

1/506; Spec. 4 Tinsley Wells Jr., Charlie Company, 1/506; PFC Dennis Morrill, Bravo Company, 326th Engineers; PFC Robert Thompson, Bravo Company, 326th Engineers.

March 21, 1970

S.Sgt. John Wanto, Alpha Company, 1/506.

March 22, 1970

PFC John Sams Jr., Charlie Company, 1/506.

March 24, 1970

PFC Donald McKee, Charlie Company, 1/506.

March 26, 1970

Sgt. Marvin Shell, Bravo Company, 2/506.

March 31, 1970

1st Lt. Harry Hayes, Bravo Company, 2/506; S.Sgt. Thomas Shriner, Bravo Company, 2/506; PFC Newton Tapp, Bravo Company, 2/506.

April 1, 1970

Cpl. Carl Barnett, Charlie Company, 2/506; Sgt. Don Heimark, Charlie Company, 2/506; Cpl. Donald Ragsdale, Charlie Company, 2/506; S.Sgt. Terry Ratcliff, Charlie Company, 2/506; Sgt. George Underdown, Charlie Company, 2/506; 2nd Lt. William Wall III, Charlie Company, 2/506; Spec. 4 Milton Swain, Bravo Company, 326th Engineers.

April 3, 1970

1st Lt. John Wilson, Bravo Company, 2/506.

April 6, 1970

1st Lt. Lawrence Christman, Charlie Company, 2/506; Spec. 4 Carl Goodson, Charlie Company, 2/506; Sgt. Steve Seward, Charlie Company, 2/506.

April 7, 1970

Sgt. Paul Frink, Delta Company, 1/506.

April 8, 1970

Spec. 4 Lynn Osborn, Delta Company, 2/506.

April 9, 1970

Cpl. Herman Clay, Bravo Company, 2/501; S.Sgt. James Mace, Bravo Company, 2/501; Cpl. Leroy Nelson, Bravo Company, 2/501; Cpl. Charles Selman, Echo Company, 2/501.

April 10, 1970

S.Sgt. Donald Sistrunk, Bravo Company, 2/501; PFC David Kays, Alpha Company, 1/506.

April 15, 1970

Sgt. Walter Bartley Jr., Alpha Company, 2/506; Sgt. Dean Dafler, Alpha Company, 2/506; Sgt. Charles Steffler, Alpha Company, 2/506; Sgt. Bobby Young, Alpha Company, 2/506.

April 16, 1970

Cpl. Dennis Heinz, Delta Company, 2/506.

April 17, 1970

Cpl. Norman Peery, Bravo Company, 2/506

April 18, 1970

Sgt. William Haakinson III, Alpha Company, 1/506.

April 19, 1970

S.Sgt. Dean Frey, Alpha Company, 2/501; S.Sgt James Jarrett, Bravo Company, 2/501; S.Sgt. Jeffrey Joseph, Bravo Company, 2/501.

April 20, 1970

S.Sgt. James Lockett, Charlie Company, 1/506; Sgt. Kent Longmire, Charlie Company, 1/506.

April 23, 1970

Sgt. Benjamin Nicks III, Echo Company, 2/501; Cpl. Garry Worley, Alpha Company, 2/501.

April 25, 1970

PFC Ronald Cline, Bravo Company, 1/506; Sgt. Boyd Magee, Charlie Company, 1/506; Cpl. Billy Sebastian, Bravo Company, 1/506.

April 26, 1970

Cpl. Eudell Kotrous, Bravo Company, 1/506.

April 29, 1970

CWO Edgar Berner, Headquarters Company, 3rd Brigade; Spec. 4 Jeffrey Klaves, Headquarters Company, 3rd Brigade; Cpl. Robert Boggs, Alpha Company, 2/501; Cpl. Dennis Hunter, Alpha Company, 2/501; Cpl. Carl Patten, Alpha Company, 2/501; Sgt. Roy Snyder, Alpha Company, 2/501; Sgt. William Stieve, Alpha Company, 2/501; Cpl. Linwood Walker, Echo Company, 2/501; Sgt. Frederick Wortmann, Alpha Company, 2/501.

April 30, 1970

Sgt. Larry Jones, Echo Company, 2/501; Sgt. Robert Shannon, Alpha Company, 2/501; Sgt. Donnie Horton, Alpha Company, 2/502; SFC Leon Tetkoski, Alpha Company, 1/506.

May 1, 1970

Spec. 4 John Barrett, Bravo Company, 1/506; S.Sgt. Robert Collett Jr., Bravo Company, 1/506; Sgt. Larry Henshaw, Bravo Company, 1/506; Sgt. Jimmy Hill, Bravo Company, 1/506; PFC Thomas Kaufman, Bravo Company, 1/506; PFC Samuel Lance, Bravo Company, 1/506; Spec. 4 Calvin Nolt, Bravo Company, 1/506.

May 6, 1970

Sgt. Michael Antle, Charlie Company, 2/501; Cpl. George Bennett Jr., Alpha Company, 2/501; Sgt. Melvin Bowman, Charlie Company, 2/501; Sgt. Gregory Chavez, Alpha Company, 2/501; Cp. Douglas Day, Alpha Company, 2/501; S.Sgt. Robert Denton, Alpha Company, 2/501; Sgt. Jay Diller, Charlie Company, 2/501; S.Sgt. Jon Doolittle, Charlie Company, 2/501; S.Sgt. Kenneth Foutz, Charlie Company, 2/501; Cpl. Lawrence Gordon, Alpha Company, 2/501; Cpt. Richard Hawley Jr., Echo Company, 2/501; Cpl. Tommy Hindman, Charlie Company, 2/501; Sgt. James Jennings, Headquarters Company, 3rd Brigade; Sgt. Frank Lewis, Alpha

Company, 2/501; CSM Raymond Long Jr., Headquarters Company, 3rd Brigade; S.Sgt. David Ogden, Echo Company, 2/501; Sgt. Dickie Reagan, Echo Company, 2/501; SFC Gary Snyder, Alpha Company, 2/501; Spec. 4 Ronald Van Beukering, Alpha Company, 2/501; Sgt. Edward Veser, Echo Company, 2/501; Cpl. Phillip Warfield, Charlie Company, 2/501; Sgt. John Widen, Alpha Company, 2/501; S.Sgt. John Willey, Alpha Company, 2/501; S.Sgt. Frederick Ziegenfelder, Alpha Company, 2/501.

May 7, 1970

Cpl. Robert Berger, Delta Company, 1/506; PFC Peter Cook, Delta Company, 1/506; 1st Lt. Lawrence Fletcher, Delta Company, 1/506; Cpl. Jose Gonzalez, Delta Company, 1/506; Sgt. Lloyd Jackson, Alpha Company, 2/506; Cpl. Robert Lohenry, Delta Company, 1/506; Sgt. David McCranie, Alpha Company, 1/506; S.Sgt. Joseph Redmond, Delta Company, 1/506.

May 10, 1970

1st. Lt. Ronald Smiley, Delta Company, 1/506.

May 11, 1970

S.Sgt. Alber Milburn, Delta Company, 2/506.

May 14, 1970

Sgt. Robert Lowe, Alpha Company, 2/506.

May 16, 1970

Cpl. David Christopherson, Alpha Company, 2/506; S.Sgt. David Jones, Alpha Company, 2/506; Cpl. John Mariani, Alpha Company, 2/506; Sgt. Gerald Mauney, Alpha Company, 2/506; Sgt. Billy McCullough, Alpha Company, 2/506.

May 18, 1970

1st Lt. John Darling Jr., Headquarters Company, 2/506; Sgt. Harry Stone, Headquarters Company, 2/506.

May 19, 1970

Cpl. Thomas Johnson, Delta Company, 1/506.

May 23, 1970

Cpl. Alan Gross, Alpha Company, 1/506; SFC Cecil Schofield, Alpha Company, 1/506; 1st Lt. Frank Verlihay Jr., Alpha Company, 1/506.

May 25, 1970

1st Lt. Jerry Smith, Delta Company, 1/506

June 3, 1970

PFC Wieland Norris, Alpha Company, 2/506.

June 8, 1970

Sgt. Winfred Smith, Alpha Company, 2/506.

June 16, 1970

Cpl. Marcus Maddox, Delta Company, 2/501.

June 22, 1970

Sgt. Mark Bush, Headquarters Company, 1/506

June 23, 1970

Cpl. Michael Baldini, Delta Company, 1/506; Cpl. Donald Rowley, Delta Company, 1/506.

June 24, 1970

Sgt. George Capuano, Alpha Company, 1/506; Sgt. James Hicks, Alpha Company, 1/506; Cpl. John Ringholm, Alpha Company, 1/506.

June 25, 1970

Cpl. Richard Barnes, Alpha Company, 1/506; Cpl. Dale Meehan, Alpha Company, 1/506; Cpl. Dennis Ritter, Alpha Company, 1/506; Cpl. Marvin Snider, Alpha Company, 1/506.

June 26, 1970

S.Sgt. Victor Cambas, Bravo Company, 1/506; S.Sgt. Halqua Cliburn, Bravo Company, 1/506; Cpl. John Garza, Bravo Company, 1/506; Cpl. Rodney Koerner, Bravo Company, 1/506.

June 27, 1970

Sgt. Gerald McDowell, Bravo Company, 1/506.

July 2, 1970

PFC Richard Conrardy, Charlie Company, 2/506; Sgt. Thomas Herndon, Charlie Company, 2/506; Cpt. Thomas Hewitt, Charlie Company, 2/506; Sgt. Lee Lenz, Echo Company, 2/506; Spec. 4 Robert Radcliff, Charlie Company, 2/506; Sgt. Roger Sumrall, Echo Company, 2/506; Spec. 4 Robert Zoller II, Charlie Company, 2/506.

July 3, 1970

Robert Utecht, Bravo Company, 2/506.

July 4, 1970

Cpl. Carl Mickens, Charlie Company, 2/501; Sgt. Jimmie Robinson, Charlie Company, 2/501; 1st Lt. William Sullivan, Charlie Company, 2/501; Sgt. Gary Thaden, Charlie Company, 2/501; Spec. 4 William Lyons, Alpha Company, 2/502; Sgt. William Ray, 58th Infantry Platoon, Scout Dogs, 101st Airborne.

July 5, 1970

Spec. 4 Forest Stone, D Troop, 2nd Squadron, 17th Cavalry; Sgt. Michael Waymire, Charlie Company, 2/501.

July 6, 1970

S.Sgt. Sandy Porter, Delta Company, 2/506.

July 7, 1970

Cpl. Michael Grimm, Delta Company, 2/506; Sgt. Gerald Risinger, Delta Company, 2/506.

July 8, 1970

Sgt. Stanley Cruse, Troop D, 2nd Squadron, 17th Cavalry; Sgt. Harold Frank, Troop D, 2nd Squadron, 17th Cavalry; Spec. 4 Joseph McDermott III, Troop D, 2nd Squadron, 17th Cavalry; PFC Harry McEwing, Troop D, 2nd Squadron, 17th Cavalry; S.Sgt. Allen Stroud, Troop D, 2nd Squadron, 17th Cavalry; Sgt. 1st Class Walter Waker, Troop D, 2nd Squadron, 17th Cavalry; Spec. 4 James Hupp, Delta Company, 2/506; Cpl. Rickey Scott, Delta Company, 2/506.

July 9, 1970

Sgt. Gregory Dodge, Echo Company, 2/506.

July 10, 1970

PFC Patrick Bohan, Troop D, 2nd Squadron, 17th Cavalry; Cpl. Victor DeFoor, Troop D, 2nd Squadron, 17th Cavalry; Spec. 4 Fredrick Raymond Jr., Troop D, 2nd Squadron, 17th Cavalry; Sgt. Daniel Hively, Bravo Company, 2/506.

July 14, 1970

S.Sgt. Paul Guimond, Delta Company, 2/501; S.Sgt. James Hembree, Delta Company, 2/501; Sgt. Dennis Huffine, Delta Company, 2/501; S.Sgt. William Jones, Delta Company, 2/501; Sgt. John Keister, Delta Company, 2/501; 1st Lt. Terry Palm, Delta Company, 2/501; S.Sgt. Gary Schneider, Delta Company, 2/501; Cpl. Keith Utter, Delta Company, 2/501.

July 18, 1970

Cpl. Burke Miller, A Battery, 2/11 Artillery; Sgt. David Beyl, Delta Company, 2/501; Sgt. William Rollason, Echo Company, 2/501; Sgt. Michael Walker, Alpha Company, 159th Aviation Battalion.

July 20, 1970

PFC Larry Plett, B Battery, 2/319 Artillery; Cpl. Bill Browning, Delta Company, 1/506; Sgt. Samuel Carroll Jr., Delta Company, 1/506; Cpl. Patrick DeWulf, Delta Company, 1/506; Cpl. John Knott, Delta Company, 1/506; Spec. 4 Eloy Valley, Delta Company, 1/506; Sgt. Durl Calhoun, Bravo Company, 326th Engineers; Sgt. Dennis Fisher, Bravo Company, 326th Engineers.

July 21, 1970

Sgt. David Johnson, A Battery, 2/11 Artillery; 1st Lt. James Kalsu, A Battery, 2/11 Artillery; Cpl. Frank Asher, Delta Company, 1/506; Sgt. Roberto Flores, Bravo Company, 2/506; Cpl. Robert Hays, Delta Company, 1/506; Cpl. Peter Huk, Delta Company, 1/506; Cpl. Francis Maune, Bravo Company, 2/506; Capt. Donald Workman, Delta Company, 1/506; Sgt. Brent Law, 326th Medical Battalion.

July 22, 1970

Cpl. John Babich, Alpha Company, 2/506; Cpl. Virgil Bixby, Alpha Company, 2/506; Cpl. Robert Brown Jr., Alpha Company, 2/506; S.Sgt. Stanley Diehl, Delta Company, 2/506; Sgt. Mark Draper, Alpha Company, 2/506; Cpl. Danny Fries, Alpha Company, 2/506; Spec. 4 Robert Journell III, Alpha Company, 2/506; S.Sgt. John Kreckel, Alpha Company, 2/506; 2nd Lt. Steven Olson, Alpha Company, 2/506; 1st Lt. William Pahissa, Alpha Company, 2/506; Sgt. Thomas Schultz, Alpha Company, 2/506; Spec. 4 Donald Severson, Alpha Company, 2/506; S.Sgt. Gerald Singleton, Alpha Company, 2/506.

July 23, 1970

Sgt. Wilfred Warner Jr., Delta Company, 2/501; Cpl. Gus Allen, Alpha Company, 2/506; Lt. Col. Andre Lucas, Headquarters Company, 2/506.

As this book was being finalized, it was learned that John Mihalko died on Sept. 18, 2015. Mihalko was a founding member of the Ripcord Association and his writings and a brief interview were important components in the foundation of this book.

Bibliography

Books

Keith Nolan, Ripcord – Screaming Eagles Under Siege. Presido, Ballantine Books, 2003

Maj. Gen. Benjamin Harrison, Hell on a Hilltop, America's Last Major Battle In Vietnam, On The Flank Of The A Shau Valley March-July 1970, The 324B Division Surrounds the 101st Airborne's Currahee Battalion, iUniverse Inc., 2004.

John Del Vecchio, The 13th Valley, Bantam Books, 1982

Peter Maslowski and Don Winslow, Looking For A Hero: Staff Sergeant Joe Ronnie Hooper and the Vietnam War, University of Nebraska Press, 2004

Keith Nolan, Into Laos, Dell Publishing, 1988

Arthur Wiknik Jr., Nam Sense, Surviving Vietnam with the 101st Airborne Division, Casemate, 2005

Doug Bonnot, The Sentinel and the Shooter, WingSpan Press, 2010

Sam Adams, War of Numbers: An Intelligence Memoir, Steerforth Press, 1994

Periodicals

Chuck Hawkins, "From Ripcord to Recon," VFW Magazine, April 1996, pages 36-38.

William Nack, "A True All-American," Sports Illustrated, July 23, 2001.

W. Earlston Andrews, "Conversations and Hill 927 (Ripcord), A Vietnam Memoir, 2014.

James Fairhall, Ph.D., "The Air Force and Ripcord," Ripcord Report, October 1987, p. 4-6.

John Mihalko, "The Ides of March," Ripcord Report, August 1985, p. 8-10.

Walt Smith, correspondence, Ripcord Report, Dec. 1985, p. 4.

Frank Gonzales, "Retrospective," Ripcord Report, December 1985, no pages listed.

Gen. Sidney Berry, "Late Incoming," Ripcord Report, June 1986, no pages listed.

John Mihalko, "Retrospective," Ripcord Report, June 1986, no pages listed.

Chip Collins, "The April Fools," Ripcord Report, May 1986, no pages listed.

Ray Blackman, "Hill 805," Ripcord Report, July 1987, p. 16-20.

Documents

Robin Graham, "An Annotated History of the 2nd Battalion (Airmobile), 506th Infantry (1 March 1970 – 1 August 1970), 2010

The 101st Airborne Division, "Combat Operations After Action Report, Operation TEXAS STAR, 1 April 1970-5 September 1970"

Interviews

The brunt of this book came from the men who served. Interviews, by phone, in person and via email, were conducted from November 2013 through June 2015. Around 200 interviews with those who served in the 101st Airborne were conducted and dozens more with those who served in the Marines, Air Force and Navy were also conducted during this timeframe.

Index

Aanonsen, James, 27, 41, 42, 89, 190
Ackerman, John, 312, 325
Adams, Joseph, 171
Alexander, Floyd, 3, 9, 272, 278, 280, 287
Allen, Gus, 312
Ames, Richard, 42, 277
Anckaitis, Robert, 137, 138, 236, 237, 240
Andrasson, Aaron, 133
Andrews, Earlston, 30-33
Arkangel, Carmelito, 20, 47
Aronson, Marc, 10, 12, 83, 109, 219
Babich, John, 289
Baldwin, William, 265, 285, 286
Barnes, Barry, 167
Baron, Red, 56
Barrowcliff, Robert, 219, 226
Beals, Charles, 183, 208, 210
Berry, Sidney, vi, vii, x, xi, 59, 109, 110, 126, 204, 265, 266, 309, 316, 317
Beyl, David, 174
Biggs, Dan, 16, 17, 101-104
Bixby, Virgil, 289

Blackman, Ray, 160, 161, 165-172, 174, 176
Blakely, Lenard, 80
Bloomingdale, Dennis, 190-195
Bodnar, Mike, 105-107
Bohan, Patrick, 156
Bond, Bruce, 149-154
Bonnot, Doug, 94, 202
Bradley, William, 22
Brady, Bruce, 13, 21, 42, 43, 46, 105, 162, 163, 279, 327, 332
Brown, John, 274, 275
Brown Jr., Robert, 289
Bruce, Mike, 141-145, 147
Brumbelow, Jackie, 167
Buhr, Paul, 23, 34, 40
Burckard, Albert, 22-26, 35, 36, 40, 51-54, 56, 58-61, 83-92, 97
Burkey, Paul, 69, 128, 133, 194, 195
Caballero, Gabino, 303, 305, 320, 323
Cafferty, Gerry, 117, 118, 125
Campbell, James, 64, 68, 69, 71, 101, 112, 128, 195-198, 201, 202
Carnes, Edward, 3, 142, 143, 145, 147, 148
Carr, Johnny, 295, 296
Chandler, Bruce, 171
Chase, Thomas, 308
Claxson, Ernest, 70, 90
Clay Jr., Herman, 80, 81
Cluff, Keith, 167
Colbert, Howie, 63, 64, 69, 71, 111, 113
Collins, Rodger, 16, 49, 50, 321
Collins, Rodney, 171
Conrad, John, 97, 98
Conrardy, Richard, 125
Cooksley, Mike, 174
Cooper, Dale, 108, 113, 121, 122, 127
Cooper, Terry, 171

Corradetti, David, 75, 76, 190

Crawford, James, 314

Critchlow, Anthony, 155, 156

Crowell, Howard, 24, 61, 63

Darling, John, 44, 61, 90

Davis, Dudley, 24-26, 33

Davis, George, 202

De Foor, Victor, 156

Diehl, Stanley, 289

Donning, Charles, 56, 57

Draper, Mark, 163, 279, 280, 289

Dreher, Jack, 113

Edwards, John, 50

Epps, Neal, 250, 251, 256, 257

Ertel, Larry, 167

Fairhall, Jim, 326

Flaherty, Jack, 66, 181, 182, 184-189, 291-292, 294, 298, 299

Flansburg, Rex, 177, 180, 182, 185, 187, 188

Flores, Roberto, 232, 240

Foster, Gary, 273-276, 282

Fotias, Nicholas, 2, 220, 224, 231, 237-239

Fowler, John, 63, 68, 75, 112, 113, 128, 129

Fox, John, 266, 309, 316, 317

Freeman, Leigh, 99, 100

Fries, Danny, 289

Galindo, Tony, 273, 274, 231

Gaskin, Dixie, 178

Gaster, Drew, 174

Gates, Thomas, 80

Gaut, Tom, 182, 184-189

Gilbert, Fred, 190, 291, 295-297

Glennon, Martin, 273-275, 281

Glennon, William, 251, 304-306

Godwin, Jack, 171

Graham, Robin, 95
Grimm, Michael, 181, 182, 187
Grove, Edwin, 219, 223, 226
Grubidt, Ron, 124
Guimond, Paul, 169-170, 174
Gunn, Steve, 67
Hand, William, 135, 136, 222, 227, 228, 232, 236, 302, 309, 318, 323
Hanrahan, Warren, 171
Harbor, Stephen, 115, 124, 125, 208
Harris, James, 134, 135, 138, 300, , 301, 314, 315
Harrison, Ben, 15, 87, 202, 204, 260, 261, 266, 309, 323, 330, 331
Hawkins, Chuck, 19, 64, 65, 67-70, 119, 159, 162, 164, 261-265, 269-278, 280, 282, 284-289, 290, 293, 294, 297, 298, 330
Heater, Daniel, 26
Heath, Bill, 22, 28, 34, 35, 53, 82, 83, 312-314
Hembree, James, 170
Hennessey, John, 176, 267, 326
Herndon, Thomas, 115
Hewitt, Tom, 112, 114-116, 118, 125, 128
Hill, Bobby, 171
Hines, Raymond, 23
Hinman, Chris, 320
Holmen, Charles, 220, 221, 224, 226
Holthausen, Donald, 115, 120, 122, 123, 125
House, Randy, 7, 11, 18, 24, 70, 87, 136, 137, 291, 293-294, 298-299, 302, 304, 306, 310-312, 315-316, 318, 319
Howard Jr., Lewis, 180, 182, 207-216
Howard, Ted, 207-216
Howton, Jimmy, 299, 300, 303-306, 322
Hudson, Ronald, 329
Ireland, Dale, 141, 146, 301, 306
Ireland, Dale, 302-303, 306
Ives, Burl, 131
Janezic, Ron, 269, 271, 282, 283

Jensen, Christopher, 10, 139, 217, 300

Johnson, David, 232, 236, 237, 240

Joliet, Tim, 26, 28, 29, 34, 36-38

Jones, William, 170

Journell, Robert III, 264, 272, 274, 281, 289

Judd, Robert, 133, 192, 195

Kalsu, James Robert, 230-241

Kalsu, Jan, 230-241

Kays, Kenneth, 88

Keister, John, 170

Kelly, Gary, 25

Kenyon, David, 74

Kern, Larry, 144, 148, 149, 225, 249, 250

Kiekintveld, Greg, 74

Koenigsbauer, Herbert, 119, 128, 159, 200

Koger, Arvel, 27, 89

Kohmetscher, Lyle, 76, 77, 79-81

Kohr, William, 299, 300, 304, 322

Kuennen, John, 120, 124, 125

Lane, Dale, 35, 53, 270, 271, 312, 315

Law, Lawrence, 51, 53, 61

Layton, Robert, 11, 75-79, 81, 82, 203, 332-333

Leib, Charles, 127, 259

Leibecke, Robert, 111, 116, 118, 122, 123, 132

Lemon, Robert, 75

Lenz, Lee, 124, 125

Lewis, Willie, 167

Lilly, Ken, 36

Little, Skip, 284-285

Livingston, Otis, 204

Lowe, Bob, 89, 90

Lucas, Andre, 12, 22, 24, 52, 59, 65, 85, 88, 95, 101, 108, 129, 136, 172, 173, 178, 180, 187-189, 196, 197, 200-202, 206, 223, 261, 264, 270, 299, 300, 303, 305, 309, 313-317, 335

Mace, James, 80
Manthei, Steve, 108, 110, 112, 114, 115, 120-123, 125, 126
Maresca, Greg, 333
Marshall, Frank, 5, 9, 26-28, 35, 190, 277, 286, 289, 292, 298, 329-331
Martin, Alfred, 239
Maslowski, Peter, 159
Matsumoto, Steven, 331
Mauney, Gerald, 89
Mayberry, Kenneth, 140, 141, 291, 292, 293, 306-309, 311, 312, 324, 325
McCall, Jim, 66, 67, 177, 182, 188, 199, 202, 203
McCoy, Gary, 27, 35
McFarland, William, 250-152, 254, 257
McGhan, Oscar, 153
McMenamy, Charles, 158
McSwain, Peter, 44, 71
Meloro, Peter, 63, 73, 74, 127, 190
Messenger, Kemett, 94, 95
Meyer, Uwe, 222, 225, 226, 321
Michaud, Phillip, 237
Miller, Kenneth, 331
Mitchell, David, 165-168, 176
Moore, Leonard, 331
Morales, Jose, 80
Motta, Ralph, 96, 97
Moyer, Amy, 333
Mulvey, William, 274, 275
Neiderer, Clem, 154-156
Nelson, Leroy, 80
Newman, Tim, 1, 41, 42
Newton, George, 229
Noll, James, iv, xv, 20, 21, 25, 30, 34-36, 40, 42, 84, 85, 87, 89, 160-164
Norris, Wieland, 98-101
Olson, Steve, 272, 278, 280, 284, 289
Pahissa, William, 289

Palm, Terry, 170
Patchell, Tom, 80
Peters, Ben, 103, 104, 204-206, 302-304, 315, 317-318, 321-323
Plenderleith, James, 171
Poulard, James, 167
Pounds, Jerry, 182
Pullen, Steve, 308
Radcliff Jr,. Robert, 125
Radcliff, Terry, 49-51
Ray, William, 153
Raymond Jr., Frederick, 156
Rice, Andre, 320
Rich, David, 47, 48, 114, 119, 138, 139
Ridge, Tom, 211
Risinger, Gerald, 195
Robinson, Carl, 167
Rollison, Rembert, 47, 65-67, 113, 180, 185, 187, 189, 197, 202, 291-294, 298
Romig, Robert, 96, 97
Rose, William, 38
Rubsam, Tom, 136
Saller, James, 6, 48
Sanders, James, 250, 254-257
Sartin, Dennis, 80
Schnarr, John, 54-56, 58, 59, 178-180
Schneider, Gary, 171
Schultz, Thomas, 275, 282, 289
Scott, Rickey, 200
Selman, George, 80
Selveggi, Ralph, 170
Senft, Peter, 93-95
Severson, Don, 282-284, 289
Singleton, Gerald, 272, 284, 289
Sistruck, Wayne, 81
Skaggs, Ricky, 239, 240

Skinner, Mark, 104-106, 182, 294-296
Smith, Danny, 115
Smith, Jody, 265
Smith, John, 242-249, 259, 261
Smith, Walt, 228
Smither, Dr. James, 331
Smoker, Bob, 115,
Spaulding, Fred, 14, 188, 196, 197, 199, 200, 202, 204, 268, 290, 291-292, 296-297, 306
Spruill, Ovell, 289
Stanger, Terry, 218, 221-224, 226-229
Stanton, Bob, 79
Stefler, Charlie, 37, 38
Steward, Steve, 75, 76
Stone, Larry, 90
Stortz, Dennis, 181, 188, 190
Strasburg, George, 182
Straub, Chris, 159, 165, 168, 171, 172, 174-176
Sumrall, Roger, 125
Tallman, Richard, 159
Tanner, Kenneth, 313-314
Tarbuck, Robert, 108, 110, 115, 121
Tolson, Phil, 44-46, 308, 317, 321-324
Thomas, Rick, 99, 100, 129, 130
Thomas, Sheryl, 129, 130
Thompson, Randall, 246
Utecht, Robert, 133
Utter, Keith, 170
Van Cleve, Charles, 113-120, 125, 126, 128
Van Hout, Craig, 49-51
Vazquez-Rodriguez, Isabelino, 19, 62-65, 6873, 104, 127, 303, 319, 320
Wagnon, Bill, 272
Walker, Michael, 222-224, 226, 228
Walker, Russel, 264, 273, 274

Walker, Van, 56, 59
Wall, Wilburn, 329
Wall, William, 51
Wallace, Robert, 68
Wallace, Steve, 134, 323
Warner, Wilfred, 174
Wasilk, Wayne, 312, 325
Weaver, David, 171
Webster, Tommy, 283
Westervelt, George, 27
Whitler, Neil, 56, 57, 59
Widjeskog, Lee, 17, 85, 90, 97, 98, 100, 101, 190, 261, 269, 271-276, 297-298, 330-331
Wiknik Jr., Arthur, 330
Wilcox, Jeff, 84, 89, 128, 129, 132, 133, 160, 192, 195-202
Williams, Bill, 47, 51, 61, 101, 132, 133, 136, 190
Wilson, John, 55-59
Winslow, Don, 159
Winters, Jeff, 80
Wold, James, 212
Workman, Don, 242, 243, 246-249, 255, 259, 261, 263
Worrall, Robert, 11, 76, 78
Wyrosdick Jr, Carl, 319-321
Zoller, Robert, 125